QA
76.585
.D56
2018

Diogenes, Yuri,
author.

Microsoft Azure
security center

P9-DUA-024

Mi
Security Center

AUG 1 3 2018

Yuri Diogenes
Dr. Thomas W. Shinder

Microsoft Azure Security Center

Published with the authorization of Microsoft Corporation by:
Pearson Education, Inc.

Copyright © 2018 by Pearson Education, Inc.

All rights reserved. This publication is protected by copyright, and permission must be obtained from the publisher prior to any prohibited reproduction, storage in a retrieval system, or transmission in any form or by any means, electronic, mechanical, photocopying, recording, or likewise. For information regarding permissions, request forms, and the appropriate contacts within the Pearson Education Global Rights & Permissions Department, please visit www.pearsoned.com/permissions/. No patent liability is assumed with respect to the use of the information contained herein. Although every precaution has been taken in the preparation of this book, the publisher and author assume no responsibility for errors or omissions. Nor is any liability assumed for damages resulting from the use of the information contained herein.

ISBN-13: 978-1-5093-0703-6
ISBN-10: 1-5093-0703-6

Library of Congress Control Number: 2018938489

1 18

TRADEMARKS

Microsoft and the trademarks listed at http://www.microsoft.com on the "Trademarks" webpage are trademarks of the Microsoft group of companies. All other marks are property of their respective owners.

WARNING AND DISCLAIMER

Every effort has been made to make this book as complete and as accurate as possible, but no warranty or fitness is implied. The information provided is on an "as is" basis. The authors, the publisher, and Microsoft Corporation shall have neither liability nor responsibility to any person or entity with respect to any loss or damages arising from the information contained in this book or from the use of the CD or programs accompanying it.

SPECIAL SALES

For information about buying this title in bulk quantities, or for special sales opportunities (which may include electronic versions; custom cover designs; and content particular to your business, training goals, marketing focus, or branding interests), please contact our corporate sales department at corpsales@pearsoned.com or (800) 382-3419.

For government sales inquiries, please contact governmentsales@pearsoned.com.

For questions about sales outside the U.S., please contact intlcs@pearson.com.

CREDITS

EDITOR-IN-CHIEF
Greg Wiegand

EXECUTIVE EDITOR
Laura Norman

DEVELOPMENT EDITOR
Kate Shoup/Polymath Publishing

MANAGING EDITOR
Sandra Schroder

SENIOR PROJECT EDITOR
Tracey Croom

COPY EDITOR
Scout Festa

INDEXER
Valerie Perry

PROOFREADER
Elizabeth Welch

TECHNICAL EDITOR
Mike Martin

EDITORIAL ASSISTANT
Cindy J. Teeters

COVER DESIGNER
Twist Creative, Seattle

COMPOSITOR
Jeff Lytle, Happenstance Type-O-Rama

GRAPHICS
Vived Graphics

Contents

Foreword   *ix*
Introduction   *xi*

Chapter 1   The threat landscape   1

Understanding cybercrime. 1

Understanding the cyber kill chain 2

Common threats 4

Building a security posture. 5

Adopting an assume-breach mentality 6

Cloud threats and security 7

    Compliance   8

    Risk management   9

    Identity and access management   9

    Operational security   9

    Endpoint protection   10

    Data protection   10

Azure Security. 11

    Host protection   12

    Network protection   12

    Storage protection   14

Chapter 2   Introduction to Azure Security Center   17

Understanding Security Center. 17

    Security Center architecture   18

    Security Center dashboard   21

Considerations before adoption. 22

    Role-based access control   22

    Security policy   23

    Storage   23

    Recommendations   23

Incorporating Security Center into your security operations 24

Onboarding resources 25

Initial assessment 30

Chapter 3   Policy management   33

Legacy Azure Security Center security policy 33

Next-generation Azure Security Center security policy 38

    The Data Collection blade   38

    The Policy Management blade   40

    The Email Notifications blade   41

    The Pricing Tier blade   42

Azure Policy 43

    Policy definitions and assignments   44

    Initiative definitions and assignments   44

    Exploring Azure Policy   45

    Customizing your Security Center security policies   49

Azure Security Center RBAC and permissions 49

Chapter 4   Mitigating security issues   51

Compute recommendations 51

    Setting up endpoint protection   52

    Remediate Security Configurations   56

Networking recommendations 58

    NSGs on subnets not enabled   59

    Restrict access through internet-facing endpoint   61

Storage and data 63

    Server auditing and threat detection not enabled   64

    Storage encryption not enabled   66

Applications 68

    Web application firewall not installed   68

Chapter 5   Using Security Center for incident response   73

Understanding security alerts 73

Detection scenarios 75

    Detecting spam activity   75

    Crash-dump analysis   76

Accessing security alerts 77

    Security incidents   79

    Custom alerts   81

Investigating a security issue 84

Responding to a security alert. 89

    Creating a playbook   89

    Building the workflow   91

    Executing a playbook   94

    Auditing playbook execution   95

Chapter 6   **Advanced cloud defense**   **99**

Threat prevention versus threat detection 99

Methods of threat detection 100

    Atomic detection   101

    Threat-intelligence feeds and integrated security solutions   102

    Behavioral analysis   104

    Anomaly detection   106

The cyber kill chain and fusion alerts 108

Application whitelisting: adaptive application controls. 111

Just-in-time VM access. 114

Chapter 7   **Security incident and event management (SIEM)**
          integration with Splunk   **121**

Integrating SIEM solutions 122

Splunk integration with Azure Security Center 123

    Confirming accessible logs in Azure Monitor   124

    Configuring the subscription for the Splunk SIEM pipe   124

    Creating and configuring a resource
    group for the Splunk SIEM pipe   124

    Setting up an Azure AD application to provide
    an access control identity   125

    Creating an Azure key vault   127

    Copying the app password into Key Vault   130

    Making an event hub   131

    Creating a shared access key for event hub access control   133

Placing the event hub shared access key in Azure Key Vault **134**

Hooking up the event hub to Azure Monitor **136**

Spinning up the virtual machine that
hosts the Splunk enterprise VM **138**

Installing and configuring the Azure Monitor add-on
for Splunk **139**

Chapter 8 **Monitoring identity and access** **141**

Monitoring identity-related activities 141

  Identity posture 143

  Failed logons 144

  Logons over time 147

Integrating Security Center with Azure
Active Directory Identity Protection 148

Customizing your search 149

Chapter 9 **Using threat intelligence to identify security issues** **153**

What is threat intelligence and why use it? 153

Using threat intelligence reports in Security Center. 155

Using the Threat Intelligence dashboard
in Security Center. 157

Hunting security issues in Security Center. 159

Virtual Analyst 163

Appendix A **Using multiple workspaces in Security Center** **164**

Creating a new workspace 164

Moving computers and VMs to a new workspace. 165

Appendix B **Customizing your operating
system security baseline assessment** **168**

General considerations 168

Customizing operating system configuration 169

  Downloading the JSON file 169

  Editing the JSON file 170

  Uploading the new rule 173

Index *174*

Acknowledgments

The authors would like to thank Laura Norman and the entire Microsoft Press team for their support in this project, Hayden Hainsworth for writing the foreword of this book, and also other Microsoft colleagues that contributed by writing a sidebar for this book: Laura Hunter, Nicholas DiCola, Koby Koren, Sarah Fender, Tomer Teller, Miri Landau, Ben Kliger, Ajeet Prakash, and John Kemnetz. We would also like to thank Mike Martin (Microsoft MVP) for reviewing this book.

Yuri would also like to thank: my wife and daughters for their endless support and understanding; my great God for giving me strength and guiding my path on each step of the way; my great friend and co-author Tom Shinder for another awesome partnership; and Adwait Joshi (AJ) and the entire Azure Security Center Team, especially all the Security Center PMs at Microsoft Israel for their ongoing collaboration and contribution. Thanks to my manager, Nicholas DiCola, and my coworkers Laura Hunter, Ty Balascio, Andrew Harris, Marie Groove, Gershon Levitz, and Yoann Mallet for inspiring me to do more. Last but not least, thanks to my parents for working hard to give me an education, which is the foundation I use every day to keep moving forward in my career.

Tom would also like to thank: so many people that it's very difficult to name them all in the space allocated. Probably most important is Yuri Diogenes, who motivated me to partner up on another book with him. I don't know why he asks me, because I know I drive him crazy each time we write a book together. Nevertheless, Yuri is a blessing to me and all those around him, and he keeps me from resting on my prodigious laurels. I want to thank David Cross, who brought me into Azure Security Engineering and all the fascinating opportunities it's offered; while David is now with Google, he's still an inspiration. I also want to give major props to Avi Ben-Menahem and Ramesh Chinta, both of whom have always been supportive of my efforts, and who are models of the best that Microsoft has to offer. And of course, the entire Azure Security Engineering PM team—the dedication, diligence, intelligence, and number of hours worked per week by this team is unmatched, and the results of these attributes show in the fact that Azure is the most secure public cloud service platform in the industry. Finally, eternal thanks to my wife—my lifetime love, partner, and confidant—and to God, who has given me much more in life than I deserve.

About the authors

Yuri Diogenes, MsC

With a master of science in cybersecurity intelligence and forensics investigation (UTICA College), Yuri is senior program manager in Microsoft CxP Security Team, where he primarily helps customers onboard and incorporate Azure Security Center as part of their security operations/incident response. Yuri has been working for Microsoft since 2006 in different positions, including five years as senior support escalation engineer in CSS Forefront Edge Team, and from 2011 to 2017 in the content development team, where he also helped create the Azure Security Center content experience since its launch in 2016. Yuri has published a total of 20 books, mostly around information security and Microsoft technologies. Yuri also holds an MBA and many IT/Security industry certifications, such as CISSP, E|CND, E|CEH, E|CSA, E|CHFI, CompTIA Security+, CySA+, Cloud Essentials Certified, Mobility+, Network+, CASP, CyberSec First Responder, MCSE, and MCTS. You can follow Yuri on Twitter at @yuridiogenes or read his articles at his personal blog: http://aka.ms/yuridio.

Tom Shinder

Tom Shinder is a cloud security program manager in Azure Security Engineering. He is responsible for security technical content and education, customer engagements, and competitive analysis. He has presented at many of the largest security industry conferences on topics related to both on-premises and public cloud security and architecture. Tom earned a bachelor's degree in neuropsychobiology from the University of California, Berkeley, and an MD from the University of Illinois, Chicago. He was a practicing neurologist prior to changing careers in the 1990s. He has written over 30 books on OS, network, and cloud security, including *Microsoft Azure Security Infrastructure* and *Microsoft Azure Security Center* (IT Best Practices series, Microsoft Press). Tom can be found hugging his Azure console when he's not busy hiding his keys and secrets in Azure Key Vault.

Foreword

I was so pleased to hear that Yuri and Tom were teaming up to write another book on security. I found their first book about Azure core security, *Microsoft Azure Security Infrastructure*, riveting—I read it cover to cover twice, recommending it to anyone interested in learning more about security in Azure.

This book extends that work. It will teach you all you want to know about how to use Azure Security Center—the security solution to get visibility and control and prevent and detect threats in your Azure subscriptions. Security Center is a critical solution for protecting a cloud workload, and, as indicated by Gartner in their Cloud Workload Protection (CWP) Magic Quadrant, modern hybrid datacenters require a unique protection strategy. And since the classic security perimeter we relied upon is gone with the migration of datacenter workloads into public clouds, a new security paradigm is required. Moreover, with the integration with Log Analytics, and as long as the monitoring agent is installed on your machines, Azure Security Center can be used for your machines on-premises, in a private datacenter, or in another cloud as well. This will simplify your life and I trust you'll come to rely on Azure Security Center as your primary dashboard and alerting engine for years to come.

No industry is immune to cyberattacks. This book is relevant for everyone around the world. Given the cybersecurity landscape as it exists today and the criticality of the information digital age, we need to assume breach as a mindset and think about what capabilities we need to detect adversarial activity or malicious insiders inside our networks rather than over-relying on thwarting attackers at the front door. Gone are the days when it was acceptable to turn a blind eye to risk. If you don't know what you don't know, it's impossible to take action. Prevention is of the utmost importance, true. However, the ability to detect and control is paramount. Simple, intuitive, and intelligent investigation capabilities are a must to support SecOps teams flooded in a sea of alerts, as well as to support incident response teams.

This book will help you plan, onboard, and learn how to effectively use Security Center to detect and investigate threats in your Azure subscriptions (or in your datacenter workloads). You'll also learn how to integrate with other solutions, like Azure Active Directory Identity Protection Center, and export your logs to a security information and event management system should you choose to do so. I sincerely hope that you get energy from the capabilities the authors outline in this book, and that it will spur you to action to follow their best practices and recommendations while gaining confidence in the solution.

After reading this book, you will have a better understanding of what Security Center is and how to incorporate it into your security operations center. Yuri and Tom were inspired to write this book because many customers would like to have one place to go to understand what Security Center is, what its requirements are, and how to operate it. You'll find the material to be technical. It is written with security analysts, architects, and cloud operators in mind, along with any IT professional who wants to understand more about Security Center.

If you've read Tom's work, you'll know he's a long-term experienced and seasoned security veteran and author. He's also a senior program manager in the Azure Security Engineering team. Follow him on Twitter. Read his blogs if you'd like to learn more. He has a wealth of knowledge and wisdom from his days working on-premises and his journey to the cloud.

Yuri is a well-established writer in his own right, publishing document after document in his former role as a content writer for Azure Security. He's recently joined my team as a senior program manager to support customers' and partners' success using Microsoft's Cloud and Enterprise Security products and services. He has a wealth of information and excels at simplifying the complex.

Dig in.

Hayden Hainsworth
Principal Group Program Manager
Microsoft C+E Security Engineering

Introduction

Welcome to *Azure Security Center,* a book that was developed together with the Azure Security Center product group to provide in-depth information about Azure Security Center and to demonstrate best practices based on real-life experience with the product in different environments.

The purpose of this book is to introduce the wide array of security features and capabilities available in Azure Security Center. After being introduced to all of these security options, you will dig in to see how they can be used in a number of operational security scenarios so that you can get the most out of the protect, detect, and respond skills provided only by Azure Security Center.

Who is this book for?

Azure Security Center is for anyone interested in Azure security: security administrators, support professionals, developers, and engineers.

Azure Security Center is designed to be useful for the entire spectrum of Azure users. You can have no security experience, some experience, or be a security expert and will get value from Azure Security Center. This book provides introductory, intermediate and advanced coverage on a large swath of security issues that are addressed by Azure Security Center.

The approach is a unique mix of didactic, narrative, and experiential instruction. Didactic covers the core introductions to the services. The narrative leverages what you already understand and we bridge your current understanding with new concepts introduced in the book.

Finally, the experience component is presented in two ways— we share our experiences with Azure Security Center and how to get the most out of it by showing in a stepwise, guided fashion how to configure Azure Security Center to gain all the benefits it has to offer,

In this book you will learn:

- How to secure your Azure assets no matter what your level of security experience

- How to save hours, days and weeks of time by removing the trial and error

- How to protect, detect, and respond to security threats better than ever by knowing how to get the most out of Azure Security Center

System requirements

- Anyone with access to a Microsoft Azure subscription can use the information in this book.

Errata, updates & book support

We've made every effort to ensure the accuracy of this book and its companion content. You can access updates to this book—in the form of a list of submitted errata and their related corrections—at:

https://aka.ms/AzureSecurityCenter/errata

If you discover an error that is not already listed, please submit it to us at the same page.

If you need additional support, email Microsoft Press Book Support at *mspinput@microsoft.com*.

Please note that product support for Microsoft software and hardware is not offered through the previous addresses. For help with Microsoft software or hardware, go to *http://support.microsoft.com*.

Stay in touch

Let's keep the conversation going! We're on Twitter: *http://twitter.com/MicrosoftPress*.

Chapter 1

The threat landscape

On May 12, 2017, the mainstream media began covering a massive ransomware attack called WannaCry, catching the world by surprise. It was reported that in a single day, 230,000 computers in more than 150 countries were infected. The attack was carried out by exploiting computers on which the MS17-010 patch—released in March 2017 to fix a Microsoft SMB vulnerability—had not been applied. In addition to affecting home users, this attack hit organizations such as the United Kingdom's National Health Service (NHS). Computers that were patched were not affected. (This of course highlights the need to have a solid update-management process in place!)

Ransomware like WannaCry—or like Petya, which allows for lateral movement (meaning it takes only a single infected machine to potentially bring down the entire network)—is just one threat in the current landscape. There are many others. Before we dive into Azure Security Center, you need a good understanding of current threats and the motivations of the people behind them. Current threats range from old but effective techniques such as phishing emails to state-sponsored attacks and everything in between. For example, one common threat is drive-by download sites. Another is Trojans. Then there is the weaponization of cloud resources to attack on-premises assets. This chapter explores several of these threats to prepare you to use Azure Security Center. But first, it discusses cybercrime and the cyber kill chain, establishing your security posture, and the assume-breach approach.

Understanding cybercrime

The days of hacking for status are behind us. Nowadays, a main motivator behind cyberattacks is some sort of financial gain.

The Internet Crime Complaint Center (IC3) is part of the Cyber Division of the US Federal Bureau of Investigation. According to its 2016 Internet Crime Report (https://pdf.ic3.gov/2016_IC3Report.pdf), the IC3 received 2,673 complaints related to ransomware, resulting in losses of more than $2.4 million. Tech-support fraud also left a mark, with a total of $7.8 million in losses in 2016. Finally, the total financial loss in the United States exceeded $1.3 billion in 2016—up 24 percent from the previous year.

You're probably wondering how cybercriminals monetize the data they steal. That's a great question. Many of these cybercriminals work in organized crime. They have a globally distributed criminal infrastructure, which is used to launch attacks. Before they launch an attack, they start a new attack campaign. To build that campaign, they work with technically sophisticated organized crime groups, which they find on the cybercriminal marketplace online.

These technical cybercriminals have different online offerings. For example, they might offer counter-antivirus (CAV) services, which scan antivirus engines to make sure new malware can be successfully deployed without being detected. Another offering could be bulletproof hosting services for online criminal activity. (They're called "bulletproof" because the owners of these servers do not cooperate with local enforcement in case of an investigation.) There are even escrow services that act as a third party in online transactions between technical criminals and their criminal clients.

> **TIP** Visit https://aka.ms/stoppingcybercrime to see how Microsoft Cloud and advanced analytics are assisting the fight against cybercrime.

Understanding the cyber kill chain

One of the most challenging aspects of defending your systems against cybercriminals is recognizing when those systems are being used for some sort of criminal activity in the first place—especially when they are part of a botnet. A *botnet* is a network of compromised devices that are controlled by an attacker without the knowledge of their owners. Botnets are not new. As a matter of fact, a 2012 Microsoft study found that cybercriminals infiltrated unsecure supply chains using the Nitol botnet, which introduced counterfeit software embedded with malware to secretly infect computers even before they were purchased. (For more information, see https://aka.ms/nitol.)

The best way to prevent this type of attack, or any other, is to identify attack vectors—that is, how an attacker will attack your environment. To help with this, Lockheed Martin developed a cyber kill chain. Each step in this chain represents a particular attack phase. (See Figure 1-1.)

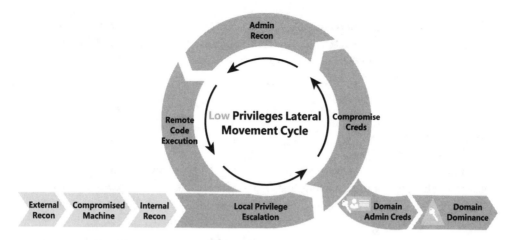

FIGURE 1-2   Typical location where QKSee is installed.

> **IMPORTANT**   Figure 1-1 is based on a Microsoft version of the cyber kill chain. You may see other versions that either summarize this chain or have an even more detailed set of steps.

The steps in this chain are as follows:

1. **External recon**   During this step, attackers typically search publicly available data to identify as much information as possible about their target. The goal of this step is to obtain intelligence, or *intel*, to better perform the attack and increase the likelihood of success.

2. **Compromised machine**   During this step, attackers leverage different techniques, such as social engineering, to entice users to do something. For example, the attacker might send a phishing email to lure the user into clicking a link that will compromise the machine. The goal is to establish a foothold on the victim's network.

3. **Internal recon and lateral movement**   During this step, the attacker performs host discovery and identifies and maps internal networks and systems. The attacker may also start moving laterally between hosts, looking for a privileged user's account to compromise.

4. **The low-privileges lateral movement cycle**   During this cycle, the attacker continues to search for accounts with administrative privileges so that he or she can perform a *local privilege escalation* attack. This cycle typically continues until the attacker finds a domain administrative user account that can be comprised.

5. **Domain admin creds**   At this point, the attacker needs complete *domain dominance*. To achieve this, the attacker will pivot through the network, either looking for valuable data or installing ransomware or any other malware that can be used for future extortion attempts.

> **IMPORTANT** Throughout this book, you will learn how Azure Security Center can be used to disrupt the cyber kill chain by detecting attacks in different phases. Therefore, it is crucial that you understand these steps.

Common threats

As mentioned, one common type of attack is the use of drive-by download sites. These are websites that host one or more exploits that target vulnerabilities in web browsers and browser add-ons. According to Microsoft Security Intelligence Report volume 22, Bing detected 0.17 drive-by download pages for every 1,000 pages in the index in March 2017.

According to the same report, in the first quarter of 2017, Trojans were the most commonly encountered type of malicious software (followed by worms and droppers). Trojans always pose as a useful application. For example, take the Win32/Xadupi Trojan, also called WinZipper (*%ProgramFiles%\WinZipper*) or QKSee (*%ProgramFiles%\qksee*). In addition to creating a shortcut to itself in the Start menu (see Figure 1-2), enabling users to zip and unzip files, this Trojan also creates a service (qkseeService) that connects to command and control (C2) servers and periodically checks for instructions using HTTP requests. Often, these instructions are to silently download new files, which could contain malware that will be executed on the local computer. This is just one example of how threats spread.

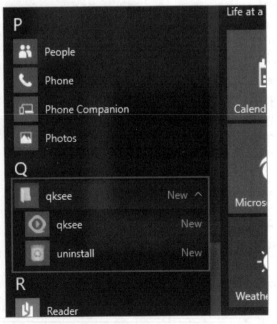

FIGURE 1-1 The cyber kill chain.

These days, the end user is almost always the target, since he or she is the weakest link. With the proliferation of mobile devices, bring-your-own-device (BYOD) models, and cloud-based apps, users are installing more and more apps. All too often, these apps are merely malware masquerading as valid apps. Many do something similar to (or even worse than) what QKSee does. For this reason, it is important to have in place not only good endpoint protection but also a detection system that can look across different sources to intelligently identify unknown threats by leveraging cutting-edge technologies such as analytics and machine learning.

Building a security posture

It used to be that cybersecurity experts recommended that organizations simply invest more in protecting their assets. Nowadays, however, simply investing in protecting your assets is not enough. Instead, organization should invest in building a solid security posture. As shown in Figure 1-3, a security posture is composed of three major pillars.

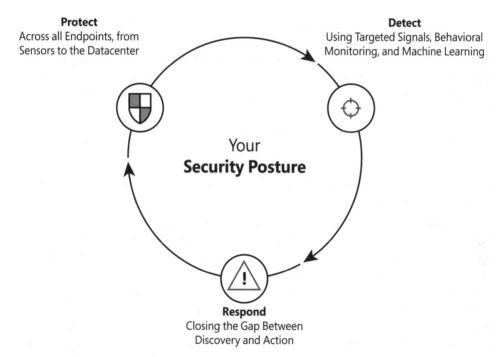

Protect
Across all Endpoints, from
Sensors to the Datacenter

Detect
Using Targeted Signals, Behavioral
Monitoring, and Machine Learning

Your
Security Posture

Respond
Closing the Gap Between
Discovery and Action

FIGURE 1-3   The three pillars of a security posture.

According to the InfoSec Institute, attackers lurk on networks for an average of 200 days without being detected. (See http://resources.infosecinstitute.com/the-seven-steps-of-a-successful-cyber-attack for more information.) No doubt, this is a huge amount of time to have an attacker inside your network. But the key word here is actually *detected*. Without a good detection mechanism, you have no way to disrupt an attack. Hence, it is imperative to invest in a holistic solution to monitor cloud-based resources as well as on-premises assets. You must be able to quickly detect an attack and to use actionable data to improve your response. All that being said, collecting data without analyzing it only delays the response process. That's why it is so important to use tools that leverage technologies such as behavior analytics, threat intelligence, and machine learning for data correlation. Azure Security Center will do all that for you, reducing false positives and showing what's relevant for you to proceed on your investigation.

> **IMPORTANT** Regardless of where your resources are, there is no doubt that threats are growing. Companies must improve their security posture to combat these threats.

Adopting an assume-breach mentality

Microsoft recognizes that it's not enough to prevent a breach. You must adopt an "assume-breach" mentality. When you adopt an assume-breach mentality, it means you *hope* that you will never be breached but you assume that you have been breached or will be soon. Then you gather the people, processes, and technology that will help you find out when a breach occurs as early as possible, discover which breach has occurred, and eject the attacker while limiting the effects of the breach as much as possible.

Taking an assume-breach approach helps you understand how attackers gain access to your system and helps you develop methods that enable you to catch the attacker as soon as possible after a breach takes place. Because attackers typically enter a system via a low-value target, if you can quickly detect when such a target has been compromised you can block the attacker from expanding to higher-value assets, which are the ultimate target.

One very effective method for doing this is through red/blue team simulations. In these exercises, the red team takes on the role of the attacker and the blue team takes on the role of a defender. To begin, you define the parameters of the exercise, including the duration. Then, the red team tries to attack your system—in this case, your Azure infrastructure. At the same time, the blue team tries to detect what the red team is doing and, if the red team manages to compromise any systems, to block the red team from compromising additional assets. At the end of the exercise, members of the red and blue teams discuss what happened, how the red team might have gotten in, and how the blue team detected and ejected the red team, and suggest technologies and operational procedures to detect attacks more quickly and easily.

Cloud threats and security

One threat is the weaponization of cloud resources to attack on-premises assets. In a typical cloud-weaponization scenario, the attacker compromises and takes control of one or more virtual machines (VMs). From there, the attacker launches attacks on other cloud or on-premises resources, including brute-force attacks and email phishing attacks. The attacker may also conduct reconnaissance—for example, port scanning to identify new targets. Figure 1-4 shows an attacker gaining access to VMs located in the cloud and leveraging compute resources from these VMs to attack on-premises assets. This is a typical cloud-weaponization scenario.

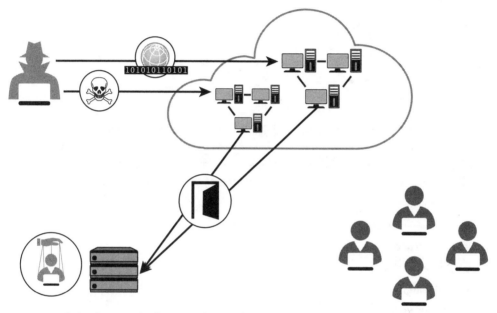

FIGURE 1-4   A cloud-weaponization scenario targeting on-premises resources.

> **IMPORTANT**   Microsoft Security Intelligence Report volume 22 shows the global outreach of these types of attacks. According to the report, more than two-thirds of incoming attacks on Azure services in the first quarter of 2017 came from IP addresses in China (35.1%), the United States (32.5%), and Korea (3.1%). All other attacks were distributed among 116 other countries and regions.

Another potential cloud threat occurs due to flaws during configuration and DevOps. One common scenario involves the public key secret shared in a public cloud. Such an event occurred in 2015, when bots scanned GitHub to steal Amazon EC2 keys. Figure 1-5 illustrates this scenario. (For more information, see https://www.theregister.co.uk/2015/01/06/dev_blunder_shows_github_crawling_with_keyslurping_bots/.)

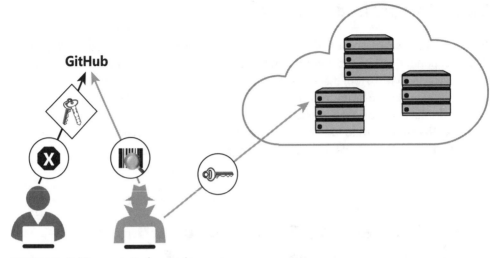

FIGURE 1-5 Public secret attack scenario.

Before adopting cloud computing, organizations must understand the security concerns inherent in the cloud-computing model. Ideally, these concerns should be addressed during the planning process. (Depending on what type of organization you're dealing with, some of these concerns may require more attention than others.) The concerns are as follows:

- Compliance
- Risk management
- Identity and access management
- Operational security
- Endpoint protection
- Data protection

The following sections describe these concerns in more detail.

Compliance

During and after migration to the cloud, organizations must continue to meet their compliance obligations. These obligations could be dictated by internal rules or by external regulations, such as industry standards.

Cloud solution providers (CSPs) must be able to assist customers in meeting these compliance requirements. Indeed, in many cases CSPs become part of the organization's chain of compliance. Work closely with your CSP to identify your organization's compliance needs and to determine how the CSP can meet them. Also verify that the CSP has a proven record of delivering reliable cloud services while keeping customer data private and secure.

MORE INFO   For more information on Microsoft's approach to compliance, visit www. microsoft.com/en-us/trustcenter/default.aspx.

Risk management

Cloud customers must be able to trust the CSP with their data. CSPs should have policies and programs in place to manage online security risks. These policies and programs may vary depending on how dynamic the environment is. Customers should work closely with CSPs and demand full transparency to understand risk decisions, how they vary depending on data sensitivity, and the level of protection required.

NOTE   To manage risks, Microsoft uses mature processes based on long-term experience delivering services on the web.

Identity and access management

Organizations planning to adopt cloud computing must be aware of the identity- and access-management methods available and of how these methods will integrate with their current on-premises infrastructure.

These days, with users working on different devices from any location and accessing apps across different cloud services, it is critical to keep the user's identity secure. Indeed, with cloud adoption, identity becomes the new perimeter—the control panel for your entire infrastructure regardless of the location, be it on-premises or in the cloud. You use identity to control access to any services from any device, and to obtain visibility and insights into how your data is being used.

As for access management, organizations should consider auditing and logging capabilities that can help administrators monitor user activity. Administrators must be able to leverage the cloud platform to evaluate suspicious logon activity and to take preventive actions directly from the identity-management portal.

Operational security

Organizations migrating to the cloud should evolve their internal processes, such as security monitoring, auditing, incident response, and forensics, accordingly. The cloud platform must enable IT administrators to monitor services in real time to observe the health conditions of these services and provide capabilities to quickly restore services that were interrupted. You should also ensure that deployed services are operated, maintained, and supported in accordance with the service level agreement (SLA) established with the CSP.

Endpoint protection

Cloud security is not only about how secure the CSP infrastructure is. It is a shared responsibility. One aspect of security for which organizations are responsible is endpoint protection. Organizations that adopt cloud computing should consider increasing endpoint security, as these endpoints will be exposed to more external connections and will access apps that may be housed by different cloud providers.

Users are the main target of attacks, and endpoints are the devices employed by users. An endpoint might be a user's workstation, a user's smartphone, or any other device that can be employed to access cloud resources. Attackers know that the end user is the weakest link in the security chain, and will continue to invest in social-engineering techniques, such as phishing emails, to entice users to perform actions that can compromise an endpoint.

> **IMPORTANT**   Securing privileged access is a critical step to establishing security assurances for business. Make sure to read more about Privileged Access Workstations at http://aka.ms/cyberpaw and know more about Microsoft's methodology for protecting high-value assets.

Data protection

With regard to cloud security, the goal when migrating to the cloud is to ensure that data is secure no matter where it is located. Data might exist in any of the following states and locations:

- **Data at rest in the user's device**   In this case, the data is located at the endpoint, which can be any device. You should always enforce data encryption at rest for company-owned devices and in BYOD scenarios.

- **Data in transit from the user's device to the cloud**   When data leaves the user's device, you should ensure that the data is still protected. There are many technologies that can encrypt data regardless of its location—for example, Azure Rights Management. It is also imperative to ensure that the transport channel is encrypted. Therefore, you should enforce the use of Transport Layer Security (TLS) to transfer data.

- **Data at rest in the cloud provider's datacenter**   When data arrives at the cloud provider's servers, their storage infrastructure should ensure redundancy and protection. Make sure you understand how your CSP performs data encryption at rest, who is responsible for managing the keys, and how data redundancy is performed.

- **Data in transit from the cloud to on-premises**   In this case, the same recommendations specified in the "Data in transit from the user's device to the cloud" bullet apply. You should enforce data encryption on the file itself and encrypt the transport layer.

- **Data at rest on-premises**   Customers are responsible for keeping their data secure on-premises. Encrypting at-rest data at the organization's datacenter is a critical step to accomplish this. Ensure that you have the correct infrastructure to enable encryption, data redundancy, and key management.

Azure Security

There are two aspects of Azure Security. One is platform security—that is, how Microsoft keeps its Azure platform secure against attackers. The other is the Azure Security capabilities that Microsoft offers to customers who use Azure.

The Azure infrastructure uses a defense-in-depth approach by implementing security controls in different layers. This ranges from physical security, to data security, to identity and access management, and to application security, as shown in Figure 1-6.

> **IMPORTANT** This book does not cover the Azure Security infrastructure in depth. For more information about this, read *Microsoft Azure Security Infrastructure,* by Debra Schinder and Yuri Diogenes, from Microsoft Press.

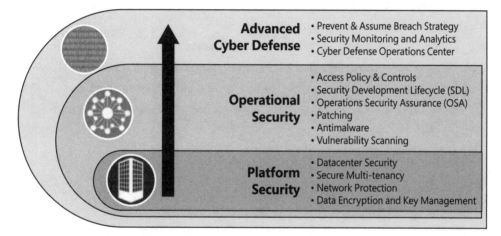

FIGURE 1-6 Multiple layers of defense.

From the Azure subscription-owner perspective, it is important to control the user's identity and roles. The subscription owner, or account administrator, is the person who signed up for the Azure subscription. This person is authorized to access the Account Center and to perform all available management tasks. With a new subscription, the account administrator is also the service administrator and inherits rights to manage the Azure Portal. Customers should be very cautious about who has access to this account. Azure administrators should use Azure's role-based access control (RBAC) to grant appropriate permission to users.

Once a user is authenticated according to his or her level of authorization, that person will be able to manage his or her resources using the Azure Portal. This is a unified hub that simplifies building, deploying, and managing your cloud resources. The Azure Portal also calculates the existing charges and forecasts the customer's monthly charges, regardless of the amount of resources across apps.

A subscription can include zero or more hosted services and zero or more storage accounts. From the Azure Portal, you can provision new hosted services, such as a new VM. These VMs will use resources allocated from compute and storage components in Azure. They can work in silos within the Azure infrastructure or they can be publicly available from the internet. You can securely publish resources that are available in your VM, such as a web server, and harden access to these resources using access control lists (ACLs). You can also isolate VMs in the cloud by creating different virtual networks (VNets) and controlling traffic between VNets using network security groups (NSGs).

Host protection

When you think about protecting VMs in Azure, you must think holistically. That is, not only must you think about leveraging built-in Azure resources to protect the VM, you must also think about protecting the operating system itself. For example, you should implement security best practices and update management to keep the VMs up to date. You should also monitor access to these VMs.

Some key VM operations include the following:

- Configuring monitoring and export events for analysis
- Configuring Microsoft antimalware or an AV/AM solution from a partner
- Applying a corporate firewall using site-to-site VPN and configuring endpoints
- Defining access controls between tiers and providing additional protection via the OS firewall
- Monitoring and responding to alerts

> **IMPORTANT** For more details about computer security, visit https://docs.microsoft .com/en-us/azure/security/security-virtual-machines-overview.

Network protection

Azure virtual networks are very similar to the virtual networks you use on-premises with your own virtualization platform solutions, such as Hyper-V or VMware. Azure uses Hyper-V, so you can take advantage of the Hyper-V virtual switch for networking. You can think of the Hyper-Virtual switch as representing a virtual network interface to which a VM's virtual network interface connects. Figure 1-7 illustrates how Azure virtual networks are distributed in a multi-tenant environment.

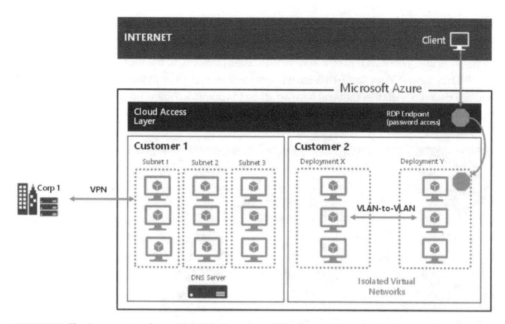

FIGURE 1-7 The Azure network provides isolation even within the same tenant virtual network.

One thing in Azure that might be different from what you use on-premises is how it isolates one customer's network from another's. On-premises, you might use different virtual switches to separate different networks from each other. That's perfectly reasonable. You can do that because you control the entire network stack and the IP addressing scheme on your network, as well as the entire routing infrastructure. Azure can't give each customer that level of control, because it needs to reuse the same private IP address space among all the different customers, and it can't tell each customer what segment of the private IP address space to use for their VMs. It can, however, apply isolation between tenants to better manage the private IP space.

Network access control is as important on Azure virtual networks as it is on-premises. The principle of least privilege applies both on-premises and in the cloud. One way to enforce net-work access controls in Azure is by taking advantage of NSGs. An NSG is equivalent to a simple stateful packet-filtering firewall or router, similar to the type of firewalling done in the 1990s. (I say this not to be negative about NSGs, but to make it clear that some techniques for network access control have survived the test of time.)

> **IMPORTANT** For more details about Azure network security, visit https://docs
> .microsoft.com/en-us/azure/security/security-network-overview.

Storage protection

Azure Disk Encryption is a technology that enables you to encrypt the VM disk files for your Azure VMs. Azure uses Windows Hyper-V as its virtualization platform, so the VMs you run on Azure use the VHD file format. With Azure Disk Encryption, you can encrypt both the operating system VHD and any data disk VHD files that you have attached to your VMs. Figure 1-8 shows the encryption options for the various Azure services that use storage.

FIGURE 1-8 Encryption options in Azure.

Keep in mind that if an attacker somehow manages to access and copy your VM disk files, he or she would not be able to mount them. This is because the disks are encrypted, and the attacker likely does not have the key required to decrypt them. Microsoft recommends that you use this powerful security technology on any VM you run on Azure. You should use similar technology on any VMs you run on-premises as well.

Another option is to use Azure Storage Service Encryption (SSE) for data at rest. This service helps you protect your data. When you use this feature, Azure Storage automatically encrypts the data prior to persisting to storage and decrypts it prior to retrieval. The encryption, decryption, and key-management processes are totally transparent to users.

> **IMPORTANT** For more details about Azure Storage security, visit https://docs.microsoft.com/en-us/azure/security/security-storage-overview.

Why Azure Security Center?

A common trope in the cybersecurity industry goes something like this: "There are only two types of companies: those that have been hacked, and those that will be." A different—and my preferred—version of that meme is, "There are only two types of companies: those that know they've been hacked, and those that don't."

This isn't meant to sound like doom and gloom or a sky-is-falling admonishment not to use the cloud. Cloud computing in all its forms—IaaS, PaaS, SaaS, microservices, and more—can provide significant advantages to any organization. I will even say that cloud computing has the potential to make you more secure than you ever had a chance to be in your on-premises environment. Skeptical? Read on.

Industry analysts (and of course cloud vendors) have long touted the advantages of the cloud in terms of easy scale-up and scale-out for your company's servers, services, and applications. But what about taking that scale-up and scale-out capability and pointing it toward the problem of cybersecurity? And what if you could use that scale-up and scale-out not just to secure your infrastructure but to increase the security of every Azure customer at large?

Enter the Microsoft Intelligent Security Graph (www.microsoft.com/en-us /security/intelligence). By applying Azure's massive computing, storage, and machine-learning capabilities to the problem of better securing our customers, Microsoft has developed a security intelligence service based on security signals that we receive from myriad sources—Office 365, Microsoft Account (formerly Windows Live ID), the Digital Crimes Unit, and the Azure cloud platform itself. By analyzing the traffic from these sources—450 million authentication events per month, 400 billion emails, and more—Microsoft can identify and respond to both existing and emerging threats originating from all over the internet and protect our customers in an extremely rapid fashion.

Azure Security Center (ASC) is not the only Microsoft service that relies on the Security Graph. But the advantages that ASC receives from the graph are numerous. We have extremely accurate data concerning new and emerging botnets, command-and-control networks, and new forms of malware that attackers are using to target our customers. And what the graph learns from one customer, it feeds into ASC so that we can use this learning to protect all our customers.

Imagine having an army of security analysts working day and night to research emerging cybersecurity threats and identify actual instances of malicious behaviors targeting your Azure resources so that you can respond and protect your critical assets in a rapid manner. With ASC, you're not imagining it—you have that capability built right into the service, with no additional work needed on your part.

Laura E. Hunter, Principal Program Manager, Security CxP

Chapter 2

Introduction to Azure Security Center

Given the threat landscape presented in Chapter 1, it is clear that there is a need for a system that can both unify security management and provide advanced threat protection for workloads running in Azure, on-premises, and on other cloud providers.

Azure Security Center gives organizations complete visibility and control over the security of hybrid cloud workloads, including compute, network, storage, and application workloads. By actively monitoring these workloads, Security Center reduces the exposure of resources to threats. Security Center also uses intelligent threat detection to assist you in protecting your environment from rapidly evolving cyberattacks.

Security Center does more than detect threats. It also assesses the security of your hybrid cloud workload and provides recommendations to mitigate threats. And it provides centralized policy management to ensure compliance with company or regulatory security requirements.

In this chapter, you will learn how you can use Security Center in your security operations, key considerations for adoption, and how to onboard resources.

Understanding Security Center

Because Security Center is an Azure service, you must have an Azure subscription to use it—even if it's just a trial subscription.

Having an Azure subscription automatically enables the free tier of Security Center. This free tier monitors compute, network, storage, and application resources in Azure. It also provides security policy, security assessment, security recommendations, and the ability to connect with other security partner solutions. Organizations that are getting started with Infrastructure as a Service (IaaS) in Azure can benefit even from this free service because it will improve their security posture.

In addition to the free tier, Security Center offers a fee-based standard tier. This tier offers a complete set of security capabilities for organizations that need more control.

Specifically, migrating your Security Center subscription from the free tier to the standard tier enables the following features:

- Security event collection and advanced search
- Just-in-time VM access
- Adaptive application controls (application whitelisting)
- Built-in and custom alerts
- Threat intelligence

Another advantage of the standard tier is that it enables you to monitor on-premises resources, VMs hosted by other cloud providers, and even nested VMs running in Azure. You achieve this by manually installing the Security Center agent in the target machine. (This is covered in more detail later in this chapter.)

When you upgrade to the standard tier, you can use it free for 60 days. This is a good opportunity to evaluate these features, see how your current environment will benefit from them, and decide whether they're worth the investment. For the latest information about Azure Security Center pricing, visit http://aka.ms/ascpricing.

> **NOTE** From here on out, this book assumes you are using the standard tier of Security Center.

Security Center architecture

When you use Security Center to monitor resources in Azure, on-premises, and hosted by other cloud providers (such as Amazon AWS), the architecture looks similar to Figure 2-1.

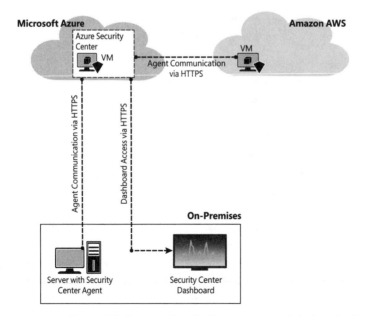

FIGURE 2-1 Connectivity between Security Center agents and the Security Center service.

Security Center uses the Microsoft Monitoring Agent, which is the same agent used by Operations Management Suite and the Log Analytics service. In Windows systems, Security Center installs the Microsoft Monitoring Agent (HealthService.exe). In Linux systems, Security Center creates the *omsagent* daemon, which runs under the *omsagent* account. This account is automatically created during agent installation.

Microsoft Monitoring Agent scans for various security-related configurations and events in Event Tracing for Windows (ETW) traces. In addition, this agent collects the following:

- Operating system logs, such as Windows events
- Operating system type and version
- Running processes
- Machine name
- IP addresses
- Logged-in user (username)
- Tenant ID
- User mode crash dump created by Windows Error Reporting (WER)

This information is sent to your workspace, which is an Azure resource used as a container to store your data. A workspace provides a geographic location for data storage, granularity for billing, and data isolation, and it helps you to better scope the configuration.

If you are using Azure Log Analytics, you already have a workspace. This workspace will be used by Security Center to store data coming from the agent. If you are not using Azure Log Analytics, a new workspace will be automatically created when you start using Security Center. The location of the workspace created by Security Center is based on the location of the VM, as follows:

- For VMs in the United States, Brazil, and Canada, the workspace location is the United States.
- For VMs in Europe and the United Kingdom, the workspace location is Europe.
- For VMs in the Asia-Pacific region, Japan, and India, the workspace location is Asia Pacific.
- For VMs in Australia, the workspace location is Australia.

If you are a global company and you need to store data in specific regions for data sovereignty or compliance reasons, you might consider creating multiple workspaces. Another scenario that might call for multiple workspaces is if you want to isolate various users. For example, you might want each customer, department, or business group to see their own data but not the data for others.

> **TIP** You need use Log Analytics to create multiple workspaces. For help performing this operation, read this article: https://aka.ms/ascworkspaces.

Figure 2-2 shows the core Security Center architecture and how these pieces come together and communicate. In this example, non-Azure machines and Azure VMs send data collected by the agent to the workspace. Security Center uses this data for advanced threat detection analysis and generates recommendations that fit within the prevention module or issues alerts that are part of the detection module. Security Center employs advanced security analytics, a method that is far more powerful than the traditional signature-based approach.

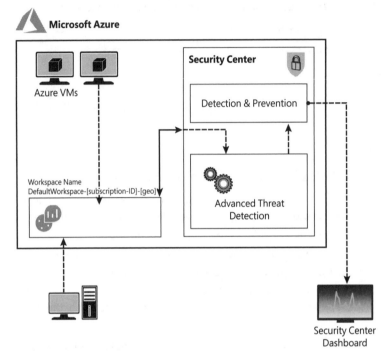

FIGURE 2-2   Security Center architecture.

Security Center uses machine-learning technologies to evaluate all relevant events across the entire cloud fabric. By using this approach, Security Center can detect threats that would be impossible to identify using manual approaches and can predict the evolution of attacks. Security Center uses the following analytics:

- **Integrated threat intelligence**   This leverages global threat intelligence from Microsoft to look for known bad actors. (You will learn more about this in Chapter 9.)

- **Behavioral analytics**   This looks for known patterns and malicious behaviors—for example, a process executed in a suspicious manner, hidden malware, an exploitation attempt, or the execution of a malicious PowerShell script.

- **Anomaly detection**   This uses statistical profiling to build a historical baseline and triggers an alert based on deviations from this baseline. An example of this is would be a VM that normally receives remote desktop connections five times a day but suddenly receives 100 connection attempts. This deviation would trigger an alert.

TIP   Read more about Security Center detection capabilities and other relevant scenarios at https://aka.ms/ascdetections.

Security Center dashboard

To access the Security Center dashboard, sign in to Azure Portal (https://portal.azure.com) and click **Security Center** in the left pane. What happens the first time you open the Security Center dashboard may vary. For the purposes of this example, the dashboard is fully populated with resources, recommendations, and alerts, as shown in Figure 2-3.

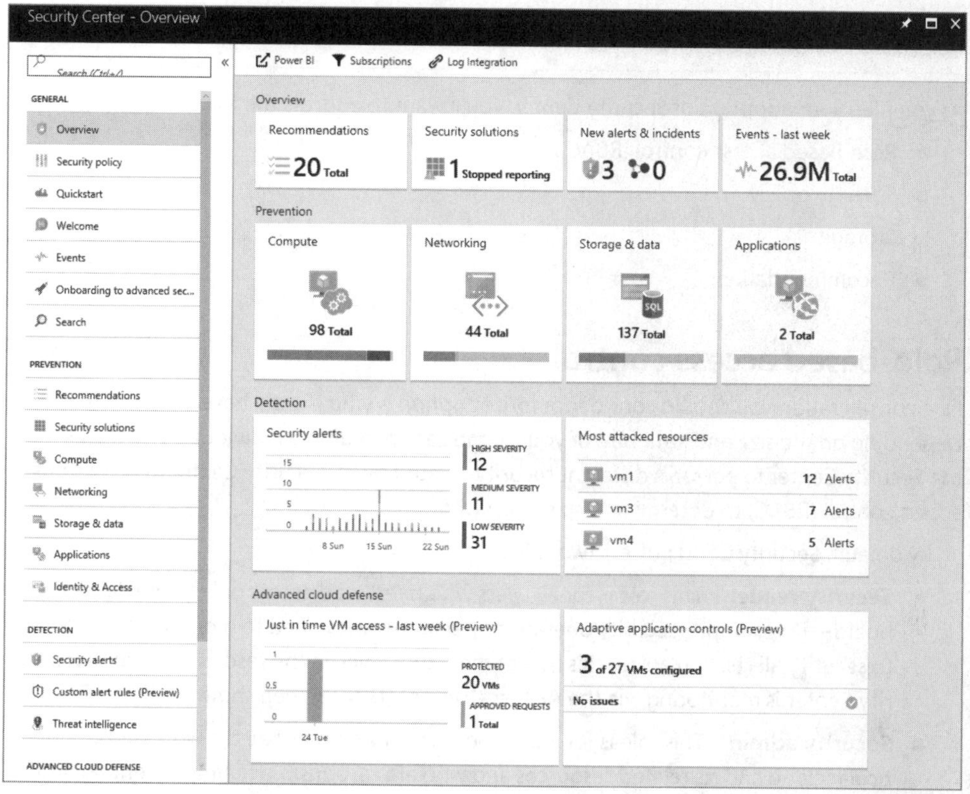

FIGURE 2-3   Security Center dashboard.

As shown in Figure 2-3, the left side of the Security Center dashboard offers access to four main groups of data relating to your workspace:

- **General**   You use the links in the General group to see information about your daily activities, to onboard non-Azure machines, and to search for alerts or events.

- **Prevention**   The links in this group offer access options to enhance your security posture. You can view a security assessment of your resources, connect with security solutions, and monitor your identity access activities.

- **Detection**   You use these options to investigate security issues and for incident-response purposes. You can also access tools for creating custom alerts and view threat-intelligence information relevant to your environment.
- **Advanced Cloud Defense**   The links in this group provide access to tools that enable you to further protect your VMs and whitelist your applications.

> **TIP**   All these options will be covered throughout this book. For now, just browse through them to familiarize yourself with them.

Considerations before adoption

As you plan your adoption of Security Center, you'll want to address the following:

- Role-based access control (RBAC)
- Security policy
- Storage
- Recommendations

Role-based access control

One consideration you should consider before adoption is who should have access to the tool. Depending on the size and structure of your organization, multiple individuals and teams may use Security Center to perform different security-related tasks. Security Center uses role-based access control (RBAC) to determine who can do what.

By default, Security Center offers two roles:

- **Security reader**   This role is for all users who need read access only to the dashboard—for example, security operations personnel who need to monitor and respond to security alerts. You assign this role at the Azure level, in the resource group that Security Center is monitoring, via the **Access Control (IAM)** screen shown in Figure 2-4.
- **Security admin**   This role is for workload owners who manage the workload of a particular cloud and its related resources and who are responsible for implementing and maintaining protections in accordance with company security policy.

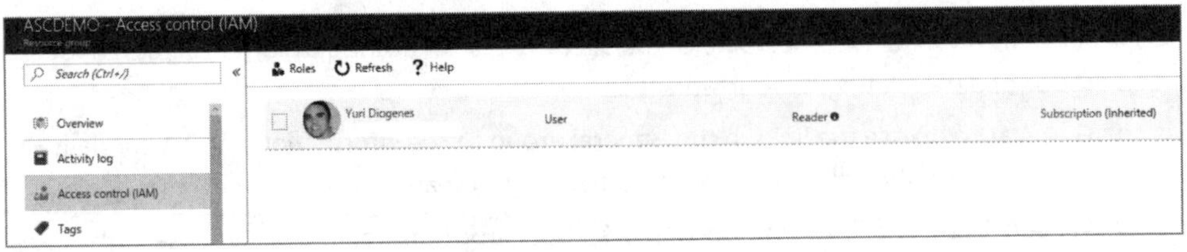

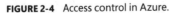

FIGURE 2-4   Access control in Azure.

IMPORTANT   Only subscription owners or contributors and security admins can edit a security policy. Only subscription and resource group owners and contributors can apply security recommendations for a resource. For more on RBAC in Azure, see http://aka.ms/azurerbac.

Security policy

Security Center uses security policies to define the configuration of your workloads. This helps to ensure compliance with company security requirements, regulatory security requirements, or both. You can define policies for your Azure subscriptions that can be personalized to the type of workload or the level of data sensitivity. As you plan your adoption of Security Center, you must identify what needs to be monitored and determine whether the default policy provided by Security Center will be adequate or if you need to create new definitions. Chapter 3 discusses security policies in more detail.

Storage

You'll need to consider your storage needs before adopting Security Center. As noted, the agent collects information and sends it to the workspace. If you are using the standard tier, you have as much as 500 MB of storage space per day across all nodes. For example, if you are monitoring five VMs in Azure and five computers on-premises, 500 MB per day will be spread across all ten of these resources. If the uploaded data surpasses 500 MB per day, additional charges will apply.

IMPORTANT   Workspaces created by Security Center retain data for 30 days. For existing workspaces, retention is based on the workspace pricing tier.

Recommendations

Security Center identifies compute, network, storage, and application resources with security issues and offers recommendations to fix them. To view a list of all security recommendations, click the **Overview** link on the left side of the Security Center dashboard and click the **Recommendations** option on the Overview screen. This opens the Recommendations screen, shown in Figure 2-5. Alternatively, you can view recommendations individually by category. You can use Security Center's severity rating to decide which recommendations to address first. Before you adopt Security Center, you should fully address all existing recommendations. Although this is not a prerequisite, it is a good practice.

DESCRIPTION	RESOURCE	STATE	SEVERITY
Enable data collection for subscriptions	1 subscriptions	Open	❗ High ...
Endpoint Protection not installed on Azure VMs	24 virtual machines	Open	❗ High ...
Endpoint protection not installed on non-Azure computers	14 computers	Open	❗ High ...
Endpoint Protection health failures	2 VMs & computers	Open	❗ High ...
Enable Network Security Groups on subnets	5 subnets	Open	❗ High ...

FIGURE 2-5 Security Center recommendations.

Incorporating Security Center into your security operations

It's critical that your IT security and IT operations departments constantly collaborate to provide better protection, detection, and response. Security operations (SecOps) describes this support function. Many organizations already have a SecOps team dedicated to maintaining the security operations of company assets.

Before using Security Center to monitor resources, you must review your organization's SecOps process and identify how you can incorporate Security Center into your routine. Figure 2-6 shows the tasks performed by a typical security operations center (SOC) and which Security Center features can be used to assist with these tasks.

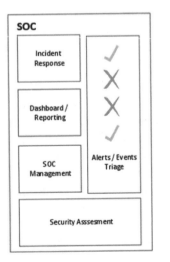
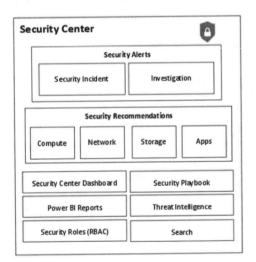

FIGURE 2-6 Mapping security operations in Security Center.

Here are a few key points for incorporating Security Center into your security operations:

- Security Center will continuously evaluate compute, network, storage, and application resources for compliance. The team responsible for ongoing security assessment should track and apply recommendations issued by Security Center on an ongoing basis.

- The security roles available in Security Center, along with Azure's RBAC capability, can help SOC management control who has access to what.

- Security Center can integrate with Power BI to create reports and graphs when more detailed analysis is needed.

- The incident response (IR) team can use security alerts and incident features during the detection and triage phases of an attack to conduct early assessments of the incident. If more in-depth research on an attack is needed, the team can use Security Center's investigation and search features. Finally, when the team is ready to respond, it can use the Security Playbook feature to customize a response to a certain alert.

> **IMPORTANT** A security assessment conducted on VMs will also look for the presence of a security configuration based on Common Configuration Enumeration (CCE) rules. To download these rules, visit https://aka.ms/ascccerules.

Onboarding resources

Now that you have learned how Security Center works and identified your needs, it's time to onboard resources. As explained, VMs located in Azure will be provisioned automatically. That is, the monitoring agent will be installed by default. To onboard non-Azure computers or VMs, follow these steps:

1. Open **Azure Portal** and sign in as a user who has Security Admin privileges.
2. In the left pane, click **Security Center**. The Security Center dashboard opens.
3. In the left pane of the dashboard, under General, click **Onboarding to Advanced Security**. A screen like the one in Figure 2-7 appears.

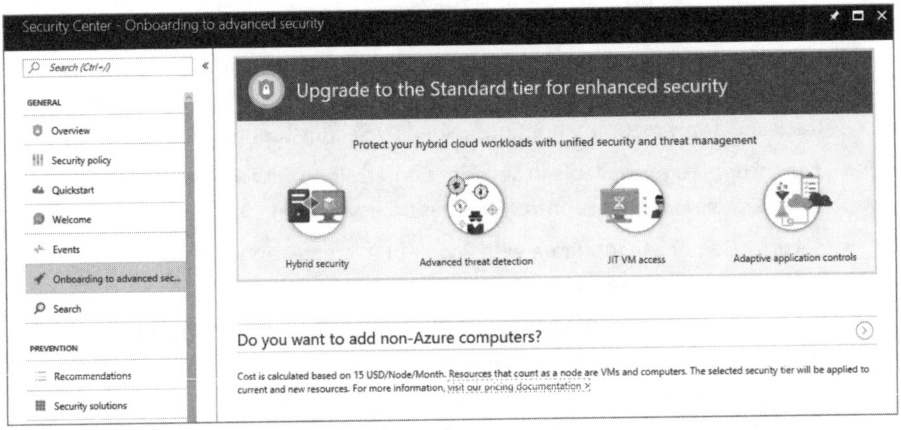

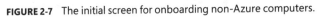

FIGURE 2-7 The initial screen for onboarding non-Azure computers.

4. Next to the **Do You Want to Add Non-Azure Computers?** text, click the right arrow. The **Add New Non-Azure Computers** page appears. (See Figure 2-8.)

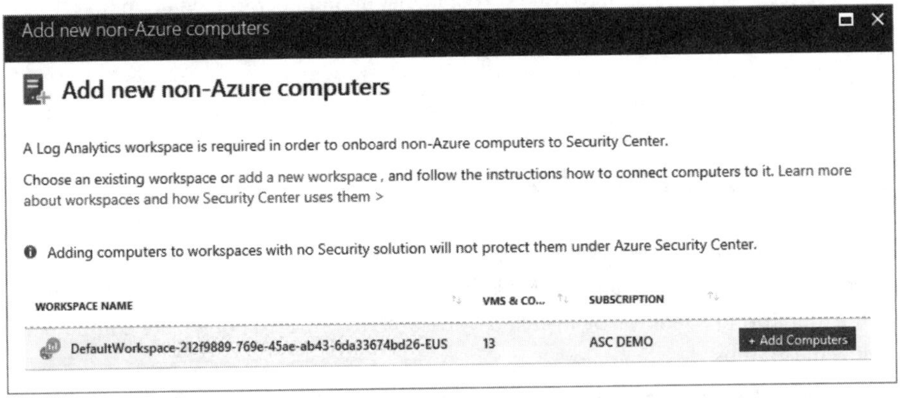

FIGURE 2-8 Add new non-Azure computers from this page.

5. If you have multiple workspaces, click the **+Add Computers** button next to the workspace to which you want to bind your non-Azure computer. The **Direct Agent** blade opens. (See Figure 2-9.)

6. In the Direct Agent blade, click the link for the appropriate Windows agent (64-bit or 32-bit).

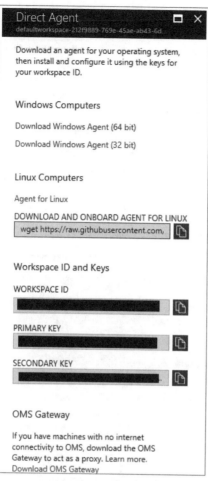

FIGURE 2-9 Agent selection.

IMPORTANT If you are installing Security Center on a Linux operating system, click the **Agent for Linux** link. See https://aka.ms/ASCLinuxAgent for more on installing Linux agents.

---

7. Copy the **workspace ID** and **primary key** values to the clipboard. You will need these values when you install the agent in the target system.

8. When the download is complete, close the Security Center dashboard (that is, close your browser).

9. Copy the agent installation file to a shared network location where the client can access it.

   For this example, the agent will be installed on a Windows Server 2012 R2 computer located on-premises. However, the same procedures apply to a non-Azure VM located in the cloud.

10. Log on to the target system.

11. Double click the **MMASetup-AMD64.exe** file.

12. If the **Open File–Security Warning** dialog box appears, click **Run**.

13. If the **User Access Control** dialog box appears, click **Yes**.

14. In the **Welcome to the Microsoft Monitoring Agent Setup Wizard** page, click **Next**.

15. Read the **Microsoft license terms** and click **I Agree**.

16. In the **Destination Folder** page of the setup wizard, leave the default selection and click **Next**. The **Agent Setup Options** page appears. (See Figure 2-10.)

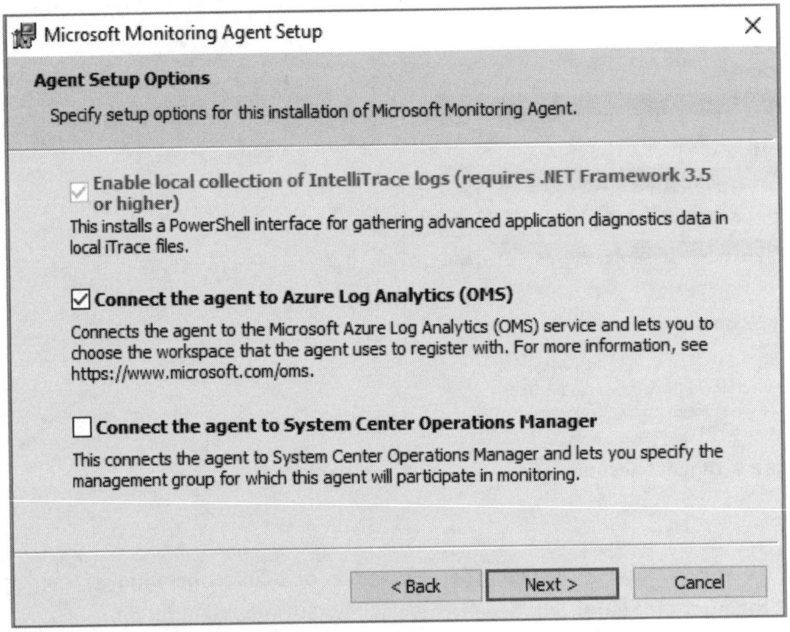

FIGURE 2-10   Selecting the target service.

17. Select the **Connect the Agent to Azure Log Analytics (OMS)** check box, as shown in Figure 2-10, and click **Next**. The **Azure Log Analytics** page opens. (See Figure 2-11.)

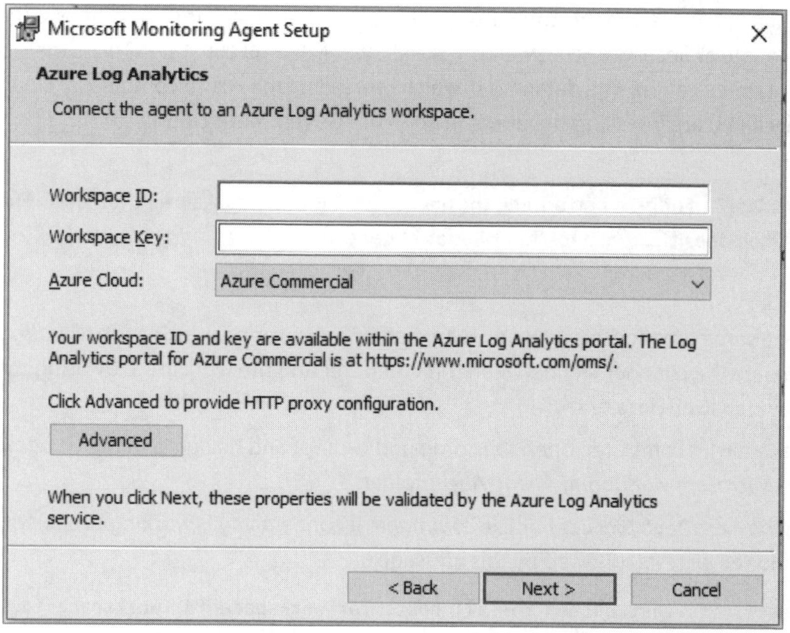

FIGURE 2-11 Providing the workspace ID and primary key.

18. Enter the workspace ID you copied in step 7 in the **Workspace ID** box.

19. Enter the primary key you copied in step 7 in the **Workspace Key** box.

20. If this computer is behind a proxy server, click the **Advanced** button and provide the proxy URL and authentication in the dialog box that appears. Then click **OK**.

21. Back in the Azure Log Analytics page, click **Next**. The Microsoft Update page opens.

22. Select **Use Microsoft Update for Updates (Recommended)** and click **Next**.

23. In the **Ready to Install** page, review the summary field and click **Install**. The **Installing the Microsoft Monitoring Agent** page shows the progress of the installation.

24. When the installation is finished, the **Microsoft Monitoring Agent Configuration Completed Successfully** page opens. Click **Finish**.

You can also perform this installation using the command-line interface (CLI) as follows:

```
MMASetup-AMD64.exe /Q:A /R:N /C:"setup.exe /qn ADD_OPINSIGHTS_WORKSPACE=1 OPINSIGHTS_
WORKSPACE_AZURE_CLOUD_TYPE=0 OPINSIGHTS_WORKSPACE_ID=<yourworkspaceID> OPINSIGHTS_
WORKSPACE_KEY=<yourworkspaceprimarykey> AcceptEndUserLicenseAgreement=1"
```

> **IMPORTANT** The /C switch in this example uses IExpress as its self-extractor. For more information about IExpress, see https://support.microsoft.com/en-us /help/262841/command-line-switches-for-windows-software-update-packages.

Most of the parameters in the agent installation are self-explanatory. The only one that may not fully resonate at first sight is OPINSIGHTS_WORKSPACE_AZURE_CLOUD_TYPE. This is the cloud environment specification. The default is 0, which represents the Azure commercial cloud. Set this to 1 only if you are installing the agent in an Azure Government cloud.

> **IMPORTANT** For help performing the agent installation using Azure Automation and PowerShell, see https://aka.ms/ASCWindowsAgent.

It can take some time for this new non-Azure computer to appear in Security Center. Still, you can validate the connectivity between this computer and the workspace by using the Test-CloudConnection tool. Here's how:

1. On the target computer, open the command prompt and navigate to the \Program Files\Microsoft Monitoring Agent\Agent folder.

2. Run the TestCloudConnection.exe *command*. If connectivity is working properly, you should see all tests followed by this message:

```
Connectivity test passed for all hosts for workspace id <workspace id>
```

Initial assessment

Chapter 4 covers the full spectrum of compute recommendations. Until then, you can follow these steps to view the initial security assessment for this new computer:

1. Open **Azure Portal** and sign in as a user with security admin privileges.

2. In the left pane, click **Security Center**. The Security Center dashboard opens.

3. In the left pane of the dashboard, under Prevention, click **Compute**. A page like the one in Figure 2-12 appears.

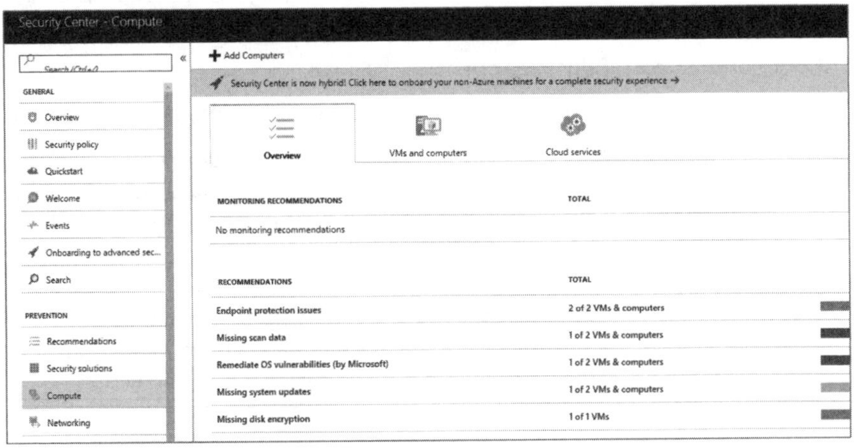

FIGURE 2-12 Accessing compute recommendations.

The **Overview** tab summarizes the current recommendations for VMs and computers, notes the number of VMs and computers to which each recommendation applies, and notes the severity of the issues that have prompted the recommendations.

4. Click the **VM and Computers** tab to see a list of individual computers and VMs and their status with regard to recommendations. (See Figure 2-13.) This list-color codes the status of each VM or machine as follows:

- **Green** This means no action is needed.
- **Yellow** This indicates a medium-priority recommendation.
- **Red** This denotes a high-priority recommendation, which must be addressed as soon as possible.
- **Blue** This is informational only.

Notice, too, that the computer icons to the left feature different colors. The purple computer (ARGOS) is a non-Azure computer, while the blue computer (ASCDEMOVM) is an Azure VM.

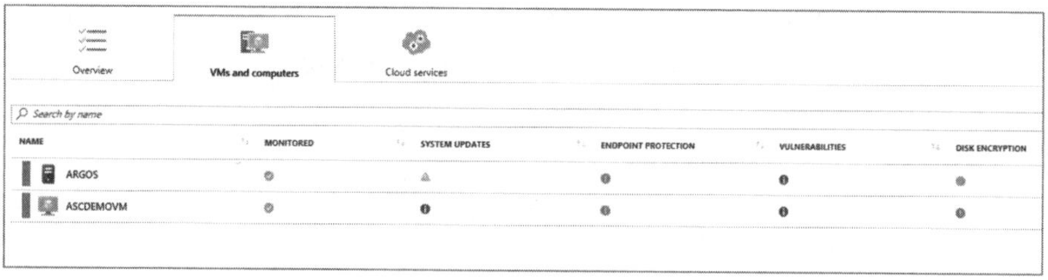

FIGURE 2-13 A list of individual VMs and computers with recommendations and their current status.

5. After you review this initial assessment, close the dashboard.

Rethinking security in the cloud

With the use of the cloud becoming ubiquitous, organizations are retooling their current security approaches to align with cloud speed, agility, and scale. Visibility takes on new importance as the management of cloud workloads is increasingly distributed across the organization and the network perimeter no longer provides a physical security barrier. While workloads are quickly moving to the cloud, most organizations operate in a hybrid mode, with some workloads on-premises and others in one or many public clouds. A unified view of security across these environments is critical to effectively managing security. This includes automatic discovery and monitoring of cloud resources.

Cloud workloads are more dynamic than traditional on-premises workloads, with resources frequently being spun up and down. These workloads consist of not only servers and virtual machines but also cloud storage, virtual networks, databases, and more. By applying security policies and continuously assessing the configuration of new and existing IaaS and PaaS resources, organizations can identify and remediate security vulnerabilities before they can be exploited.

Meanwhile, attackers continue to innovate, making it hard for organizations to keep pace. Here the cloud effect offers significant benefits. By analyzing data across cloud customers using tools like machine learning, an attack seen targeting one customer can be used to detect similar attacks against other customers. Collecting and monitoring data from hybrid cloud environments, tapping into cloud threat intelligence and advanced analytics, and providing ready access to the data and insights needed to respond quickly are all essential to combatting today's threats.

Sarah Fender, Principal Program Manager, Azure Security Center

Chapter 3

Policy management

Ever since the release of Azure Security Center, our customers have found the issue of policy management a bit confusing. It's not too hard to understand why, because the term *policy* can mean a lot of different things. The problem with ambiguous terms like this one is that people often try to lay their own meanings over them—and in most circumstances, those meanings aren't right.

The good news is that this book can steer you in the right direction when it comes to Azure Security Center policy! In fact, you'll find that Azure Security Center policy is quite simple. It can also be quite powerful, as a recent update has given it new and amazing powers. This chapter discusses this update, which, at the time of this writing, is in preview.

Legacy Azure Security Center security policy

Many say that the best way to understand the present and get a better view of the future is to understand the past. We don't know if that's necessarily true, but it sounds good and provides a nice introduction to the current view of Azure Security Center security policy. (By the time you read this book, this "current view" will in fact be the historical view, as you'll be seeing the "new" Security Center security policy.)

Follow these steps to explore the "legacy" Security Center security policy:

1. In Security Center, click **Security Center** in the left pane. Then click **Security Policy**. (See Figure 3-1.)

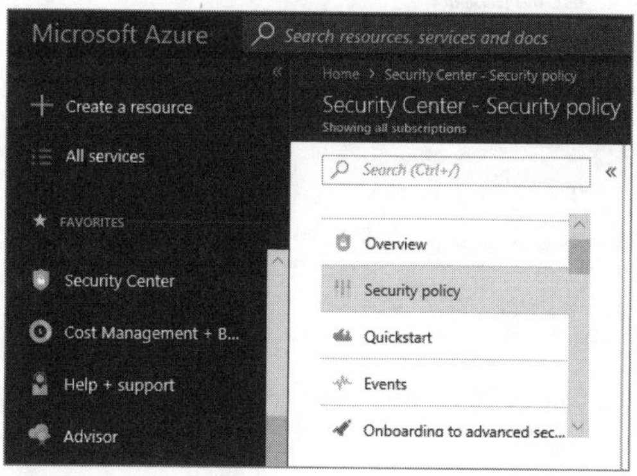

FIGURE 3-1 Accessing legacy Security Policy settings.

2. On the left side of the screen, select the subscription for which you want to configure security policy.

   As shown in Figure 3-2, the right side of the screen contains five options:

   - Data Collection
   - Security Policy
   - Email Notifications
   - Pricing Tier
   - Edit Security Configurations

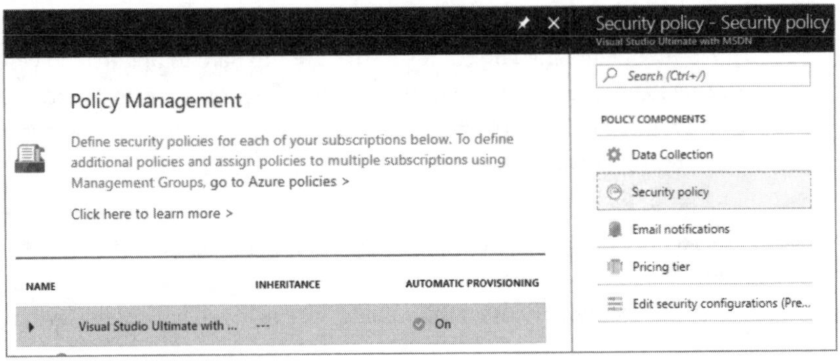

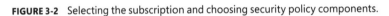

FIGURE 3-2 Selecting the subscription and choosing security policy components.

3. Click **Data Collection** to open the Data Collection blade. (See Figure 3-3.)

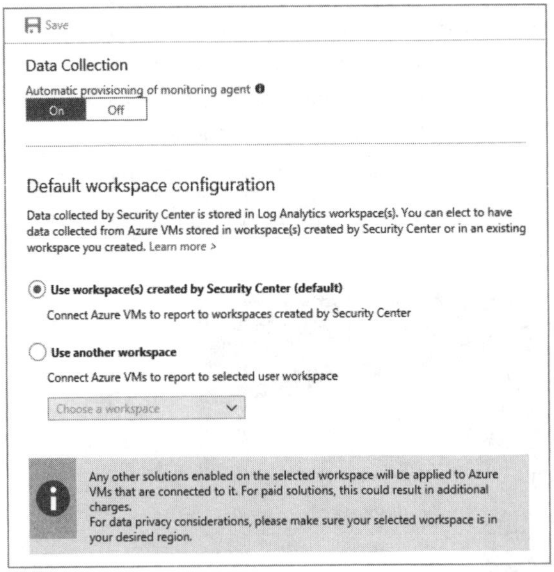

FIGURE 3-3 Configuring data collection for the subscription.

You can use the buttons in the **Data Collection** section to enable or disable the monitoring agent. The monitoring agent is automatically installed on any Azure Infrastructure as a Service (IaaS) and Platform as a Service (PaaS) resources that Security Center monitors and is enabled by default. In other words, information is collected by default.

4. If you don't want Azure Security Center to collect information, click the **Off** button.

> **NOTE** Disabling data collection doesn't mean the agent is removed. To remove the agent, you must manually uninstall Microsoft Monitoring Agent.

It used to be that Security Center kept the information it collected from Azure Storage in something called a Log Analytics workspace. If you have OMS solutions connected to a particular workspace, those solutions will apply themselves to the data coming in from Security Center. This is good if the solutions can convert that Security Center data into something you find useful—but it's bad if your solutions charge for data analysis and you aren't aware of the impact the Security Center data will have. (For more on workspaces, refer to Chapter 2 and see Appendix A.)

> **TIP** If you choose to put Security Center data into an existing workspace that already has connected solutions, monitor your costs closely.

5. If you do have OMS solutions connected to a particular workspace, select the **Use Another Workspace** option in the Data Collection blade and use the corresponding dropdown list to select the desired workspace. (See Appendix A for more details.) Otherwise, select the **Use Workspace(s) Created by Security Center (Default) option.**

6. Click the **Security Policy** option in the **Security Policy** configuration interface to open a blade like the one shown in Figure 3-4 on the next page.

This blade is where some of the confusion regarding security policy has come in. When you configure policy here—whether it's a protection policy, a detection policy, a response policy, or what have you—you're simply telling Security Center what you want recommendations for. That's it. There's no "leveling" of policy—for example, high versus medium versus low—and there's no hierarchy. It's just a "what do you want us to look at" type of policy.

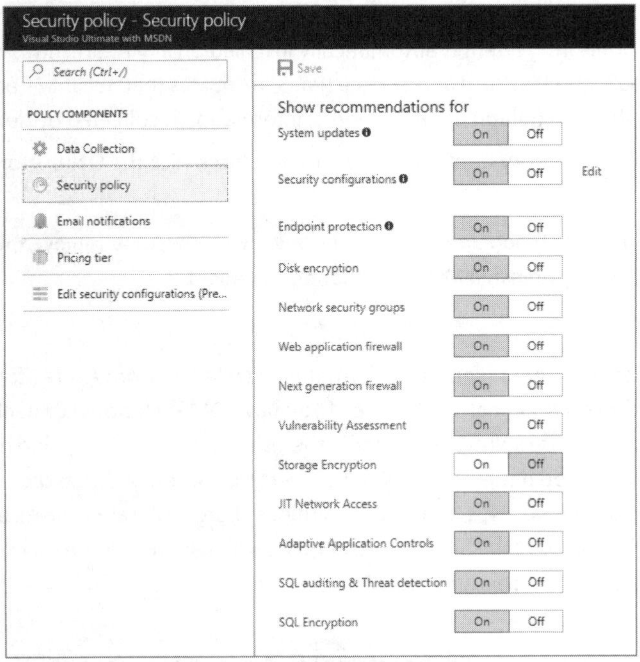

FIGURE 3-4 Configuring security policy.

Security Center uses your input in this blade to create a series of **recommendations** for you. It's like having a cybersecurity expert review your configuration and provide recommendations that you can use to significantly enhance the security of your deployment. Some recommendations have mitigations built right into Azure Security Center, making maximizing security a one-click event. Most recommendations, however, will require you to manually carry out some activities to instantiate them. In those cases, Security Center provides you with instructions on how to do it yourself.

When enabled (turned on), this is what the policies do:

- **System Updates** This policy informs you if your system is out of date when it comes to security updates. For IaaS virtual machines (VMs) that run Windows, Service Center uses Windows Update or WSUS to make the determination (based on what the Windows machine is configured to use). Linux-based VMs use a distribution-specific package-management system. This policy also checks PaaS VMs and informs you if updates are recommended.

- **Security Configurations** This is a type of vulnerability assessment (VA) that Security Center performs. You can use this VA as-is or pair it with partner solutions such as Qualys. Security Center is always working to improve VA. To get an idea of the baselines against which these VAs are compared, see https://gallery.technet.microsoft.com/Azure-Security-Center-a789e335. Appendix B explains how to customize your security configuration.

- **Endpoint Protection**   This is otherwise known as antivirus (AV) and antimalware (AM). Azure Security Center checks whether you have AV and AM installed and alerts you if you don't. It then gives you the option to automatically install Microsoft Antimalware for Azure. Alternatively, you can install any of a number of partner AV/AM solutions.

- **Disk Encryption**   A lot of Service Center customers assume that this policy pertains to Azure Storage Encryption, but it doesn't. Rather, it refers to Azure Disk Encryption, which you can use to encrypt the virtual disks that compose a VM. For more information about Azure Disk Encryption, see https://aka.ms/AzDiskEncry.

- **Network Security Groups**   A network security group (NSG) is essentially a basic stateful packet filter that enables you to control inbound and outbound traffic based on a 5-tuple. It is not application layer–aware. Although the NSG is very basic, it gets the job done. Security Center checks your configuration to determine whether your system is allowing inbound connections from the Internet to your VMs. Because all VMs will always be on an Azure virtual network, it's important that you have NSGs in place to control traffic. Security Center will help ensure you haven't forgotten.

- **Web Application Firewall**   There are two circumstances in which Security Center will likely recommend that you erect a web application firewall (WAF). The first, which is unlikely, is if you have a "classic" VM assigned an instance-level IP address that accepts incoming connections on TCP port 80, TCP port 443, or both. The second (and more likely) is that you have an external load balancer that is listening on TCP port 80, TCP port 443, or both and is forwarding connections to a public-facing web server. In either scenario, Azure Security Center will tell you to get a WAF in place, which is a great idea.

- **Next Generation Firewall**   There may be times when incoming and outgoing connections of VMs and subnets use protocols other than web protocols. If so, Security Center will recommend you use something more robust than a basic WAF: a Next-Generation Firewall (NGFW). NGFWs can perform numerous sophisticated application-layer inspections, as well as protocol validation and intrusion detection and prevention.

- **Vulnerability Assessment**   Wait a minute—aren't the recommendations provided by Security Center a type of VA? Yes. But like any good doctor, Azure Security Center suggests you get a second opinion from another VA solution. Security Center supports numerous VA solutions, such as Qualys, whose findings are tightly integrated with the alerting function in the Security Center console.

- **Storage Encryption**   Azure Storage Service Encryption is an Azure Storage feature that automatically encrypts information in Azure Storage. Currently, encryption is available for binary large object (BLOB) and file storage. If Security Center finds that you haven't turned on encryption for storage, it will suggest that you do so.

- **JIT Network Access**   Security Center has a just-in-time (JIT) access feature that enables you to constrain how long access from the Internet to VMs is allowed and to constrain who is allowed access. In most cases, access to VMs from the Internet is allowed for management purposes. For example, for Windows VMs, inbound TCP port 3389 (for RDP) and inbound TCP port 22 (for Linux) are allowed. The problem is that brute-force attacks against VMs are very common, so you should allow those protocols inbound access only when required. JIT network access enables you to control who has inbound access and for how long.

- **Adaptive Application Controls** This specifies whether adaptive application controls will be used and monitored.

- **SQL Auditing & Threat Detection** Azure SQL includes a very advanced threat prevention, detection, and remediation system. You can integrate SQL's comprehensive security protections into Security Center by enabling it in policy. This tells Security Center to check what the SQL security facilities have to say about the current security configuration state of the SQL server.

- **SQL Encryption** This Security Center check ensures that SQL encryption is on at rest and on the wire. This includes SQL TDE, CLE, and SQL Always On encryption.

> **NOTE** By the time you read this book, there's a good chance this interface will look different—or maybe it won't change at all. It's impossible to predict. Regardless, be aware that security policies direct the recommendations you'll receive from Security Center.

Next-generation Azure Security Center security policy

The next version of Security Center security policy will be a lot more powerful. Here's why:

- It will be connected to Azure Policy, so you'll have more global influence over policy as it pertains to Security Center.
- Policy elements will be more configurable and customizable.
- You'll be able to define your own policy elements.

> **NOTE** At the time of this writing, the next-generation version of Security Center security policy is in public preview, so we expect some changes, especially in the appearance of its interface. We expect that the core functionality will remain intact, however.

The Data Collection blade

The first place you'll notice a change is in the **Data Collection** blade. In the previous version, your work was done after you configured the workspace configuration (as discussed in the previous section). With the updated **Data Collection** blade, you'll be asked about the data collection configuration for security events. (For more information about what is collected by Security Center, visit https://aka.ms/ASCDataSecurity.) As shown in Figure 3-5, you have four options:

- **All Events** If you select this option, Security Center will surface all security events. In other words, if you choose this option, there will be no filtering of events. You'll see them all. At times, and for some deployments, this can introduce a significant amount of noise into the system.

- **Common** When you select this option, Security Center surfaces a filtered subset of events. Microsoft considers these events—including login and logout events—to provide sufficient detail to represent a reasonable audit trail. Other events, such as Kerberos operations, security group changes, and more, are included based on industry consensus as to what constitutes a full audit trail.

- **Minimal** Choosing this setting results in the surfacing of fewer events than the **Common** setting, although we aren't sure how many fewer or what types of events are omitted. Microsoft worked with customers to ensure that this configuration surfaces enough events that successful breaches are detected and that important low-volume events are recorded, but logout events aren't recorded, so it doesn't support a full user audit trail.

> **NOTE** The key to success here is to understand the difference between **Minimal** and **Common.** We suggest you test both configurations to see which one meets your needs.

- **None** This setting doesn't really mean *none*—more like *almost none*. When you enable this option, your security dashboards in Security Center will contain information drawn from Windows firewall logs and from source assessments done by antimalware, baseline assessments, and update evaluations. It includes no security alerts and no information from the operating system logs or App Locker logs.

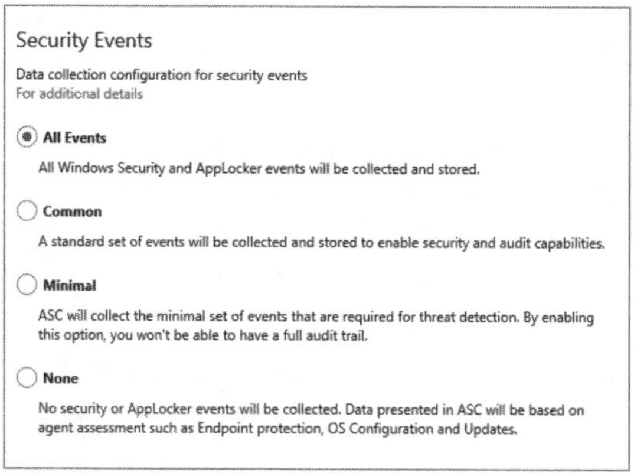

Security Events

Data collection configuration for security events
For additional details

◉ **All Events**
    All Windows Security and AppLocker events will be collected and stored.

◯ **Common**
    A standard set of events will be collected and stored to enable security and audit capabilities.

◯ **Minimal**
    ASC will collect the minimal set of events that are required for threat detection. By enabling this option, you won't be able to have a full audit trail.

◯ **None**
    No security or AppLocker events will be collected. Data presented in ASC will be based on agent assessment such as Endpoint protection, OS Configuration and Updates.

FIGURE 3-5 Setting filtering for security events.

NOTE For an up-to-date list of security and App Locker event IDs, see https://
docs.microsoft.com/en-us/azure/security-center/security-center-enable-data-
collection#data-collection-tier.

The Policy Management blade

Now we can move to the big change: security policy configuration. We'll go into more detail on Azure Policy later in this chapter; at this point, let's focus on the Azure Security Center experience. When you select the **Security Policy** option, the **Policy Management** blade opens. (See Figure 3-6.) Select the subscription whose policy you want to configure.

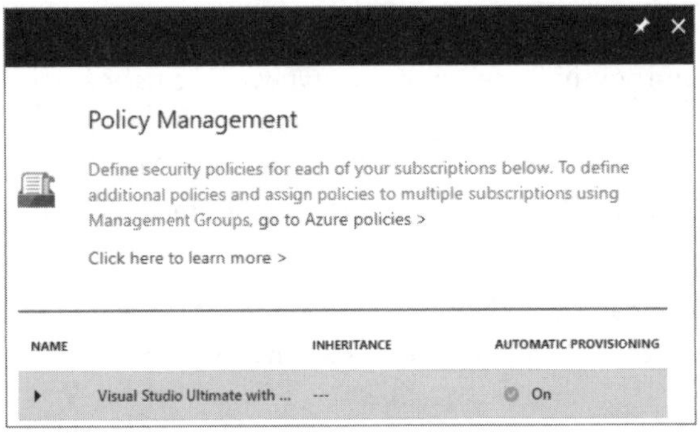

FIGURE 3-6 Selecting the subscription whose policy you want to configure.

By default, Azure Policy creates a set of policies for Security Center that is similar to those of the previous policy engine. Although policy configuration options look different, Azure Policy maps the same 13 policies as Azure Security Center. As shown in Figure 3-7, the policy-management experience is completely different from the previous version. While the default Azure Security Center policies in the new version of Security Center are likely to be the same as in the current one, there will be options for adding new policies. These might include policies created by Azure security (based on discoveries made by the Azure security team). In addition, you can create policies yourself.

Because it's likely that the appearance of the user interface will change, we won't spend much time on that here. The key things to note include the following (see Figure 3-7):

- **Policies and Parameters** This section (in the bottom left of Figure 3-7) contains all the policies that have been defined for this subscription.
- **Available Definitions** This contains a list of policy definitions that can be added to the Azure Security Center security policy. Many of these are new and weren't available until Azure Security Center security policy became integrated with Azure Policy.

FIGURE 3-7 Viewing Azure Security Center policy within the Azure Policy console.

Security Center policy as defined by Azure Policy is still somewhat in flux, so detailed information is not available at this time. Although Azure Policy can be assigned to a resource group, as of this writing that capability is not supported for Security Center security policy. This means the Azure Policy options you configure will be applied to the entire subscription. However, the information included in this chapter represents the most current information at the time of this writing.

The Email Notifications blade

In the left pane of the Security Policy screen, under Policy Components, click the **Email Notifications** option. You'll see the following options (see Figure 3-8):

- **Security Contact Emails** Microsoft uses any email addresses you enter in this box to contact you if it ascertains that one or more of your resources has been compromised. You can enter as many email addresses as you want here. Be certain, however, that any email addresses you include are secured with two-factor authentication. Information shared in these email notifications may contain confidential information, and you want to minimize your risk and exposure.

- **Phone Number** Enter your phone number (just one) here using the international format—for example, +1-415-555-5555. As with the security contact emails, this phone number will be used by Azure security to contact you about possible compromises of your resources. Write in your policies and procedures documents that this number should be audited periodically. It's easy to forget what number you entered here, and there is always a chance that this number will change. Don't put yourself in the position of having to tell your boss, "Oh, I completely forgot about that! I guess that's why we didn't hear from Microsoft."

- **Send Me Emails About Alerts** If you don't select this option, then Microsoft will contact you only if it finds that your resources have been compromised based on information available to it. If you want the email addresses you included in the list on this page to get email alerts, then enable this option.

> **NOTE** If you do not select this option, you will not receive emails for all alerts. You will receive email notifications only for high-severity alerts.

- **Send Email Also to Subscription Owners** Selecting this option adds the email addresses of any subscription owners to the list of users who will receive emails about high-priority alerts.

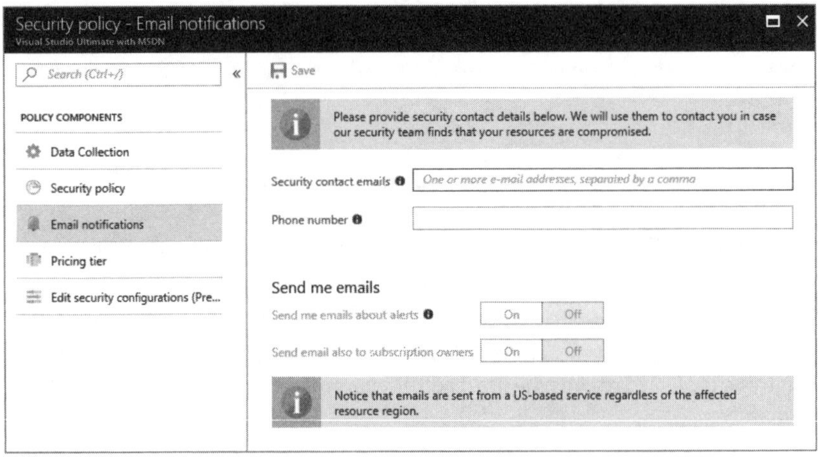

FIGURE 3-8 Configuring email notifications.

The Pricing Tier blade

The final policy component you need to configure is the **pricing tier**. (See Figure 3-9.) Pricing tiers define what features you get with Security Center. Everyone has access to the Free pricing tier and its corresponding protections. These include the following:

- **Security assessment** Security assessment includes the analysis of your subscriptions and their current security state. After Security Center assesses the security state, it creates security recommendations for your review. You can automatically remediate these recommendations in the Security Center console or, if automatic remediation isn't available, carry out steps provided to you by the recommendations.

- **Security recommendations** These are security recommendations based on comparisons with a basic security policy available to all Security Center customers. Some recommendations have automatic mitigations built in, while others provide links to instructions on how you can manually instantiate the recommendation.

- **Basic security policy** A basic security policy is included with Security Center, which you'll be able to read from the Azure policy that flows down to Security Center. These policy definitions compose the basic security policy.

- **Connected partner solutions** These are security solutions that can be tightly integrated with Security Center so that Security Center can surface any security events and information they detect. Examples of such security solutions include endpoint protection, WAF, NGFW, and VA.

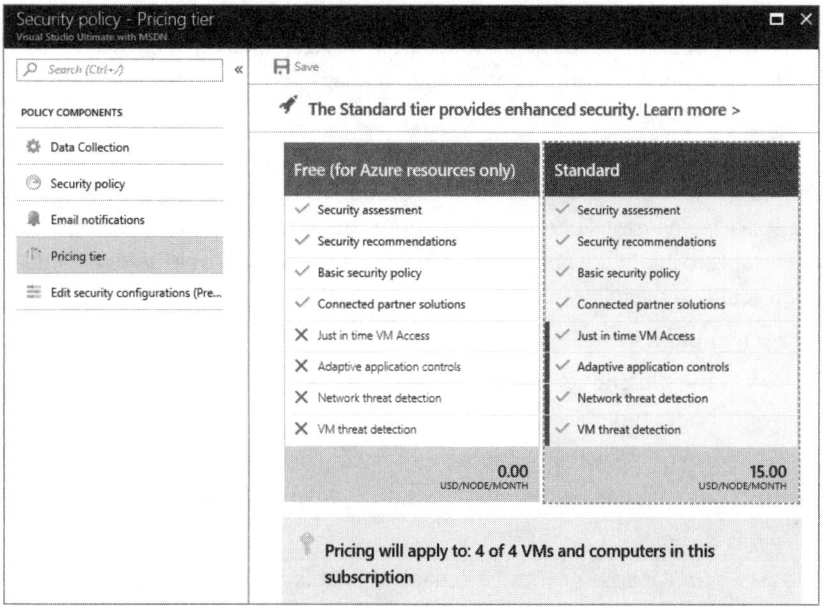

FIGURE 3-9 Pricing tier selection.

Azure Policy

Azure Security Center policies are driven by overarching Azure policies. This significantly improves the overall reach and management of your Security Center policies. In addition, centralized management of policies is now available, making the governance of your Azure solutions that much easier.

It's well known in all areas of IT—enterprise, small business, and even startup—that policy-based management streamlines and increases IT operations. This is especially true in security, where the combination of technologies and processes becomes a potent weapon. In fact, if the right policies are in place and are carried out assiduously, then even less-than-optimal technology can effectively protect an organization.

With this in mind, Microsoft has introduced Azure Policy. Azure Policy enables you to create, assign, and manage a variety of policy definitions, many of which can be applied to Security Center. When these policy definitions are in place, you can compare them to your current configuration. Any resources that do not adhere to the policy will be deemed out of compliance. You can then focus on these out-of-compliance assets to bring them into compliance.

Policy definitions and assignments

A policy assignment is a policy definition that has been assigned to take place within a specific scope. *Scope* refers to all the resource groups, subscriptions, or management groups to which a policy definition is assigned. This scope might range from an Azure management group to a resource group. (A management group enables you to manage access, policy, costs, and compliance across subscriptions.)

Policy assignments are inherited by all child resources. If a policy is applied to a resource group, it is applied to all the resources in that resource group. However, you can exclude a sub-scope from a *policy assignment*. For example, suppose you want to allow only a certain subset of users to be able to configure networking resources for your Azure virtual networks. To achieve this, you could do the following:

1. Configure a subscription scope.
2. Assign a policy to the subscription scope that prevents users within that scope from creating networking resources.
3. Exempt one resource group within the subscription scope from the policy.
4. Grant access to this resource group to users whom you trust with creating networking resources.

This provides a very granular access control mechanism, enabling support of the principle of least privilege. The use of the exclusion option actually enables you to define what might be a primary goal.

Initiative definitions and assignments

An initiative definition is *collection of policy definitions* that are tailored toward achieving a singular overarching goal. Grouping policies into an initiative definition simplifies the assignment and management of policy definitions. For example, you could create an initiative called Azure Security Center Recommendations. The policy definitions populating this initiative definition would track all the available security recommendations in your Security Center configuration. (See Figure 3-10.)

An initiative assignment is an *initiative definition assigned to a specific scope*. This scope could range from a management group to a resource group. Initiative assignments reduce the need for the creation of several initiative definitions for each scope. Returning to the Azure Security Center Recommendations example, this initiative definition could be assigned to different scopes. For example, one could be assigned to one subscription, and a second one could be assigned to another subscription.

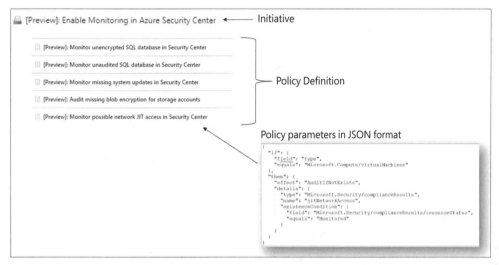

FIGURE 3-10   Azure Policy components grouped in an initiative definition.

Exploring Azure Policy

Let's explore Azure Policy. Follow these steps:

1. Open the Getting Started screen, shown in Figure 3-11, and click **Getting Started**.

> **NOTE**   Many of the screens shown here may change by the time you read this chapter.

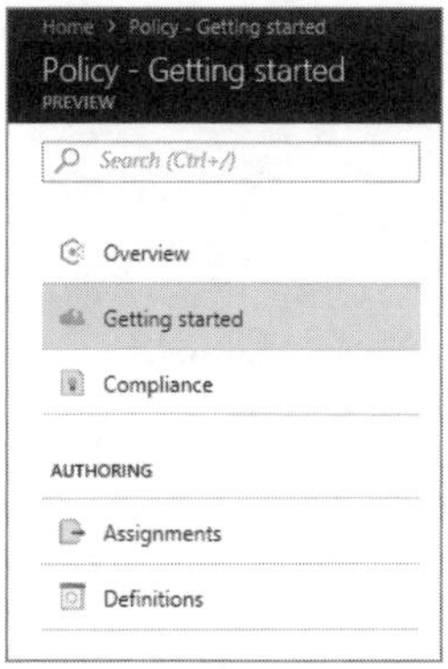

FIGURE 3-11   The Azure Policy Getting Started screen.

The **Welcome to Azure Policy** blade opens. (See Figure 3-12.) This screen includes the following sections:

- **Browse Policy and Initiative Definitions**   This section includes a View Definitions link. This link provides access to existing policy definitions and initiative definitions.

- **Assign a Definition to a Scope of Resources**   This section contains an Assign a Policy link and an Assign an Initiative link. Click these links to assign a policy or an initiative, respectively.

- **View Policy Evaluation Results**   You can click the Go to Compliance link in this section to see what resources are outside the constraints defined in your policies and policy initiatives.

- **Handle Special Cases with Exclusions**   Clicking the Go to Assignments link in this section enables you to apply exclusions to policies. You can apply exclusions to a resource, a resource group, or a scope to exempt it from policy rules. Exclusions are applied on a per-assignment basis.

As shown in Figure 3-12, the Welcome to Azure Policy blade also includes the following buttons:

- **Assign a Policy**   This assigns a single policy.
- **Assign an Initiative**   This assigns an initiative instead of a policy.

Welcome to Azure Policy

Azure Policy allows you to assess and enforce governing standards across all your resources at scale.

1   Browse Policy and Initiative Definitions

A policy definition expresses what to evaluate and what action to take. For example, you could prevent VMs from being deployed if they are exposed to a public IP address. Learn how to write Policy Definitions

An initiative definition is a set of policy definitions to help track your compliance state for a larger goal. Even if you have a single policy, we recommend to use initiative if you anticipate to increase the numbers over time.

We've already added some common Policy Definitions for you.

View Definitions

2   Assign a Definition to a scope of resources

Assign Policy or Initiative Definitions to a scope of resources to take effect. You can assign Policies to Management Groups, Subscriptions or Resource Groups.

Assign a Policy

Assign an Initiative

3   View Policy Evaluation results

Once a Policy or Initiative is assigned, we evaluate the state of compliance for all your resources. You can view these details in the Assignments tab. Learn more about compliance results

Go to Compliance

4   Handle special cases with exclusions

Individual resources, resource groups, and subscriptions within a scope can be exempted from having policy rules affect it. Exclusions are handled individually for each assignment.

Go to Assignments

Assign a Policy   Assign an Initiative

FIGURE 3-12   The Welcome to Azure Policy blade.

2. Click the **View Definitions** link in the **Browse Policy and Initiative Definitions** section of the Welcome to Azure Policy blade.

3. A screen listing initiative definitions opens. (See Figure 3-13.) Click the ellipsis to the right of the **ASC Default** entry in the list and click **View Definition** in the menu that appears to see the policies that compose the ACS Default initiative. (See Figure 3-14.)

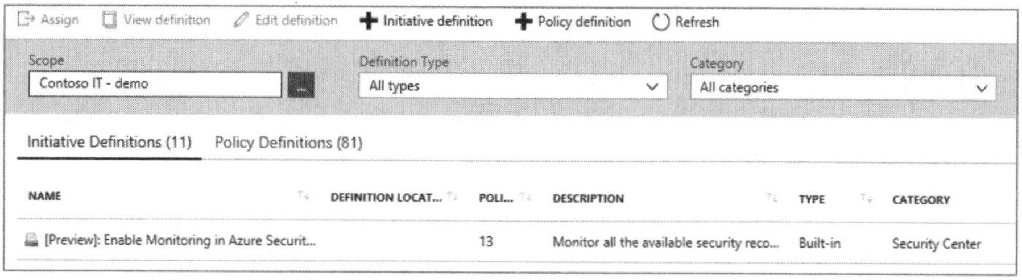

FIGURE 3-13   This screen lists initiative definitions and provides a link to a list of policy definitions.

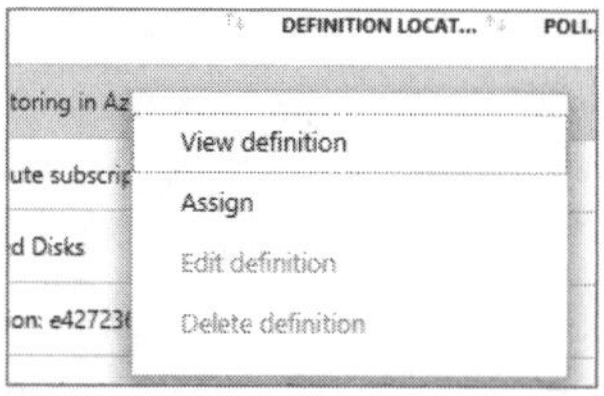

FIGURE 3-14   Selecting the View Definition option.

4. A screen appears showing the list of policy definitions that compose the selected initiative definition. (See Figure 3-15.) Click a policy definition.

FIGURE 3-15   Policy elements.

5. A properties pane opens with a **Details** tab and a **Json** tab. Under the **Details** tab, you see a description of the policy definition and other information. (See Figure 3-16.)

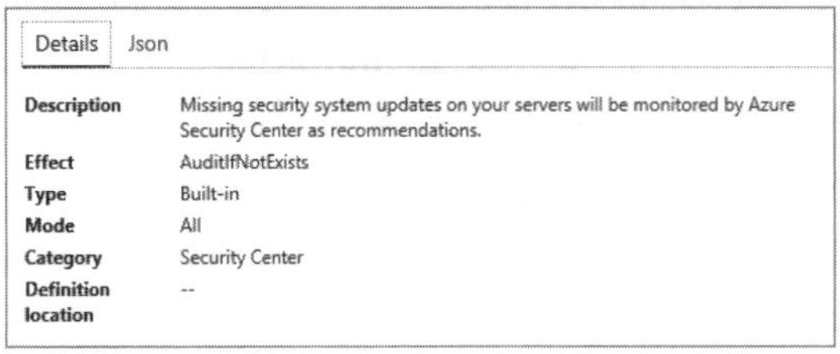

Details	Json	
Description	Missing security system updates on your servers will be monitored by Azure Security Center as recommendations.	
Effect	AuditIfNotExists	
Type	Built-in	
Mode	All	
Category	Security Center	
Definition location	--	

FIGURE 3-16   Details of an Azure Policy definition.

6. Click the **Json** tab to see the JSON information used to define the policy. (See Figure 3-17.)

TIP   If you are well versed in JSON, you can configure your own policy definitions.

```
Details | Json
1  {
2    "if": {
3      "field": "type",
4      "in": [
5        "Microsoft.Compute/virtualMachines",
6        "Microsoft.ClassicCompute/virtualMachines",
7        "Microsoft.OperationalInsights/workspaces"
8      ]
9    },
10   "then": {
11     "effect": "AuditIfNotExists",
12     "details": {
13       "type": "Microsoft.Security/complianceResults",
14       "name": "systemUpdates",
15       "existenceCondition": {
16         "field": "Microsoft.Security/complianceResults/resource
```

FIGURE 3-17   JSON configuration for an Azure policy definition.

NOTE   For more information on working with Azure Policy, see https://docs.microsoft .com/en-us/azure/azure-policy/azure-policy-introduction.

Customizing your Security Center security policies

In an environment where you have multiple subscriptions, you might need to customize your Security Center security policies to either add new definitions or remove old ones. Follow these steps to create a new initiative and apply it to your subscription:

1. Open the **Azure Portal** and sign in as a user who has **Security Admin** privileges.
2. In the left pane, click **All Services** and type **Policy**.
3. In the Policy page, under **Authoring**, click **Definitions**.
4. Click the plus sign next to the **Initial Definition** entry.
5. In the **Initiative Definition** blade, in the **Name** box, type a name for this initiative.
6. In the **Description** box, type a brief explanation of this initiative.
7. In the **Definition Location** box, select the subscription for which you want to store this policy.
8. In the **Category** section, you can link to an existing category or create a new one. In this example, create a new one and name it **Custom Policies**.
9. In the **Available Definitions** pane to the right, select a definition you want to add to your policy and click the plus sign. Repeat for as many definitions as you want to add.
10. Click **Save**.
11. Select the definition you created and click **Assign**.
12. In the New Assign Initiative blade, type the name for this definition in the **Name** box.
13. In the **Description** box, type a brief explanation of this policy.
14. In the **Scope** box, click the ellipsis button (the one with three dots).
15. In the **Scope** blade, select the subscription and click **Select**.
16. Click **Assign**.
17. In the left navigation pane of the **Policy** page, click **Assignments**. You should see your assignment in the subscription scope.

Azure Security Center RBAC and permissions

Security Center supports a somewhat coarse level of role-based access control (RBAC). The goal of any RBAC initiative is to provide users with just enough authority to get their work done, but no more. As you learned in Chapter 2, Security Center supports two key RBAC roles:

- **Security reader**   A user with security reader permissions can view recommendations, alerts, security policy, and security states. However, as the name of the role suggests, the user cannot make any changes to this information.

- **Security administrator**   A user with security administrator permissions can read anything in Security Center, make changes to security policy, and view security alerts.

These roles are relevant only to Security Center. For example, just because someone has security administrator privileges in Security Center doesn't mean he or she will have that level of access elsewhere in your system.

Many organizations consider this desirable. For example, in the DevOps world, where code moves quickly, the DevOps team might not be tightly integrated with the security team (although it should be). However, all areas in your organization need security team oversight to avoid expensive consequences. Therefore, you want to give security teams some visibility and control over the DevOps security policy (which should be designed and defined by the security team). Security Center RBAC roles allow for this kind of division of responsibility.

Azure supports numerous RBAC roles. Figure 3-18 outlines what some of the most commonly used roles can do within Security Center.

Role	Edit security policy	Apply security recommendations for a resource	Dismiss alerts and recommendations	View alerts and recommendations
Subscription Owner	X	X	X	X
Subscription Contributor	X	X	X	X
Resource Group Owner	--	X	--	X
Resource Group Contributor	--	X	--	X
Reader	--	--	--	X
Security Administrator	X	--	X	X
Security Reader	--	--	--	X

FIGURE 3-18   RBAC roles and permissions used by Azure Security Center.

Chapter 4

Mitigating security issues

Recent ransomware outbreaks, such as WannaCry and Petya, reinforced the importance of having a vulnerability-management system. But they also reinforced the fact that many computers are not fully updated and do not use the most secure configuration.

To enhance your overall security posture, you need to increase your protection. A security assessment is critical to identifying the current security state of your assets—and what you need to do to improve it. Azure Security Center can perform a security assessment for all major workloads: compute, network, storage, and applications. The result of this security assessment is a set of recommendations that will help you enhance the security posture of your workloads.

In this chapter, you will learn how to use Security Center to perform a security assessment for major workloads, and how to use the result of this assessment to improve your defense system.

Compute recommendations

In Chapter 2, you learned about the Security Center agent and how it performs an initial security assessment. As part of your onboarding process, you should make sure to address all critical (high-priority) recommendations first, evaluate all other recommendations, and apply the recommendations according to your environment's needs.

Some recommendations may require system downtime—for example, to apply certain security updates. This means that after you identify the changes that need to be made in the target system, you may need to start a change-control process to maintain compliance with the security assessment.

> **TIP** Recommendations are applicable only for operating systems that are supported in Security Center. Visit the latest version of supported operating systems at https://aka.ms/ASCSupportedOS.

Compute recommendations include recommendations for Azure virtual machines (VMs) and non-Azure computers. These recommendations vary depending on the environment. For this reason, it is important to be aware of the full list of recommendations that might apply to your environment:

- **Endpoint Protection Issues** This shows a list of computers that are missing an endpoint protection. Alternatively, it can serve as a warning about endpoint protection not being fully updated in a target system.

- **Missing Scan Data** This shows the systems that are missing the most current scan data collected by the agent.

- **Remediate Security Configurations** This shows a list of computers (Windows and Linux) that are not using the most secure configuration according to Common Configuration Enumeration (CCE) standards.

- **Missing System Updates** This shows a list of computers that are missing security and critical updates.

- **Missing Disk Encryption** This shows a list of Azure VMs that don't have disk encryption enabled.

- **Vulnerability Assessment Not Installed** In some scenarios Security Center may recommend the installation of a vulnerability-assessment solution, such as Qualys, on one or more Azure VMs.

- **VM Agent Is Missing or Not Responding** When Security Center recognizes that a VM is missing the agent, or that the agent is installed but not responding, Security Center will list all Azure VMs that are exhibiting this behavior.

- **Restart Pending** This appears when Security Center identifies that there is a restart pending in one or more Azure VMs.

- **Apply a Just-in-Time Network Access Control** This suggests that you apply just-in-time network access for one or more Azure VMs.

- **OS Version Not Updated** This is specifically for Platform as a Service (PaaS). It recommends that you update the operating system (OS) version for your cloud service to the most recent version available for your OS family.

> **TIP** Keep in mind that new recommendations may be included without further notice. For the latest list of compute recommendations, see https://aka.ms/ASCComputeRec.

The following sections cover the implementation of some of these recommendations.

Setting up endpoint protection

Security Center can detect whether your VM or computer has endpoint protection installed on it, and whether this endpoint protection is up to date. However, this capability will detect only a certain number of supported endpoint protection partners. At the time of this writing, the supported partners are as follows:

- Windows Defender (Microsoft Antimalware)
- System Center Endpoint Protection (Microsoft Antimalware)
- Trend Micro – All versions
- Symantec v12.1.1100+

> **TIP** The list of partners is always in revision, and new partners may be included without further notice. For the latest list of supported endpoint protection, visit https://aka.ms/ASCPartners.

If a recommendation suggests the installation of endpoint protection in non-Azure VMs and computers, you will need to do this manually, following the instructions from the anti-malware vendor of your choice. For VMs in Azure, System Center will guide you through the installation process, and you can choose the endpoint protection based on the options available in the Azure marketplace. Follow these steps to remediate a compute recommendation by deploying Windows Defender (Microsoft Antimalware) in an Azure VM:

1. Open the **Azure Portal** and sign in as a user who has **Security Admin** privileges.
2. In the left pane, click **Security Center**.
3. In the left pane of the Security Center window, under **Prevention**, click **Compute**.
4. Click the **Endpoint Protection Issues** recommendation. The dashboard shown in Figure 4-1 appears.

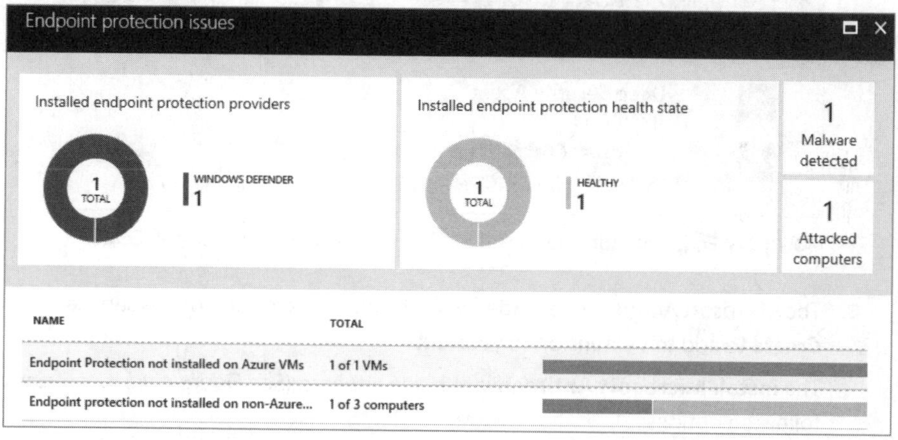

FIGURE 4-1 The Endpoint Protection Issues dashboard.

5. Click the **Endpoint Protection Not Installed on Azure VMs** recommendation. The blade shown in Figure 4-2 appears.

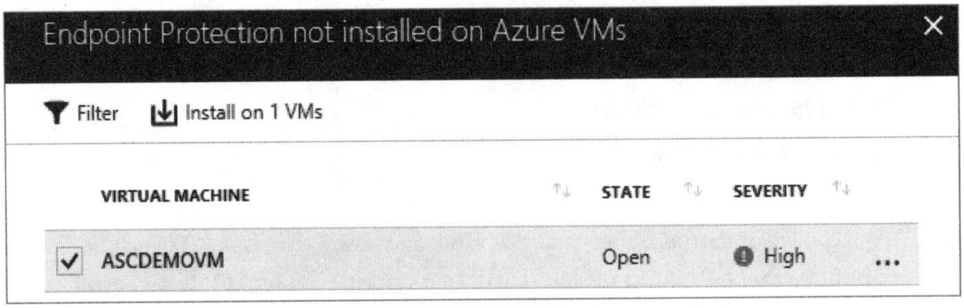

FIGURE 4-2 List of Azure VMs that need endpoint protection.

6. Leave the VM selected and click **Install on 1 VMs**.

> **NOTE** If there is more than one VM in the list, select only the ones for which you want to install an endpoint protection solution.

7. The **Select Endpoint Protection** blade opens. (See Figure 4-3.) It contains two options:
   - **Microsoft Antimalware** This is a free solution from Microsoft.
   - **Deep Security Agent** This is a fee-based solution from TrendMicro. If you select this option, you'll need to provide your license information.

   In this case, click **Microsoft Antimalware**.

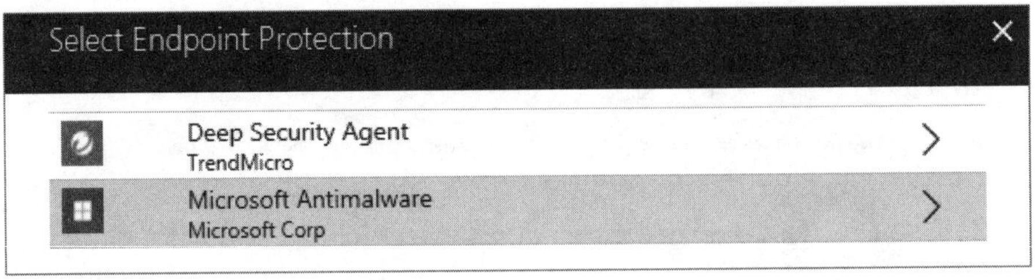

FIGURE 4-3 Endpoint protection solutions that are integrated with Security Center.

8. The Microsoft Antimalware blade appears, with a description of this service. Click **Create** to add this extension to your VM.

   The **Install Microsoft Antimalware** blade appears. (See Figure 4-4.) It contains the following options:
   - **Excluded Files and Locations** Here, you can specify any paths or locations to exclude from the scan. To add multiple paths or locations, separate them with semi-colons. This is an optional setting.
   - **Excluded Files and Extensions** This box lets you specify file names or extensions to exclude from the scan. Again, to add multiple names or extensions, you separate them with a semicolon. Note that you should avoid using wildcard characters.

- **Excluded Processes**   Use this box to specify any processes that should be excluded from the scan—again, using semicolons to separate multiple processes.
- **Real-Time Protection**   By default, this check box is enabled. Unless you have a good business reason to do otherwise, you should leave it that way.
- **Run a Scheduled Scan**   Selecting this check box enables you to run a scheduled scan.
- **Scan Type**   If you selected the Run a Scheduled Scan check box, you can use this drop-down list to specify the type of scan. (A quick scan is run by default.)
- **Scan Day**   If you selected the Run a Scheduled Scan check box, you can use this drop-down list to specify the day that the scan will run.
- **Scan Time**   If you selected the Run a Scheduled Scan check box, you can use this drop-down list to specify what time the scan will run. The time is indicated in increments of 60 minutes (60 = 1 AM, 120 = 2AM, and so on).

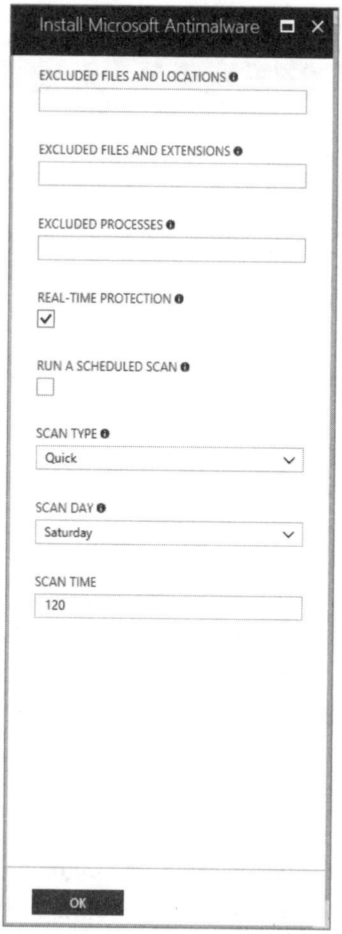

FIGURE 4-4 Options to customize the Microsoft Antimalware installation.

9. Leave the default selections and click the **Create** button. In the upper-right corner of the dashboard, you will see a notification that the installation has started in the target system, as shown in Figure 4-5.

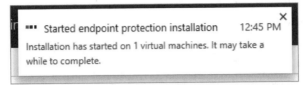

×
■■■ Started endpoint protection installation   12:45 PM
Installation has started on 1 virtual machines. It may take a while to complete.

FIGURE 4-5 Notification that endpoint protection installation has started.

10. Close all blades and go back to the main **Security Center** dashboard. The installation time varies depending on the environment.

11. To verify whether the Microsoft Antimalware extension was installed, open the VM properties in Azure and click the **Extensions** options. (See Figure 4-6.)

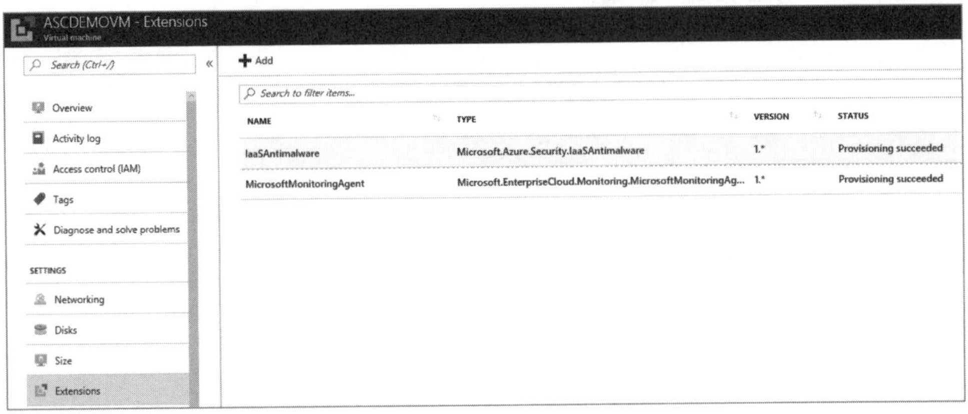

FIGURE 4-6 Validation that the antimalware extension was installed.

Remediate Security Configurations

Security Center uses Common Configuration Enumeration (CCE) standards to validate the security state of a VM or computer's configuration. If a VM or computer is not compliant with the CCE standard that was tested, Security Center will generate a security recommendation. Follow these steps to get a sense of how these recommendations work:

1. Open the **Azure Portal** and sign in as a user who has **Security Admin** privileges.

2. In the left pane, click **Security Center**.

3. In the left pane of the Security Center window, under **Prevention**, click **Compute**.

4. Click **Remediate security configurations**. The **Remediate security configurations** blade appears. (See Figure 4-7.)

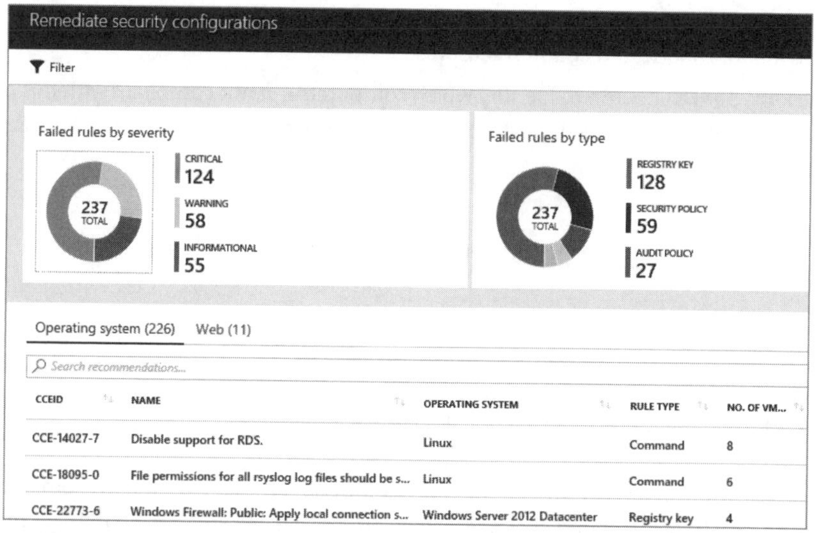

FIGURE 4-7 List of OS vulnerabilities according to CCE standards.

5. In this blade, you can quickly see the number of resources that do not comply with various CCE standards, and the type of standard in question (registry, security policy, or audit policy). For more information on any of these vulnerabilities, click the associated resource to view a comprehensive description. (See Figure 4-8.)

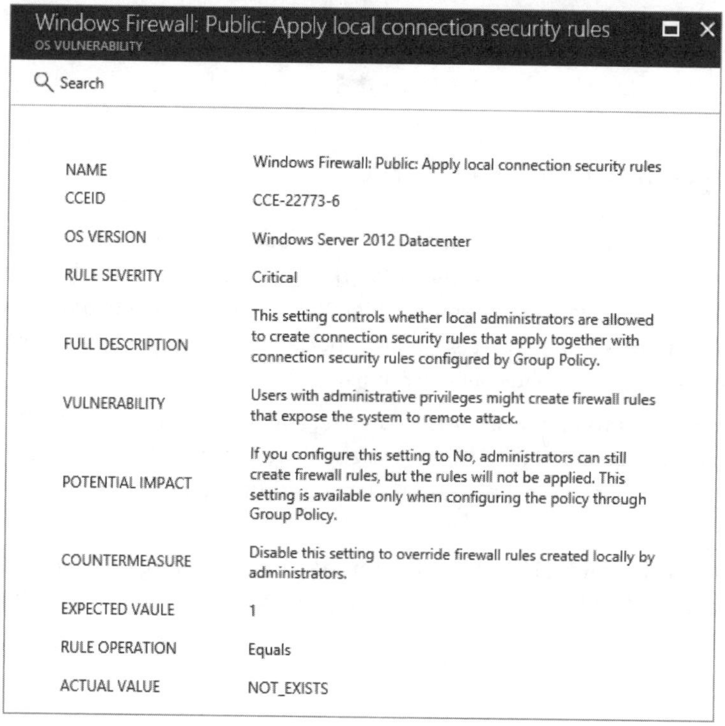

FIGURE 4-8 Details about a vulnerability and how to mitigate it.

6. Read the description to better understand the vulnerability, gauge its potential impact, and identify suggested countermeasures.

7. Click the **Search** button to identify which computers are not compliant with this rule. Azure launches Log Analytics and displays the query result. (See Figure 4-9.)

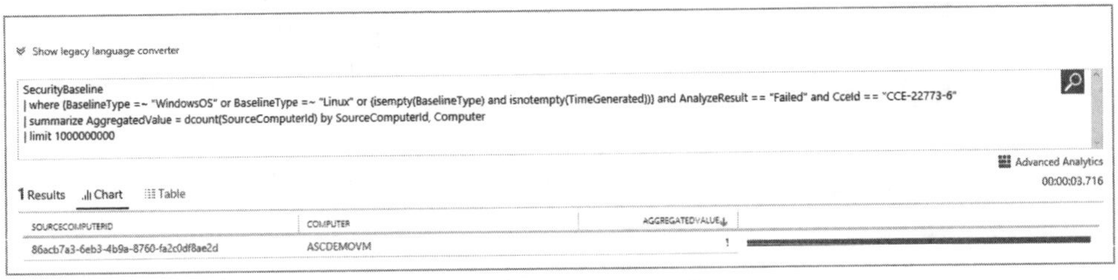

FIGURE 4-9 A list of computers that are not compliant with this rule.

This is an example of a recommendation that cannot be remediated directly from Security Center. The intent here is to bring awareness that some machines are missing the security best practices and to help you identify these machines. From there, you will need to deploy the countermeasure using other tools. Most of these recommendations can be addressed using Group Policy in Active Directory if you are using Windows-based, domain-joined virtual machines.

> **TIP** For information about which CCE rules are tested, visit https://gallery.technet.microsoft.com/Azure-Security-Center-a789e335.

Networking recommendations

An Azure virtual network is a logical isolation of the Azure cloud dedicated to your subscription. Security Center identifies the Azure virtual networks available in your subscription and provides recommendations to improve overall security. Networking recommendations vary depending on the environment. For this reason, it is important to be aware of the full list of recommendations that might apply to your environment:

- **Add a Next Generation Firewall** After scanning your virtual network, Security Center may recommend that you install a Next Generation Firewall (NGFW) in your environment. Because this option is not natively available, Security Center will recommend various partners that can help you with this.

- **Route Traffic Through NGFW Only** This setting suggests that you configure network security group (NSG) rules to force inbound traffic to your VM through your NGFW.

- **NSGs on Subnets Not Enabled**   After scanning your virtual network, Security Center may recommend that you enable an NSG on subnets or VMs.

- **Restrict Access Through Internet Facing Endpoint**   After scanning your virtual network, Security Center may recommend that you configure inbound traffic rules for NSGs.

The following sections cover the implementation of some of these recommendations.

NSGs on subnets not enabled

An NSG contains a list of security rules that allow or deny network traffic to resources connected to Azure Virtual Networks (VNets). You can associate NSGs with VMs, NICs, and subnets. Security Center will verify whether your subnet needs to have an NSG to be more secure. If so, it will create a network recommendation for it. Follow these steps to access the network recommendations:

1. Open the **Azure Portal** and sign in as a user who has **Security Admin** privileges.

2. In the left pane, click **Security Center**.

3. In the left pane of the Security Center window, under **Prevention**, click **Networking**. The **Networking** blade appears. (See Figure 4-10.)

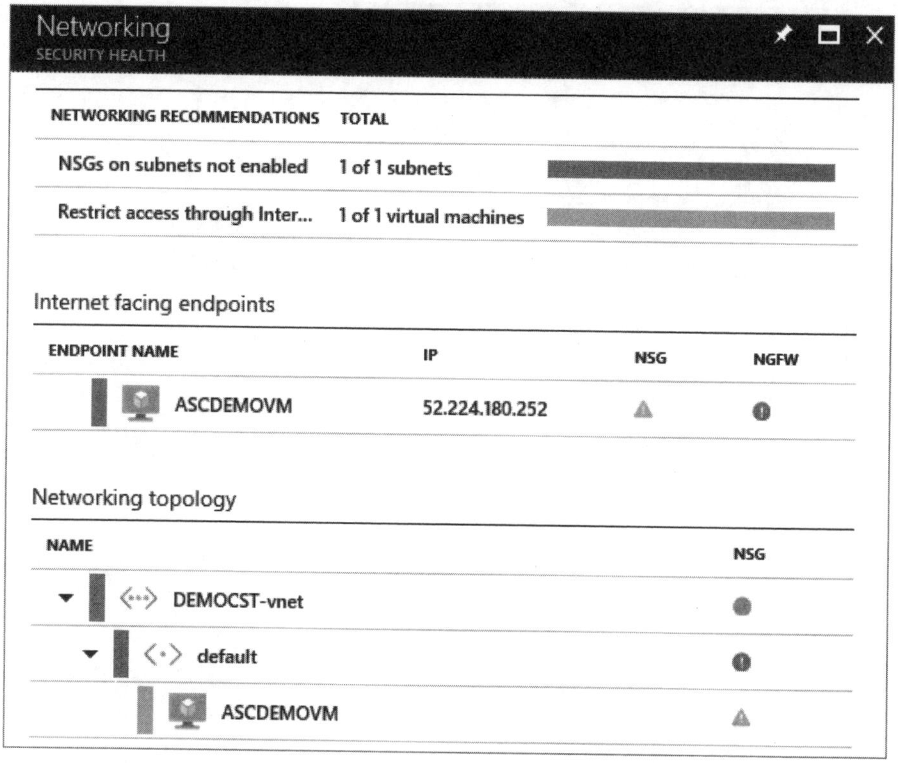

FIGURE 4-10 Networking recommendations vary depending on the Azure Virtual Network environment.

The top of the blade features a list of recommendations specifically for your Azure VNet environment. Below that are recommendations pertaining to endpoints that are exposed to the internet. Finally, the bottom of the blade shows the virtual network topology.

4. Click the **NSGs on Subnet Not Enabled** recommendation. The **Configure Missing Network Security Groups** for Subnets blade appears. (See Figure 4-11.)

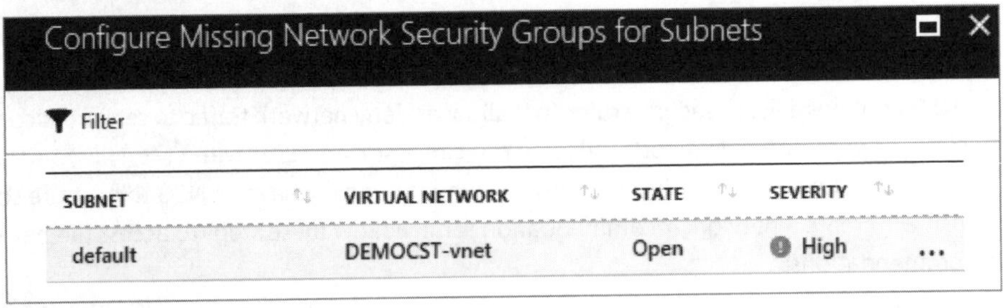

FIGURE 4-11 Subnets that are currently missing network security groups.

5. Select the subnet for which you want to enable the security group. The **Choose Network Security Group** blade appears. (See Figure 4-12.)

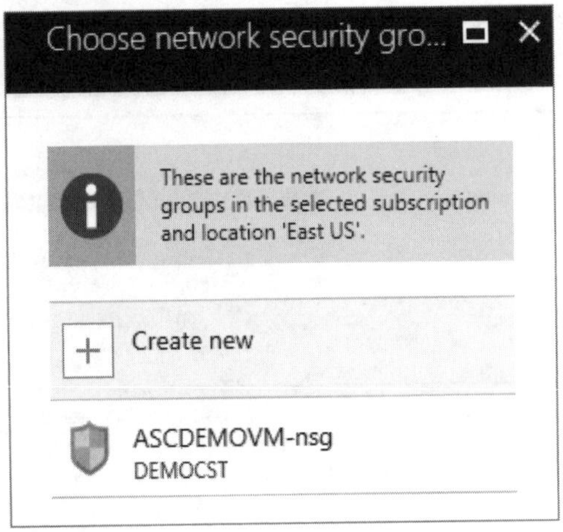

FIGURE 4-12 Usable NSGs.

6. You can select an NSG from the list or click Create New to create a new one. In this case, click **ASCDEMOVM-nsg**. You'll see a notification like the one in Figure 4-13.

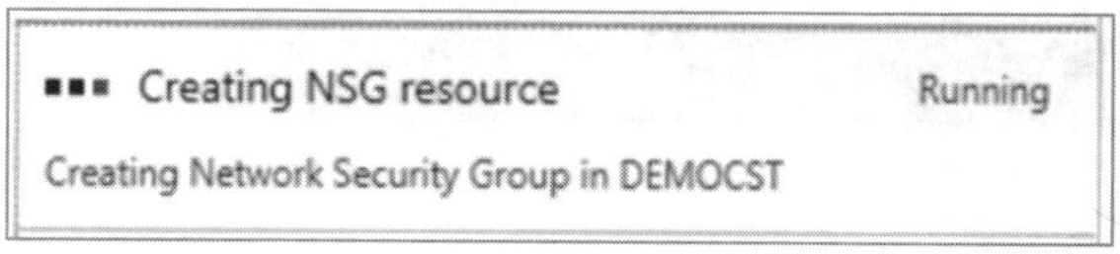

> ■■■ Creating NSG resource   Running
>
> Creating Network Security Group in DEMOCST

FIGURE 4-13 The Creating NSG Resource notification.

When this process is complete, the recommendation will disappear, and you can move on to the next one.

Restrict access through internet-facing endpoint

Security management and control are imperative when dealing with cloud resources. When new VMs are provisioned in your IaaS environment, you need to ensure that these VMs are not fully exposed to the internet. This can be difficult in a large environment. Fortunately, Security Center provides full visibility of internet-facing endpoints in a single location. Follow these steps to access this network recommendation:

1. Open the **Azure Portal** and sign in as a user who has **Security Admin** privileges.

2. In the left pane, click **Security Center**.

3. In the left pane of the Security Center window, under **Prevention**, click **Networking**. The **Networking** blade appears.

4. Click the **Restrict Access Through Internet Facing Endpoint** recommendation. The **Restrict Access Through Internet Facing Endpoint** blade appears. (See Figure 4-14.)

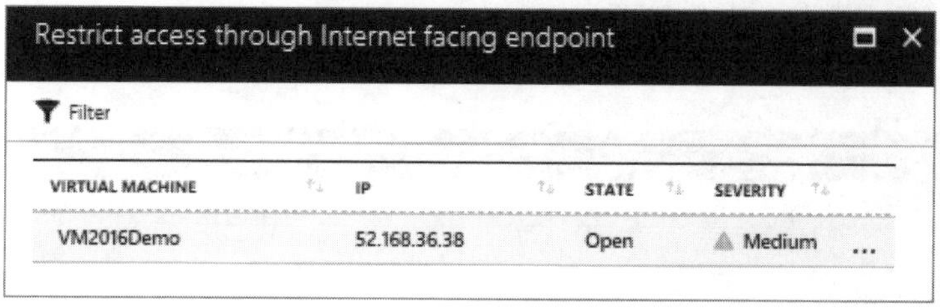

VIRTUAL MACHINE	IP	STATE	SEVERITY	
VM2016Demo	52.168.36.38	Open	⚠ Medium	...

FIGURE 4-14 The Restrict Access Through Internet Facing Endpoint blade.

5. Click a VM in the list. The NSG blade appears. (See Figure 4-15.) Notice that the current inbound rule allows any source (*) to connect to this VM using TCP.

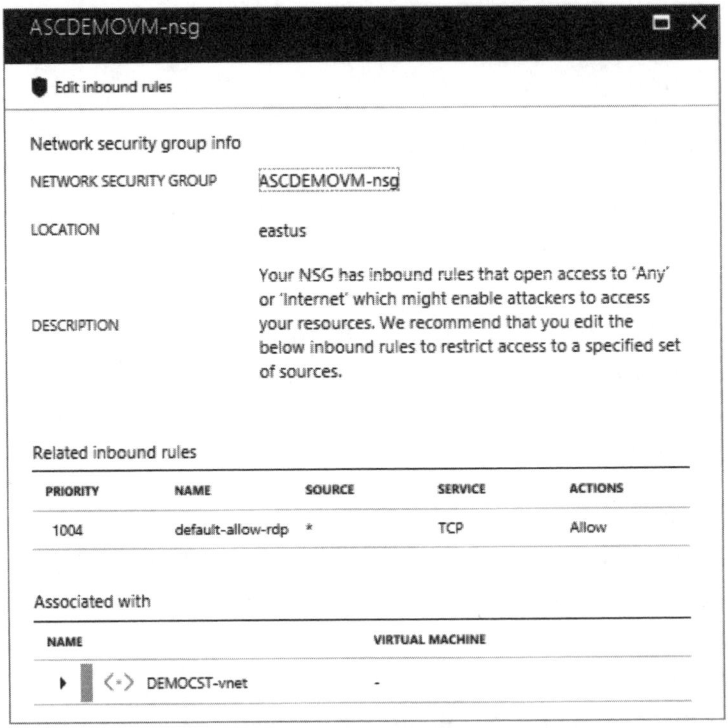

ASCDEMOVM-nsg

🛡 Edit inbound rules

Network security group info

NETWORK SECURITY GROUP	ASCDEMOVM-nsg
LOCATION	eastus
DESCRIPTION	Your NSG has inbound rules that open access to 'Any' or 'Internet' which might enable attackers to access your resources. We recommend that you edit the below inbound rules to restrict access to a specified set of sources.

Related inbound rules

PRIORITY	NAME	SOURCE	SERVICE	ACTIONS
1004	default-allow-rdp	*	TCP	Allow

Associated with

NAME	VIRTUAL MACHINE
▶ ⟨·⟩ DEMOCST-vnet	-

FIGURE 4-15 The NSG blade with the current inbound rules.

6. Click **Edit Inbound Rules** (at the top of the page). The **Inbound Security Rules** page opens. (See Figure 4-16.)

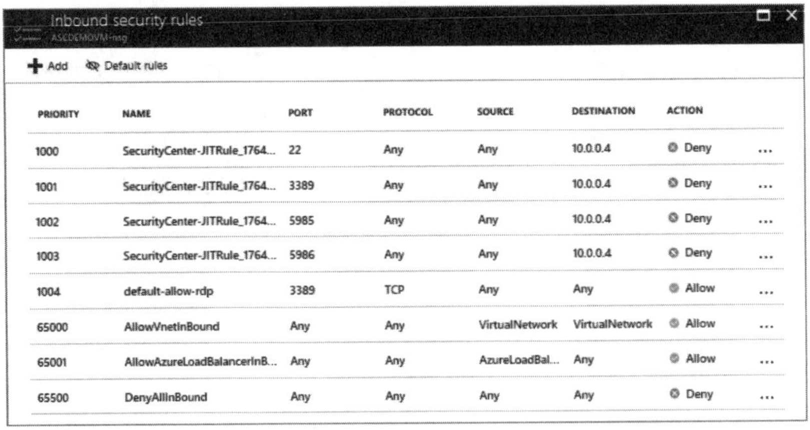

Inbound security rules
ASCDEMOVM-nsg

➕ Add   🏷 Default rules

PRIORITY	NAME	PORT	PROTOCOL	SOURCE	DESTINATION	ACTION	
1000	SecurityCenter-JITRule_1764...	22	Any	Any	10.0.0.4	⊘ Deny	...
1001	SecurityCenter-JITRule_1764...	3389	Any	Any	10.0.0.4	⊘ Deny	...
1002	SecurityCenter-JITRule_1764...	5985	Any	Any	10.0.0.4	⊘ Deny	...
1003	SecurityCenter-JITRule_1764...	5986	Any	Any	10.0.0.4	⊘ Deny	...
1004	default-allow-rdp	3389	TCP	Any	Any	⊘ Allow	...
65000	AllowVnetInBound	Any	Any	VirtualNetwork	VirtualNetwork	⊘ Allow	...
65001	AllowAzureLoadBalancerInB...	Any	Any	AzureLoadBal...	Any	⊘ Allow	...
65500	DenyAllInBound	Any	Any	Any	Any	⊘ Deny	...

FIGURE 4-16 Current list of inbound security rules.

7. You can change the default rule (default-allow-rdp) by altering the source port to a specific IP or IP range. To do so, click **default-allow-rdp**. The **default-allow-rdp** blade appears. (See Figure 4-17.) The settings that you will harden in this page will vary depending on your organization's needs.

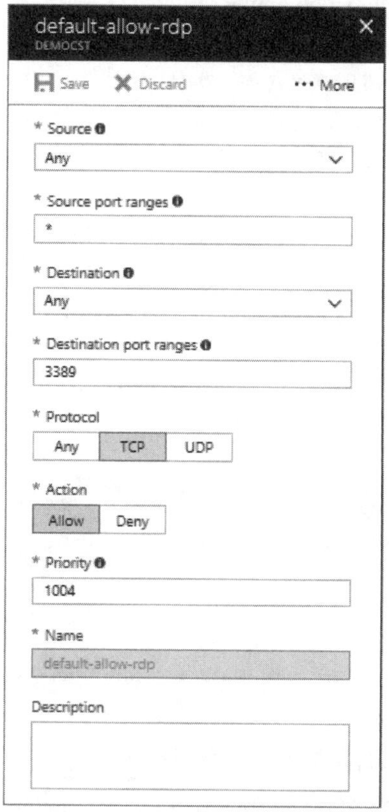

FIGURE 4-17 Creating an inbound rule.

8. To address the Security Center recommendation, you should at least change the value in the **Source** field to a specific IP address or an IP address range.

9. Click **Save**, and close all other blades.

Storage and data

One of the ultimate goals of an attacker is to gain access to a target's data. Therefore, it is important to address all security recommendations for storage (where the data is located) and for the data itself. Security Center meets these requirements by providing security recommendations for Azure SQL databases and for Azure Storage, which includes each VM's virtual hard disk (VHD).

Storage and data recommendations vary depending on the environment. For this reason, it is important to be aware of the full list of recommendations that might apply to your environment:

- **Server Auditing and Threat Detection Not Enabled**   This setting is specific for Azure SQL and is available only if you currently have an Azure SQL workload. It recommends that you enable auditing and threat detection on the server level.
- **Database Auditing and Threat Detection Not Enabled**   This setting recommends that you turn on auditing and threat detection for Azure SQL databases.
- **TDE Not Enabled**   This setting recommends that you turn on Transparent Data Encryption (TDE) for your Azure SQL database. TDE protects your data and helps you meet compliance requirements by encrypting your database.
- **Healthy Databases**   This setting shows which Azure SQL databases are healthy. (It offers no further security recommendations.)
- **Storage Encryption Not Enabled**   This setting shows which storage accounts do not have encryption enabled.
- **Healthy Storage Accounts**   This setting shows which storage accounts are healthy. (It offers no further security recommendations.)

> **NOTE** After you enable Storage Encryption, only new data will be encrypted. Any existing files in this storage account will remain unencrypted. Once encryption is enabled, it cannot be disabled.

The following sections cover the implementation of some of these recommendations.

Server auditing and threat detection not enabled

Security Center can perform a security assessment to verify whether you are leveraging Azure SQL auditing and threat detection security capabilities. Auditing and threat detection can assist you in the following tasks:

- Maintaining regulatory compliance
- Understanding database activity
- Gaining insight into discrepancies and anomalies
- Identifying security violations

After you turn on auditing, you can configure threat detection settings and set up email security alerts. Threat detection detects anomalous database activities indicating potential security threats to the database. This enables you to detect and respond to potential threats as they occur. Follow these steps to address this recommendation:

1. Open the **Azure Portal** and sign in as a user who has **Security Admin** privileges.
2. In the left pane, click **Security Center**.

3. In the left pane of the Security Center window, under **Prevention**, click **Storage and Data**. The **Data Resources** blade appears. (See Figure 4-18.)

FIGURE 4-18 The Data Resources blade.

4. Click the **Server Auditing & Threat Detection Not Enabled** recommendation. The **Enable Auditing & Threat Detection on SQL Servers** blade appears. (See Figure 4-19.)

FIGURE 4-19 List of Azure SQL Servers that are not using the most secure configuration.

5. Click the server for which you want to change this setting. The **Auditing & Threat Detection** blade appears. (See Figure 4-20.)

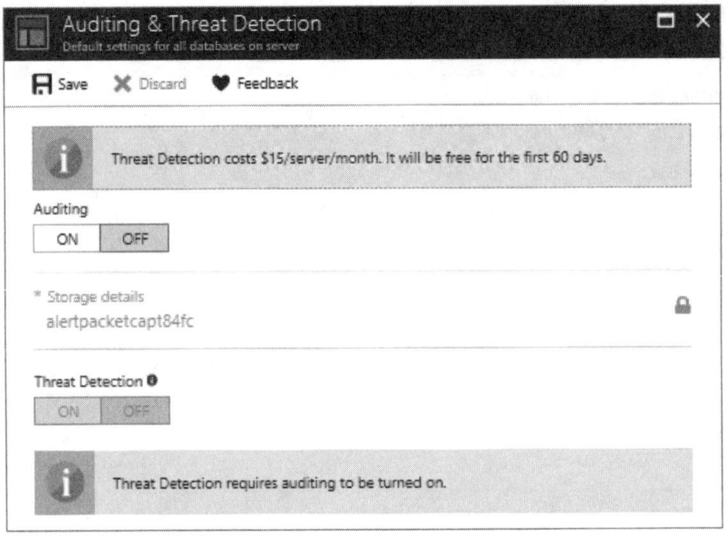

FIGURE 4-20 The Auditing & Threat Detection blade.

> **TIP** Be sure to read the information about the charges that will apply if you enable these options.

6. Under **Auditing**, click **ON**.
7. Under **Threat Detection**, click **ON**.
8. Click **Save** and close all pages.

> **TIP** For more information about Azure SQL database threat detection, visit https://aka.ms/AzureSQLTD.

Storage encryption not enabled

Security Center can perform a security assessment to verify whether your Azure Storage account is encrypted. Azure Storage Service Encryption (SSE) for Data at Rest can help you protect and safeguard your data in Azure. When this feature is enabled, Azure Storage automatically encrypts your data before persisting to storage and decrypts it before retrieval. Follow these steps to address this recommendation:

1. Open the **Azure Portal** and sign in as a user who has **Security Admin** privileges.

2. In the left pane, click **Security Center**.

3. In the left pane of the Security Center window, under **Prevention**, click **Storage and Data**. The **Data Resources** blade appears.

4. Click the **Storage Encryption Not Enabled** recommendation. The **Enable Storage Encryption** blade appears. (See Figure 4-21.)

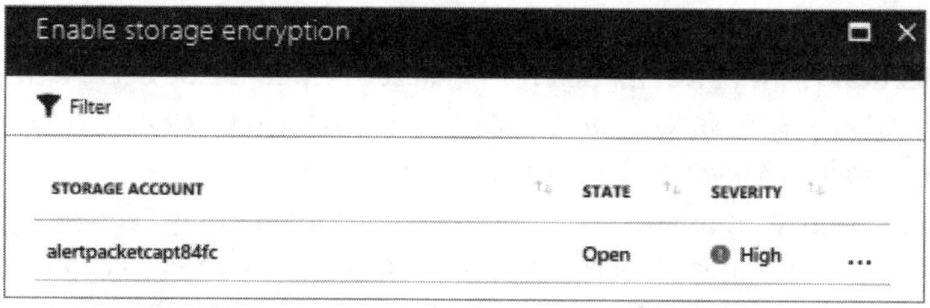

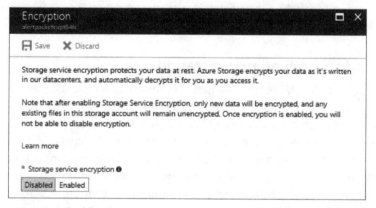

FIGURE 4-21 List of storage accounts that are not using encryption.

5. Click the storage account that needs to be encrypted. The **Encryption** page opens. (See Figure 4-22.)

FIGURE 4-22 Enabling storage service encryption for your storage account.

6. Click **Enabled**. Then click **Save**.

> **TIP** For more information about Azure Storage Service Encryption for Data at Rest, visit https://aka.ms/AzureSSE.

Applications

Many customers host their web applications in VMs running on Azure, which means they need to ensure that the security states of these VMs are well configured. This should be done not only on the operating system side (which was done under the **compute** recommendations) but also at the web application level.

Application recommendations include security recommendations for Internet Information Services (IIS) web applications running on Azure VMs. Application recommendations vary depending on the environment. For this reason, it is important to be aware of the full list of recommendations that might apply to your environment:

- **Web Application Firewall Not Installed** When Security Center detects a web application that needs advanced protection, it will recommend that you install a web application firewall (WAF) from a Microsoft partner.

- **Finalize Application Protection** After you install the WAF, Security Center will generate another recommendation to finalize the protection of your web application. Here you will see a list of additional recommendations, such as changing the web application DNS record to match the WAF IP address, and will also suggest traffic restriction using NSGs.

- **Healthy Web Applications** This shows you which web applications are healthy. (It includes no further security recommendations.)

The following section covers the implementation the web application firewall recommendation in more detail.

Web application firewall not installed

Web applications are increasingly becoming targets of cyberattacks such as SQL injection, cross-site scripting (XSS), and many others documented at the OWASP Top 10. (For more information, see www.owasp.org/index.php/Category:OWASP_Top_Ten_Project.) Although many of these attacks are preventable via code that has been put through a full Security Development Lifecycle, or SDL (www.microsoft.com/en-us/sdl/), it can be hard to prevent some of these attacks in the application code itself, as it may require rigorous maintenance, patching, and monitoring on multiple layers. A web application firewall can enhance the protection of your web application from web vulnerabilities and attacks without modification to application code. Follow these steps to address this recommendation:

1. Open the **Azure Portal** and sign in as a user who has **Security Admin** privileges.

2. In the left pane, click **Security Center**.

3. In the left pane of the Security Center window, under **Prevention**, click **Applications**. The **Applications** blade appears. (See Figure 4-23.)

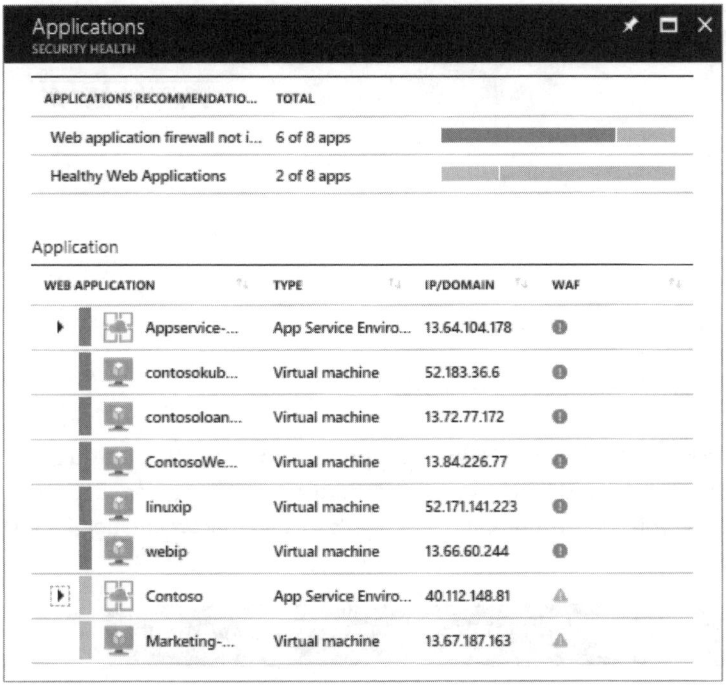

FIGURE 4-23 The Applications blade.

4. Click the **Web Application Firewall Not Installed** recommendation to open the **Web Application Firewall Not Installed** page. (See Figure 4-24.)

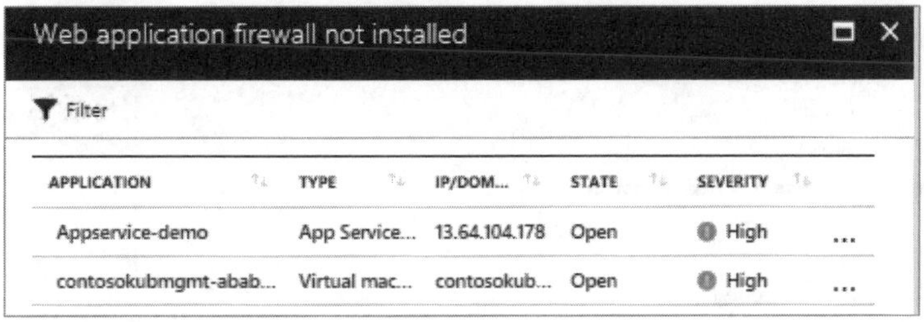

FIGURE 4-24 List of web applications that need a web application firewall.

5. Click an application that needs a WAF. The **Add a Web Application Firewall** blade appears. (See Figure 4-25.)

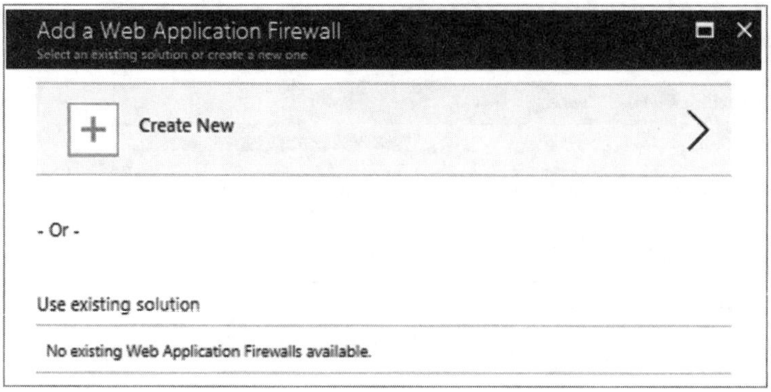

FIGURE 4-25 Adding a Web Application Firewall.

6. Click **Create New**. The **Create a New Web Application Firewall Solution** blade appears. (See Figure 4-26.) From this point forward, the steps may vary depending on the solution you choose. Consult the partner's solution documentation for further information.

FIGURE 4-26 Adding a new web application firewall.

Real World: The Importance of Prevention

In today's age of cybersecurity, prevention is just as important as detection and response. One of 2017's largest attacks, WannaCry, could have been prevented with patching. Mitigating vulnerabilities—including applying patches—can significantly reduce the likelihood of an attack.

Azure Security Center provides recommendations across compute, network, data, and apps that you can easily remediate from right inside the Security Center blades. These recommendations cover security best practices, missing configurations and patches, and other vulnerable areas of datacenter workloads. Security Center provides a simple way to identify risks and to resolve them quickly, reducing your attack surface.

Nicholas DiCola, Principal Program Manager, C+E Security Engineering

Chapter 5

Using Security Center for incident response

In the previous chapter, you learned how to address security recommendations using Azure Security Center, which is part of the overall enhancement of your security posture. However, protection is just one of the pillars of your security posture. You also need to enhance your detection and response.

On the detection front, Security Center constantly monitors your assets. When it identifies suspicious activities, it raises an alert. Importantly, it also reduces false positives, which is very important for your security operations.

In this chapter, you will learn how to use Security Center to detect threats against your environment, and how to investigate security issues as part of your incident-response process.

Understanding security alerts

The information gathered by Security Center in conjunction with network data and feeds from connected partners is used to detect threats and suspicious activities. Security Center analyzes this information by correlating the data from these sources to identify threats. Security alerts are prioritized in Security Center along with recommendations on how to remediate the threat.

> **IMPORTANT** Security alerts are not available in the free tier version of Security Center; the standard tier is required.

Security Center uses advanced security analytics and machine-learning technologies to evaluate events across the entire cloud fabric. The security analytics include data from multiple sources, including Microsoft products and services, the Microsoft Digital Crimes Unit (DCU), the Microsoft Security Response Center (MSRC), and external feeds. Security Center also applies known patterns to discover malicious behavior, which is called behavioral analysis.

Security Center uses statistical profiling to build a historical baseline, which is called anomaly detection. This triggers alerts when it detects deviations from established baselines that conform to a potential attack vector.

Detection capabilities in Azure Security Center

The Azure Security Center Threat Detection module helps identify active threats targeting your Microsoft Azure resources or on-premises computers and provides you with the insights needed to respond quickly.

The detection engine collects data from multiple data sources including but not limited to endpoint logs, network traffic, and cloud services activity, and applies atomic, behavioral, and machine learning-based logic to detect active threats.

Customers can extend the capabilities of the detection engine by authoring their own custom alert rules using a powerful search language. When a threat is detected, an alert is generated and undergoes a series of enrichment stations. These include the following:

- **Comparing against threat intelligence feeds**
- **Using an innovative confidence score and reasoning system**
- **Using a sophisticated fusion engine that correlates alerts into incidents**

To help triage the alerts, Security Center provides advanced incident-response tools that help customers investigate the threat scope and apply custom playbooks to remediate them automatically.

Tomer Teller, Principal Security Program Manager, Azure Security

Regardless of which capability Security Center uses to identify a threat, the result will be externalized in the dashboard via a security alert. A security alert contains valuable information about what triggered the alert, the resources targeted, the source of the attack, and suggestions to remediate the threat.

Security alerts are divided in four categories:

- **Virtual Machine Behavioral Analysis (VMBA)**   This type of alert uses behavioral analytics to identify compromised resources based on an analysis of the virtual machine (VM) event logs, such as process creation events and login events.
- **Network analysis**   This type of alert collects security information from your Azure Internet Protocol Flow Information Export (IPFIX) traffic and analyzes it to identify threats. An example of an alert that belongs to this category is the Suspicious Incoming RDP Network Activity from Multiple Sources alert.
- **Resource analysis**   This analyzes your Platform as a Service (PaaS) services, such as Azure SQL, and triggers alerts based on this analysis. An example of an alert that belongs to this category is the *Potential SQL Injection* alert.
- **Contextual information**   This provides extra context to reach a verdict about the nature of the threat and how to mitigate it.

TIP Because the list of alerts is constantly evolving, we recommend that you visit https://aka.ms/ASCAlerts to obtain the latest list of security alerts.

Detection scenarios

There are many scenarios in which Security Center will rapidly warn you about a suspicious activity. The following sections cover a couple of important scenarios to give you an idea of how powerful Security Center detections are and the advantage of using multiple data sources to enhance the confidence level of an alert.

Detecting spam activity

In this detection scenario, the attacker compromises an Azure VM and uses it to send spam emails. Using machine learning, Security Center can detect a spike in SMTP traffic. It then queries other data sources to make sure this spike is due to malicious behavior. Finally, it correlates this traffic with the Office 365 spam database to determine whether it is legitimate traffic. If the result of this correlation is that the traffic is suspicious, Security Center triggers the alert shown in Figure 5-1. In this scenario, Security Center uses built-in analytics, machine learning, and threat intelligence from Office 365. Performing these three steps provides not only more precise detection but also a higher level of confidence in the alert.

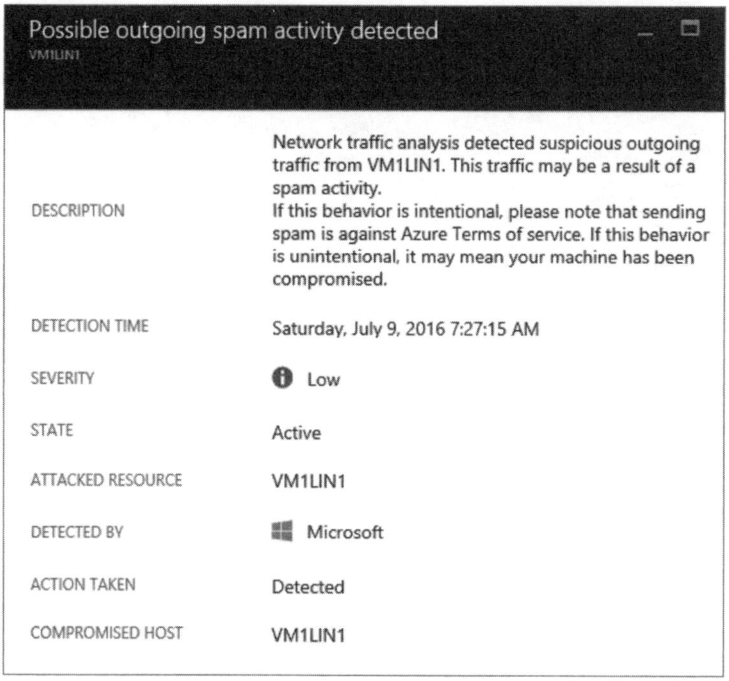

Possible outgoing spam activity detected	
VM1LIN1	
DESCRIPTION	Network traffic analysis detected suspicious outgoing traffic from VM1LIN1. This traffic may be a result of a spam activity. If this behavior is intentional, please note that sending spam is against Azure Terms of service. If this behavior is unintentional, it may mean your machine has been compromised.
DETECTION TIME	Saturday, July 9, 2016 7:27:15 AM
SEVERITY	🛈 Low
STATE	Active
ATTACKED RESOURCE	VM1LIN1
DETECTED BY	⊞ Microsoft
ACTION TAKEN	Detected
COMPROMISED HOST	VM1LIN1

FIGURE 5-1 Spam alert in Security Center.

Crash-dump analysis

In this scenario, the attacker compromises an Azure VM and installs malware that goes undetected by the antimalware installed on the VM. This malware causes a crash in a legitimate program. When a crash occurs in a Windows system, Windows Error Reporting (WER) generates a user-mode memory crash dump (.dmp file), which by default is located under *%LOCALAPPDATA%\CrashDumps*. Security Center collects an ephemeral copy of the crash dump file and scans it for evidence of exploits and compromises.

If Security Center finds such evidence, it generates an alert like the one shown in Figure 5-2. This alert indicates that the crash-dump analysis has detected executable code that exhibits behavior that is commonly performed by malicious payloads. Although non-malicious software may perform this behavior, it is not a typical development practice. Follow the remediation steps to investigate this issue further.

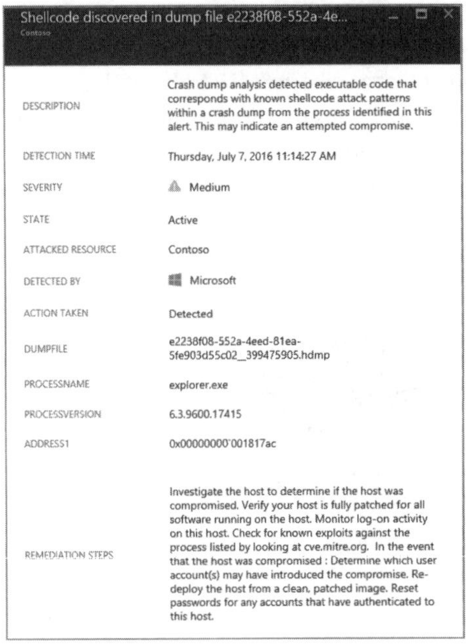

FIGURE 5-2 Crash-dump analysis alert.

Accessing security alerts

The number of security alerts you see in the Security Center dashboard may vary depending on the amount of resources that you are monitoring with Security Center and the business itself. Some organizations receive more attacks than others, and as a result have more security alerts.

If you don't have any security alerts in your environment, simulate one by following the procedures in the following article: https://aka.ms/ASCAlertValidation. Once you have an alert, follow these steps to access it:

1. Open the **Azure Portal** and sign in as a user who has **Security Admin** privileges.

2. In the left pane, click **Security Center**.

3. In the left pane of the Security Center window, under **Detection**, click **Security Alerts**. The Security Alerts dashboard appears. (See Figure 5-3.)

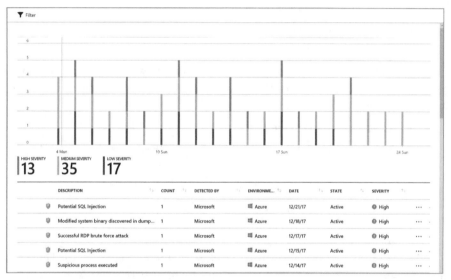

FIGURE 5-3 The Security Alerts dashboard.

4. The Security Alerts dashboard lists current alerts, organized by severity (with high-severity alerts listed first), and a bar graph showing the distribution of high-, medium-, and low-severity alerts. Click an alert type to open a new blade showing resources that have been flagged with the alert. (See Figure 5-4.)

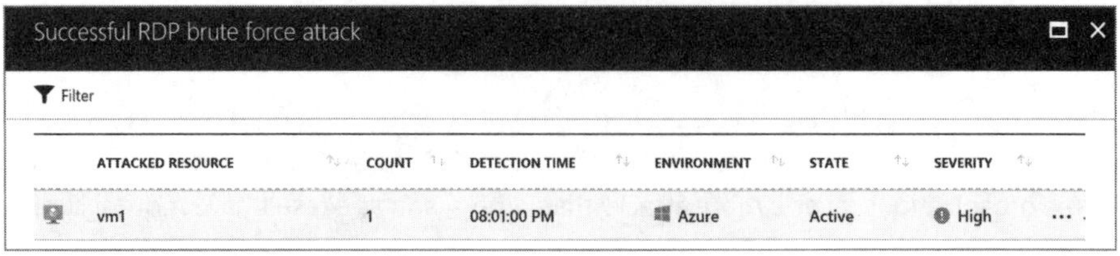

FIGURE 5-4 A list of attacked resources.

The list contains the following information about each attacked resource:

- The name of the attacked resource
- The number of times the resource was attacked
- The time at which the attack was detected
- The environment in which that the resource resides
- The state of the alert
- The severity of the alert

5. Click an attacked resource to see details about the attack, including the following. (See Figure 5-5. Note that the subscription ID has been intentionally obscured in this figure.)

- A clear description of the attack
- Attack-specific information, such as the source IP and the software used by the attacker
- A list of steps to remediate the issue

6. Return to the main **Security Center** dashboard.

> **TIP** You can use the Azure Activity Log to query security alerts originated by Azure Security Center. For more information, see https://aka.ms/ASCActivityLog. You can also use the Alert API to obtain these alerts; see https://aka.ms/ASCAlertAPI for details.

Successful RDP brute force attack
vm1

DESCRIPTION	Several Remote Desktop login attempts were detected from FreeRDP (96.81.218.10), some of which were able to successfully login to the machine. Event logs analysis shows that in the last 30 minutes there were 60 failed attempts. 20 of the failed login attempts aimed at non-existent users. 1 of the failed login attempts aimed at existing users.
DETECTION TIME	Sunday, December 17, 2017 8:01:00 PM
SEVERITY	❶ High
STATE	Active
ATTACKED RESOURCE	vm1
SUBSCRIPTION	▇▇▇▇▇▇▇▇▇▇▇
DETECTED BY	⊞ Microsoft
ACTION TAKEN	Detected
ENVIRONMENT	⊞ Azure
RESOURCE TYPE	🖥 Virtual Machine
SUCCESSFUL LOGINS	1
REPORTS	Report: RDP Brute Forcing
REMEDIATION STEPS	1. Escalate the alert to the information security team 2. If available, add the source IP to NSG block list for 24 hours (see https://azure.microsoft.com/en-us/documentation/articles/virtual-networks-nsg/) 3. Enforce the use of strong passwords and do not re-use them across multiple VMs and services (see

FIGURE 5-5 Details of a security alert.

Security incidents

Some attacks may happen in a completely isolated way. Others will be coordinated—that is, part of the same attack campaign. Security Center can identify correlations among these types of attacks and create a security incident that contains two or more related security alerts. To see how this works, follow these steps:

1. In the left pane of the Security Center window, under **Detection**, click **Security Alerts**. If Security Center has identified a security incident in your environment, it will create an alert marked by a different icon. (See the first two alerts in Figure 5-6.)

	DESCRIPTION	COUNT	DETECTED BY	ENVIRONME...	DATE	STATE	SEVERITY	
⁑●	Security incident with shared process detected	1	Microsoft	⊞ Azure	10/19/17	Active	❶ High	···
⁑●	Security incident with shared process detected	1	Microsoft	⊞ Azure	10/10/17	Active	❶ High	···
🛡	Potential SQL Injection	1	Microsoft	⊞ Azure	12/21/17	Active	❶ High	···
🛡	Modified system binary discovered in dump...	1	Microsoft	⊞ Azure	12/18/17	Active	❶ High	···

FIGURE 5-6 Security incidents appear in the Security Alert dashboard with a different icon.

2. Click a security incident. A new blade opens with more details about the incident. In the blade shown in Figure 5-7, the incident contains two alerts and two notable events. These notable events are contextual information that can help you during an investigation. (Note that the subscription ID and attacked resources have been intentionally hidden in the figure.)

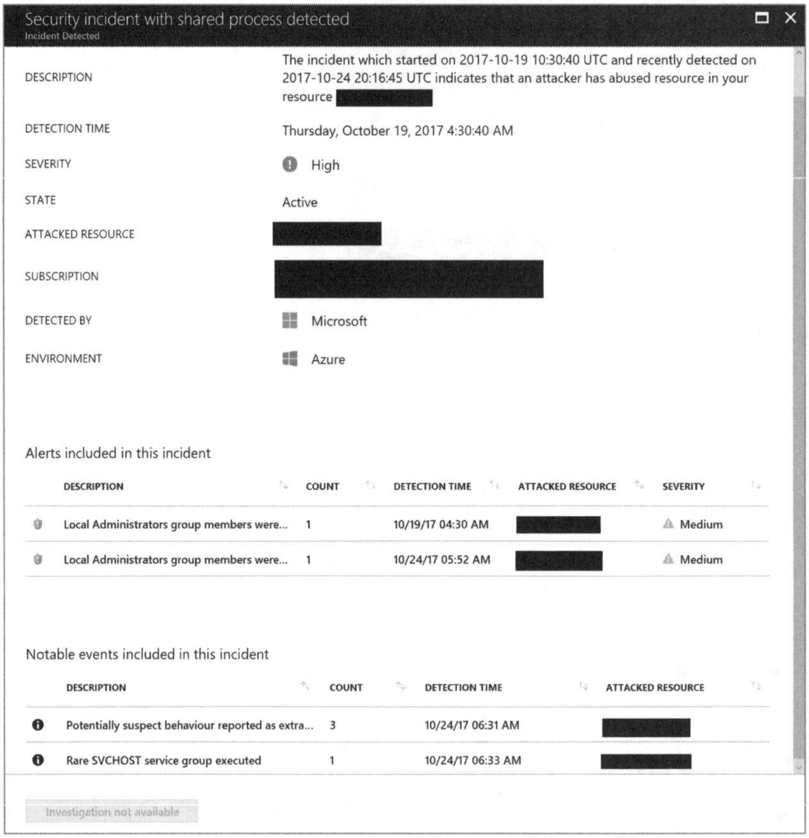

FIGURE 5-7 Details about a security incident.

> **NOTE** The advantage of using the Security Incident blade is that it tells you which alerts are related. This can help you to track down the perpetrator and identify compromised systems.

3. Click an alert to see details about the alert. The details will be similar to those shown in Figure 5-5.

4. Click a notable event. This opens a page containing contextual data about the event. (See Figure 5-8.) This page shows the suspicious process name and the command

line that was executed, and emphasizes other information that is relevant to your investigation.

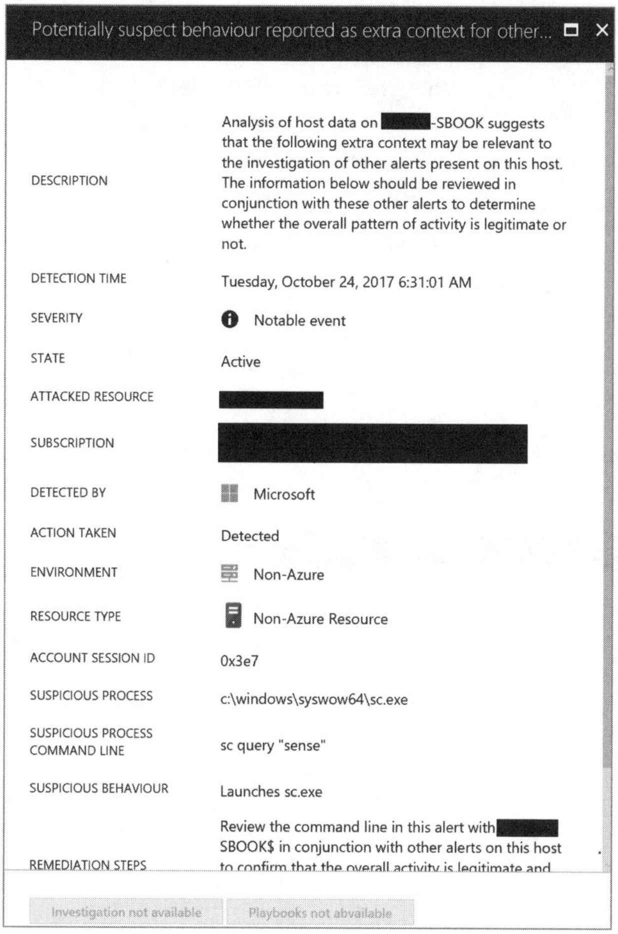

FIGURE 5-8 Contextual information with more details about an event.

5. Return to the main **Security Center** dashboard.

Custom alerts

Each environment may have its own unique processes that can be identified as suspicious. For example, your organization might consider it suspicious to run a particular executable file, but Security Center might not. To address this type of scenario, Security Center enables you to create your own custom alerts. Follow these steps to create a new custom alert:

1. In the left pane of the Security Center window, under **Detection**, click **Custom Alert Rules**. The **Custom Alert Rules** blade appears. (See Figure 5-9.)

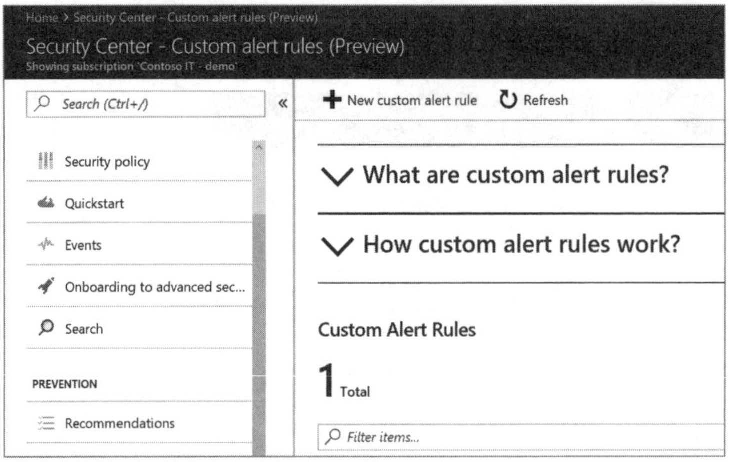
Home > Security Center - Custom alert rules (Preview)
Security Center - Custom alert rules (Preview)
Showing subscription 'Contoso IT - demo'
Search (Ctrl+/)
New custom alert rule
Refresh
Security policy
Quickstart
Events
Onboarding to advanced sec...
Search
PREVENTION
Recommendations
What are custom alert rules?
How custom alert rules work?
Custom Alert Rules
1 Total
Filter items...

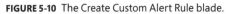

FIGURE 5-9 Creating a custom alert.

2. Click the **New Custom Alert Rule** button. The **Create a Custom Alert Rule** blade appears. (See Figure 5-10.)

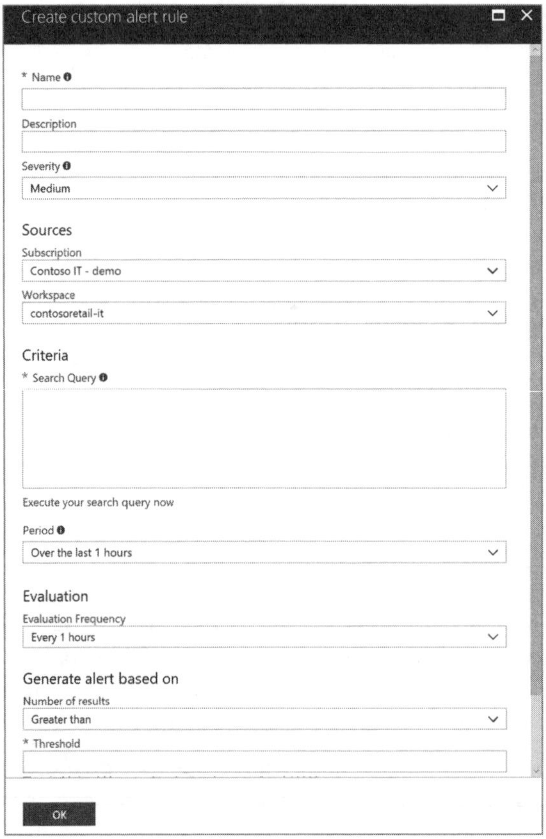
Create custom alert rule
* Name
Description
Severity
Medium
Sources
Subscription
Contoso IT - demo
Workspace
contosoretail-it
Criteria
* Search Query
Execute your search query now
Period
Over the last 1 hours
Evaluation
Evaluation Frequency
Every 1 hours
Generate alert based on
Number of results
Greater than
* Threshold
OK

FIGURE 5-10 The Create Custom Alert Rule blade.

3. In the **Name** field, type the name for this rule.

4. In the **Description** field, type a brief description of the rule's intent.

5. In the **Severity** drop-down list, select the severity level—High, Medium, or Low. Choose a level that reflects the priority of this alert for your security operations team.

6. In the **Sources** section, open the **Subscription** drop-down list and select the subscription that will be used by this custom rule.

7. Open the **Workspace** drop-down list and choose the workspace against which this rule should be running.

8. In the **Search Query** box in the **Criteria** section, search for the event you want to monitor. For example, if you want to monitor all security events whose identifier is *4688* and whose command line contains the word *diskpart*, type the following query and click the **Execute Your Search Query Now** link:

```
SecurityEvent | where EventID==4688 and CommandLine contains "diskpart"
```

> **TIP** The query language used for this search is the Log Analytics language. For more information about this language, and for more examples, see https://aka.ms /laquerylan.

9. In the **Period** drop-down list, select the time interval that should be used for this query. (By default, it will test over the last hour.)

10. In the **Evaluation** section, open the **Evaluation Frequency** drop-down list and specify how frequently this custom rule should be executed.

11. The **Generate Alert Based On** section contains two settings that are directly correlated: **Number of Results** and **Threshold**. Open the **Number of Results** drop-down list and choose **Greater Than.** Then, in the **Threshold** box, type **2**. The alert will be triggered if the result for the query is greater than 2.

12. Select the **Enable Suppress Alerts** option if you want to set a time to wait before Security Center sends another alert for this rule.

13. Click **OK** to create the new rule. It will appear in the **Custom Alert Rules** section of the **Custom Alert** blade. (See Figure 5-11.)

Custom Alert Rules

1 Total

🔍 Filter items...

ALERT NAME		DESCRIPTION
ⓘ ASCBook		Testing Rule for the ASC Book

FIGURE 5-11 The new custom rule.

14. Now that you've created the new rule, alerts pertaining to this rule will appear with other alerts in the **Security Alerts** dashboard. (See Figure 5-12.)

	DESCRIPTION	COUNT	DETECTED BY	ENVIRONME...	DATE	STATE	SEVERITY	
NEW ⬛	ASCBook	1	Alert Rule	⬛ Azure	12/25/17	Active	⚠ Medium	•••

FIGURE 5-12 A new security alert based on the custom rule that was created.

Investigating a security issue

In some scenarios, the information you obtain from a security alert can be enough for your incident-response team to conduct an investigation and identify the root cause of the issue. However, in some circumstances, you may need more details to understand the correlation between alerts and how the attack was performed. In Security Center, you can use the **Investigation** feature to obtain this information. Follow these steps:

1. In the left pane of the Security Center window, under **Detection**, click **Security Alerts**.

2. In the **Security Alerts** dashboard, click the security alert that you want to investigate.

3. Select the attacked resource you want to investigate. Then click the **Investigate** option at the bottom of the security alert page. (After you click the Investigate option for an alert, it changes to a **Continue an Investigation** option.) The **Investigation** dashboard appears. (See Figure 5-13.)

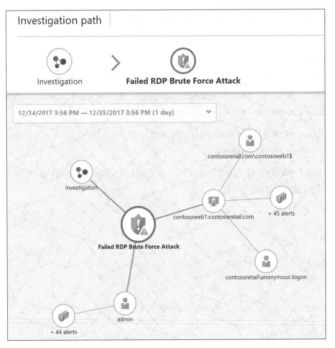

FIGURE 5-13 The Investigation dashboard with a security incident selected.

On the left side of the Investigation dashboard is the **investigation path** and **map**. The relevant entities (security alerts, computer, users, and security incidents) appear correlated in the map, and the timeline shows the current data interval for this investigation. On the right side are the attributes for the selected entity in the map. For example, Figure 5-14 shows the attributes for the entity selected in Figure 5-13.

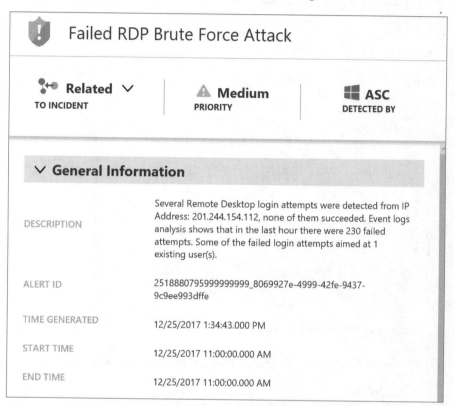

FIGURE 5-14 Security incident detected attributes.

The approach you take when investigating a security issue may vary depending on the attack, the amount of information available, and what you already know about the attack. For this example, one option would be to analyze the information available from the resource that was attacked—in this case, *contosoweb1*.

4. In the investigation map, click **contosweb1** to see more details about it. Notice that the investigation map also changes. (See Figure 5-15.) As you can see, there are more than 45 alerts on this server, and there have been anonymous login attempts from the *contosoretail* domain.

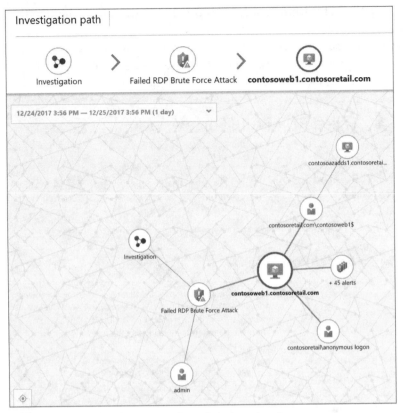

FIGURE 5-15 The investigation map reflects the selected entity.

5. To explore further, click the **Exploration** option in the right pane. (See Figure 5-16.)

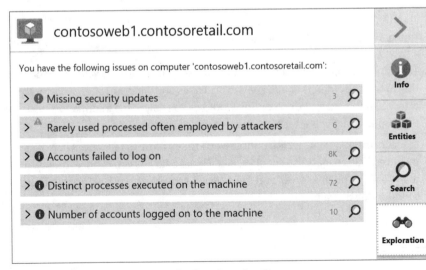

FIGURE 5-16 Exploring more options for the selected entity.

6. Review all the events in the **Exploration** page. These will be very important for your investigation and can help you understand how the attack took place.

7. Repeat steps 4–6 for each relevant entity in the investigation map. As the map redraws itself, it will become clearer how the attack took place and which systems were compromised.

   As you click each entity, the options available to you may change depending on the entity type.

8. To see all entities correlated with the entity you've selected on the map, click the **Entities** option. The example shown in Figure 5-17 displays two entities (Alerts and Computers) that are correlated with the selected user on the map.

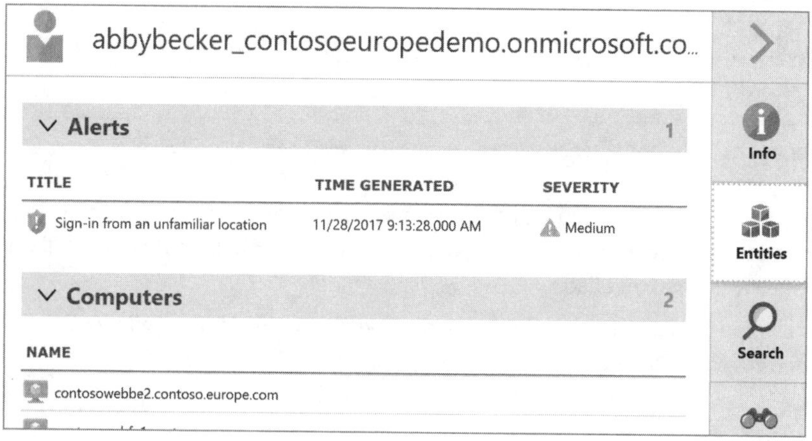

FIGURE 5-17 Entities correlation.

9. To visualize events correlated with the selected entity, click the **Search** option. The example in Figure 5-18 shows the events correlated with a server.

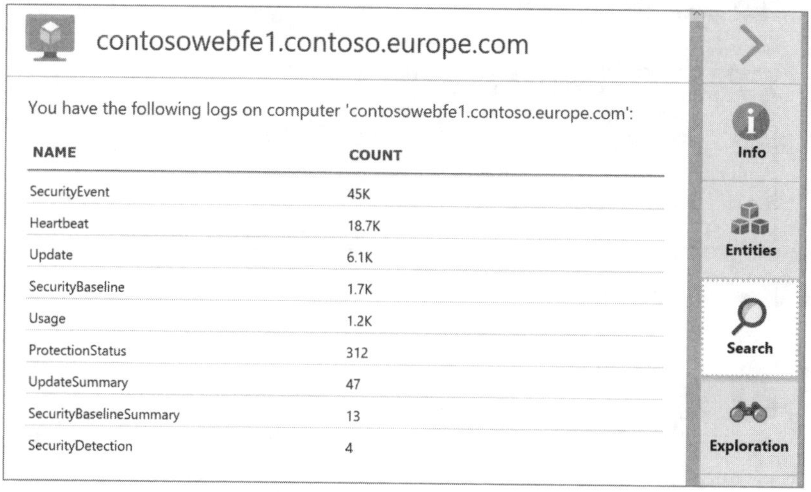

FIGURE 5-18 Events correlated with the selected entity.

10. Click one of the events. The **Log Search** dashboard from **Log Analytics** opens and shows all records.

As you continue to investigate each entity, you may find that Security Center will flag an entity as **unrelated** to the incident. (See Figure 5-19.)

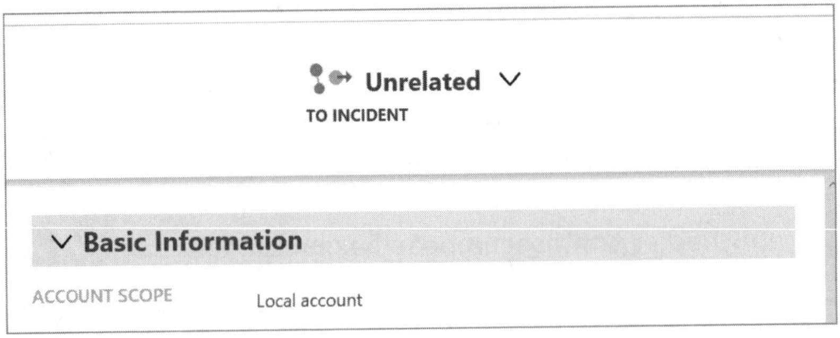

⸱⤇ Unrelated ⌄
TO INCIDENT

⌄ Basic Information

ACCOUNT SCOPE   Local account

FIGURE 5-19 Security Center may flag an entity as unrelated to the incident.

Usually, this determination is accurate. However, in some scenarios, you may find that a correlation between that entity and the incident does exist. In that case, you'll want to manually change that flag.

11. To change the flag, click the drop-down arrow next to the **Unrelated** heading, select **Related**, and choose a reason in the drop-down list. (See Figure 5-20.)

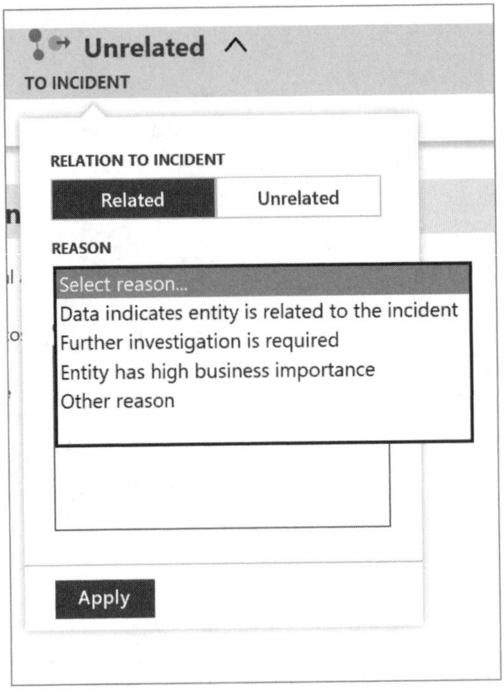

⸱⤇ Unrelated ⌃
TO INCIDENT

RELATION TO INCIDENT

| Related | Unrelated |

REASON

Select reason...
Data indicates entity is related to the incident
Further investigation is required
Entity has high business importance
Other reason

Apply

FIGURE 5-20 Changing the entity relation with the incident.

Responding to a security alert

Now that you know how to use Security Center to detect an alert and how to investigate a security issue, you can move to the next phase: responding to a security alert. To aid you in this, Security Center supports a feature called security playbook. Security playbooks enable you to create a collection of procedures that can be executed from Security Center when a certain security alert is triggered. Azure Logic Apps is the automation mechanism behind security playbooks.

Before creating a playbook, you should have in mind what you want to automate. Before implementing this feature, answer the following questions:

- For which security alert should I automate a response?
- What steps should be automated if the conditions for this alert are true?
- What steps should be automated if the conditions for this alert are false?

> **NOTE** This is only a sampling of questions to get you started. As you start creating security playbooks, other questions may be raised.

Creating a playbook

In this example, the goal is to create a security playbook that sends an email anytime a high alert is triggered. Follow these steps:

1. In the left pane of the Security Center window, under **Automation & Orchestration**, click **Playbooks**. The Playbook dashboard opens. Assuming this is the first time you've created a playbook, the dashboard will be empty, as shown in Figure 5-21.

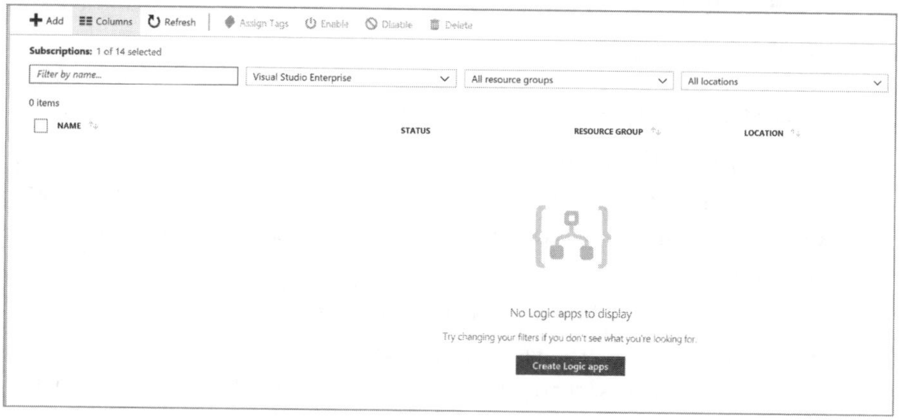

FIGURE 5-21 Creating a new security playbook.

2. Click the **Create Logic App** button. The **Create Logic App** blade appears. (See Figure 5-22.)

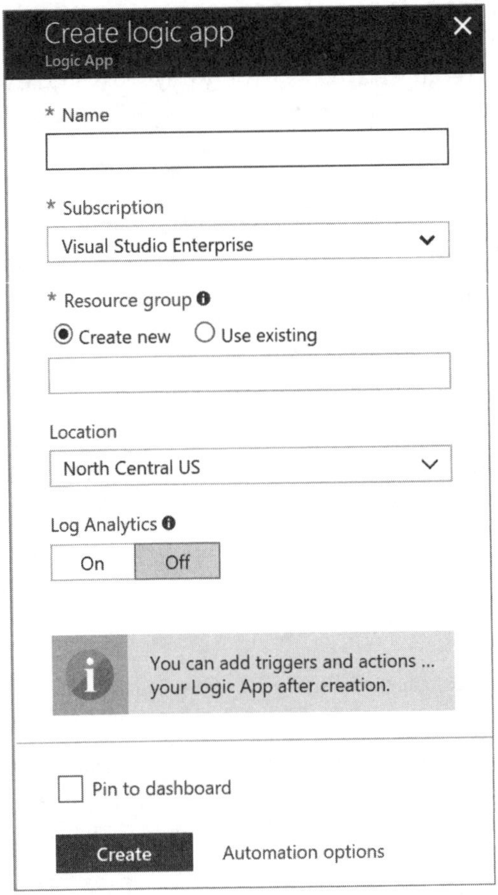

FIGURE 5-22 Creating a new logic app.

3. In the **Name** box, type a name for this playbook.

4. In the **Subscription** drop-down list, select your subscription type.

5. In the **Resource Group** section, select either the **Create New** or the **Use Existing** option. If you select the latter, type the name of the existing group in the box below the option buttons.

6. Select a location from the **Location** drop-down list.

7. If you want to monitor your workflow using Log Analytics, you can click the **On** button in the **Log Analytics** section. For this example, leave it **Off**, which is the default.

8. Click the **Create** button. The new playbook will appear in the list in the Playbook dashboard. (See Figure 5-23.) If you don't see it, click **Refresh**.

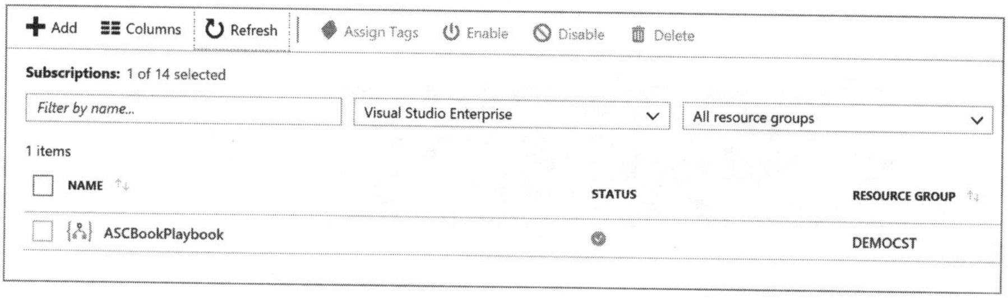

FIGURE 5-23 New playbook successfully created.

Building the workflow

You've created a playbook, but it doesn't contain any procedures yet. Your next step is to build the workflow for the playbook. Follow these steps:

1. Click the playbook you just created to edit it.
2. Under **Templates**, click **Blank Logic App**. The **Logic Apps Designer** dashboard appears.
3. In the **Search** box, type **Security Center**. (See Figure 5-24.)

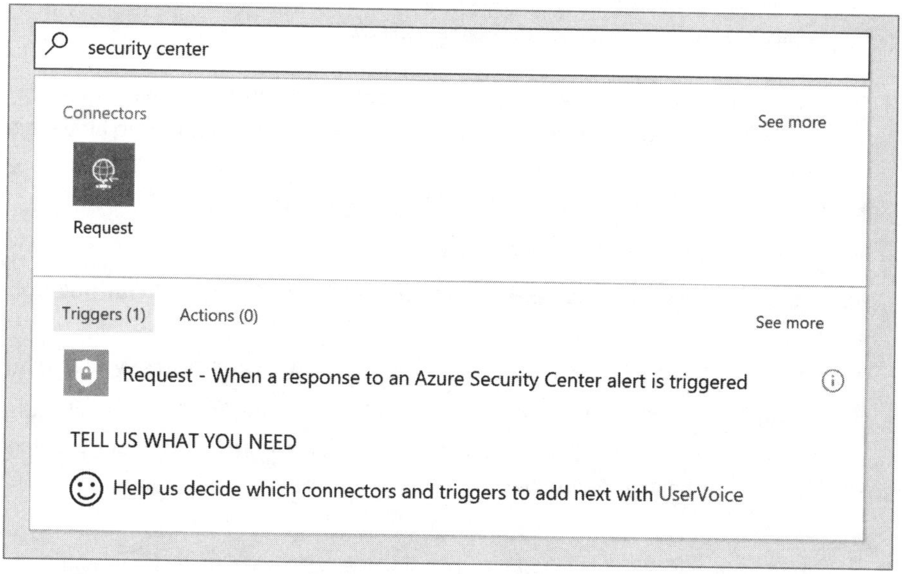

FIGURE 5-24 Using the Security Center template in Logic Apps.

4. Click the **Request – When a Response to an Azure Security Center Alert Is Triggered** option.

5. Click the **New Step** button. The options shown in Figure 5-25 appear.

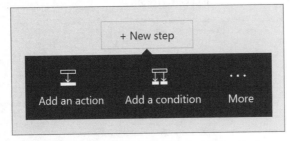

FIGURE 5-25 Adding a new step to the workflow.

6. Click **Add a Condition**. The options shown in Figure 5-26 appear.

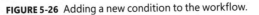

FIGURE 5-26 Adding a new condition to the workflow.

7. Under **Condition**, click the first box, and select **Alert Severity** from the drop-down list that appears. Then click the gray area outside the Condition settings to hide the drop-down list.

8. Leave the second box with the default option (**Is Equal To**).

9. Click in the third box and type **Medium**.

10. In the **If True** section, click **Add an Action**, and choose **Office 365 Outlook** from the drop-down list that appears

11. Open the **All Actions** drop-down list and choose **Office 365 Outlook – Send an Email**.

12. Sign in with your Office 365 or corporate Outlook account. This is the email address that will be used to send the email when this condition is met. You should see a dialog box like the one shown in Figure 5-27.

> **NOTE** In a real-world scenario, you could use a custom account—for example, incident@contoso.com or support@contoso.com—instead of a user email address.

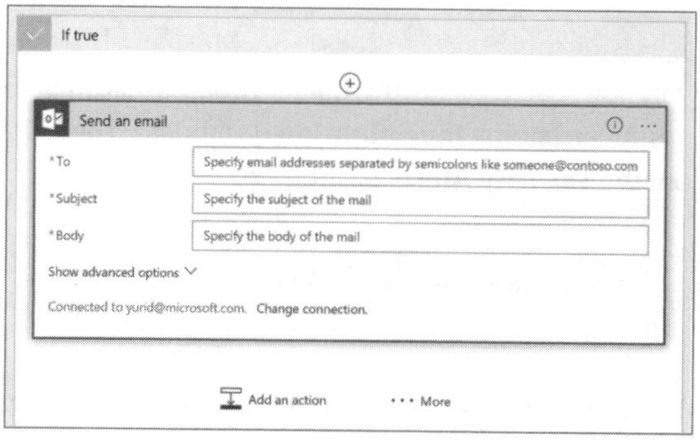

FIGURE 5-27 Email parameters.

13. Type the destination address in the **To** field. This is the mailbox that will receive the alert. If you want to send the alert to more than one mailbox, separate each address with a semicolon.

14. In the **Subject** field, type a brief message that reflects the intent of the email—for example, **High Severity Alert Detected**.

15. In the **Body** field, type a generic message, and concatenate it with the variables that appear in the drop-down list next to the **Send an Email** box. (See Figure 5-28.)

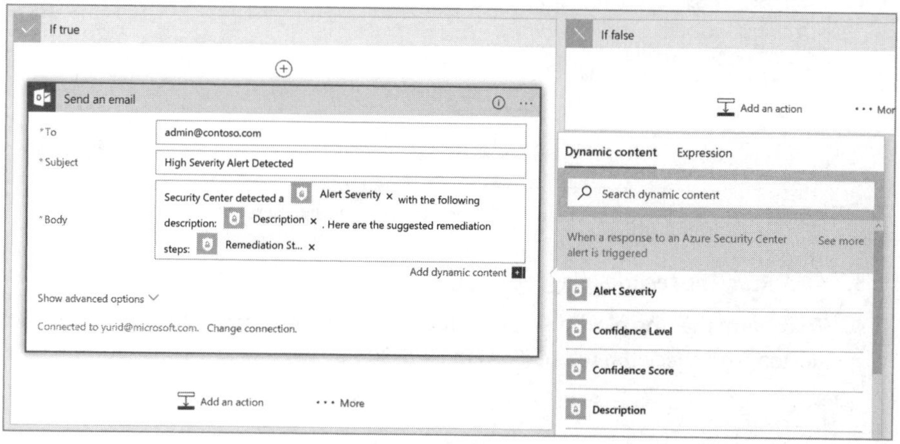

FIGURE 5-28 Description using fixed text and variables.

16. If you want to trigger an action if the alert is not a high priority, repeat steps 10–15 in the **If False** section.

17. Click **Save** in the upper-left corner of the **Logic Apps Designer** dashboard.

18. Click **Close** in the **Logic Apps Designer** dashboard and in the playbook's properties.

Executing a playbook

Now that the playbook contains a workflow, you can execute the playbook. You can do so from two locations: the **Security Alerts** dashboard or the **Investigation** dashboard. The following steps demonstrate the execution from the **Security Alerts** dashboard.

> **NOTE** As of this writing, the playbook feature is on preview and is a manual process.

1. In the left pane of the Security Center window, under **Detection**, click **Security Alerts**.

2. The playbook you created applies to high-severity alerts. To meet this condition, click a high-priority alert.

3. Click the attacked resource that corresponds to the high-priority alert. A blade for the attacked resource opens.

4. Click the **Run Playbooks** button. The Playbooks blade appears. (See Figure 5-29.)

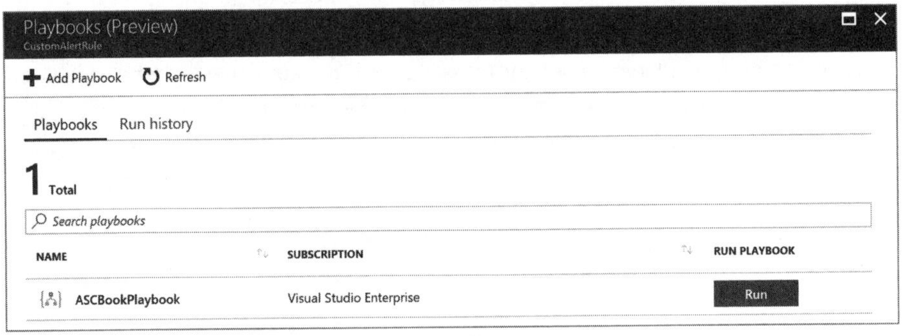

FIGURE 5-29 The Playbooks blade with the playbook you just created.

5. Click **Run**. The security playbook runs.

6. To confirm that the playbook ran correctly, click the **Run History** tab, click the **Refresh** button, and check the result. (See Figure 5-30.)

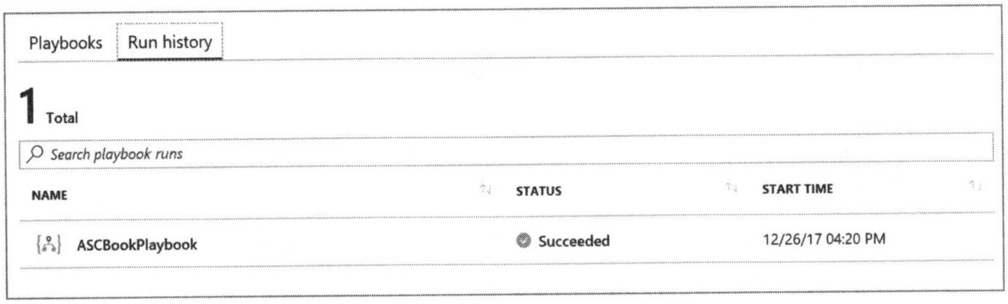

FIGURE 5-30 The Run History tab shows a history of every execution of this playbook.

7. Check the mailbox you set as the destination for the email generated by the playbook. You should have received an email from Security Center about the alert based on the parameters you set when you created the workflow.

When you click **Run History**, the log you see pertains only to the execution of the playbook against the alert you selected. Let's call it Alert A. If you run the same playbook on a different alert—Alert B—you won't see an entry for that operation in the history for Alert A. Instead, it will appear in a separate history, for Alert B.

Auditing playbook execution

As noted, you can check whether a playbook was executed against a particular alert by viewing its history. However, this won't show you whether the playbook was executed against *all* relevant alerts. For that, you should audit the playbook's execution. That way, you see its full execution log. Follow these steps to perform this operation:

1. In the left pane of the Security Center window, under **Automation & Orchestration**, click **Playbooks**.

2. Click the playbook you want to audit.

3. The playbook's properties cite the details of all executions, including the date, start time, and duration. You can also filter by date and time. (See Figure 5-31.)

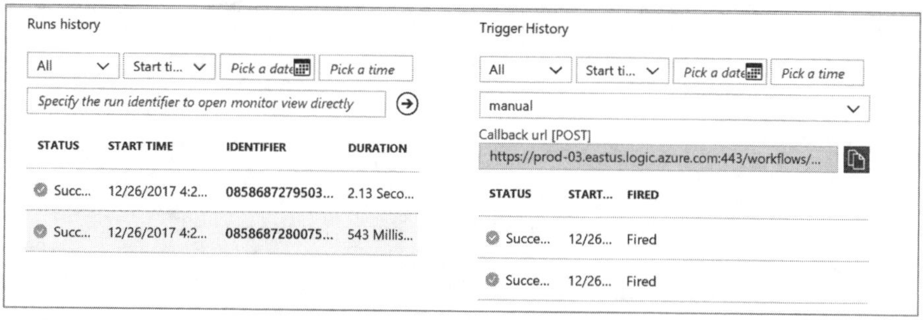

FIGURE 5-31 Complete history of executions for this playbook.

4. For more details on a particular execution, click the execution line. The **Run History** blade opens with the **Logic App Run** dashboard displayed. (See Figure 5-32.)

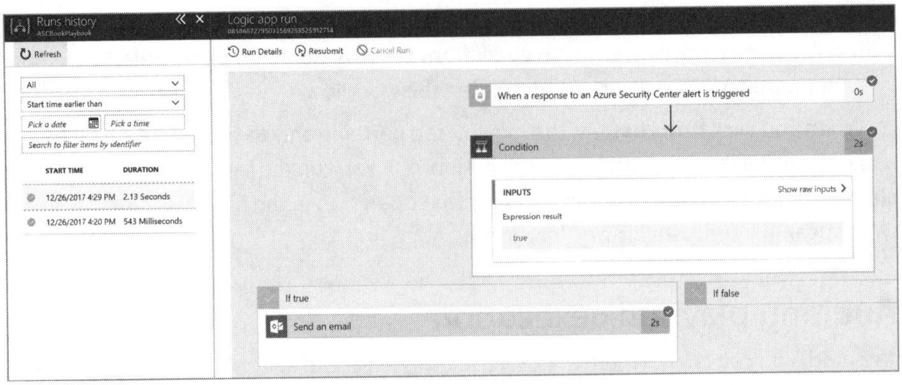

FIGURE 5-32 More details about a particular execution.

Notice that in the workflow, a small green check mark appears in the upper-right corner of each box. This indicates the successful execution of that particular step.

5. If you don't see a green check mark, click the step to view the raw data and trouble-shoot. For example, if you click the **When a Response to an Azure Security Center Alert Is Triggered** option, you will see the raw input and output received by the Logic App. (See Figure 5-33.)

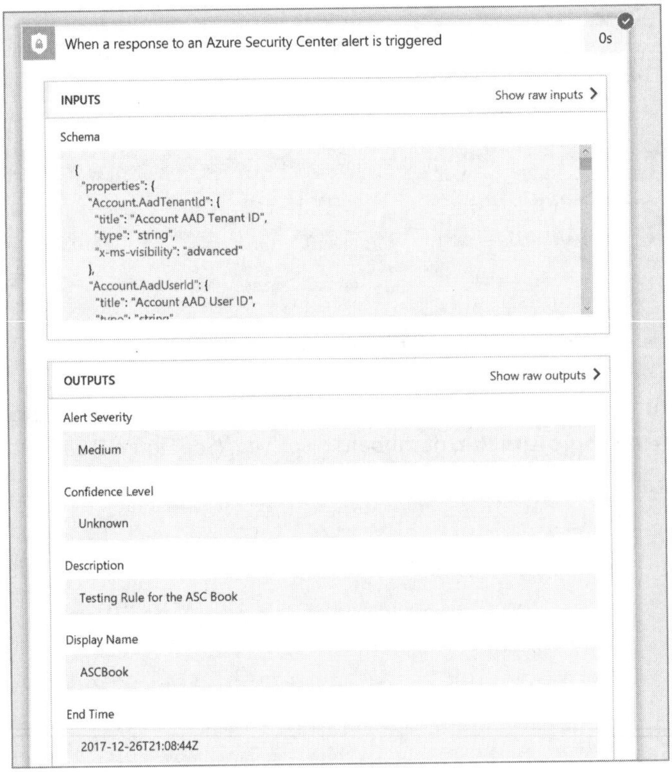

FIGURE 5-33 Raw input and output.

6. Click **Close** in the Logic App Run page and in the playbook's properties.

You can integrate the playbook with solutions from certain partners. For example, you can integrate it with Service Now to create a service ticket when an incident is detected.

> **TIP** The following presentation, delivered by co-author Yuri Diogenes at Ignite 2017, shows how to integrate playbook with Slack: https://youtu.be/e8iFCz5RM4g.

Chapter 6

Advanced cloud defense

In this chapter, you will learn how Azure Security Center works to enable advanced threat protection not only for your Azure-situated assets but also for your on-premises deployments. To help you understand the overall threat landscape and what modern cybersecurity professionals have to deal with today, this chapter begins with a discussion on how preferences are changing from threat protection to threat detection (and why this is probably a good thing). It also covers methods of threat detection and how Azure Security Center uses them to catch attackers as early as possible. After that, the chapter looks at the cyber kill chain and how Azure Security Center uses this construct to assemble fusion alerts, which are high-quality and high-fidelity alerts that enable you to focus your attention on the most pressing security issues confronting you today. Finally, the chapter covers application whitelisting, just-in-time virtual machine (VM) access, and connected security solutions.

Threat prevention versus threat detection

Historically, cybersecurity professionals have spent their careers doing most (or all) of the following to secure IT assets:

- Installing antivirus and antimalware
- Erecting firewalls at the edge of the corporate network
- Creating DMZs to limit network access to resources that belong to different security zones
- Hardening operating systems
- Configuring the registry
- Creating security-centric "golden images" that have been researched and vetted to provide the highest level of protection
- Implementing network intrusion detection systems and intrusion protection systems to detect possible network-based attacks
- Implementing unified threat gateways, web proxies, and Next-Generation Firewalls (NGFs) to locate threats at various network junction points and stop attacks at those points

Most likely, your experience and training have taught you that threat prevention is the preferred way of preventing "bad things" from happening. This view has probably prompted your company or your customers to invest heavily in threat-prevention solutions. Yet it seems as if a day doesn't go by without some kind of major attack against a large company. The outcomes of these attacks vary, but often the result is the loss of customer information, including personally identifiable information (PII), which can put the identities of those customers at risk.

Given this, you might begin to feel as if security is a hopeless endeavor—that the most you as a security professional can do is to hope attackers don't come after your company and to use preventive technologies (including those listed on the previous page) to put some bumps in the road if they do. We disagree. A simple change of focus—shifting some of your attention from protection to detection—can greatly improve your overall security posture.

This shift from threat prevention to threat detection is based on the following:

- The recognition that the previous emphasis on threat protection has not been as effective as we hoped it would be

- Lessons learned from red team exercises, in which a dedicated team of "trusted" attackers attempts to gain access to various components of the cloud infrastructure and data

- The acceptance of the fact that all organizations will be compromised to a greater or lesser extent at some point, and that early detection, ejection, and remediation are therefore the most productive use of time, money, and resources

One of this book's co-authors, Tom Shinder, is a physician. He uses a medical example to illustrate this point. Suppose medical experts believe an influenza epidemic is imminent. It is well known that an influenza vaccine delivered before the outbreak of the epidemic will prevent the virus from infecting a certain percentage of people. However, rates of effectiveness vary—sometimes as little as 10 percent of the vaccinated population will avoid infection. Because of this, it's critical that incidences of the flu are detected as early as possible. That way, people infected with the virus know to stay home or to obtain medical attention as soon as possible to prevent a longer illness or even death. Similarly, if you can detect when an attacker has infiltrated your network and resources as early as possible, you can eject the attacker before the attacker attains his or her goals, thereby reducing the amount of damage done.

Methods of threat detection

Numerous methods are used to detect threats. Some are more effective than others, but often, the less effective methods can be implemented more quickly. As a result, you'll likely end up using a variety of methods that balance each other out. (See Figure 6-1.)

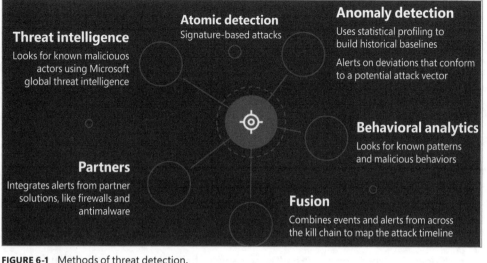

FIGURE 6-1 Methods of threat detection.

Azure Security Center uses the following methods to detect threats:

- Atomic (signature-based) detection
- Traditional threat intelligence feeds and incoming data from integrated security solutions
- Behavioral analysis
- Anomaly detection
- Detection fusion

We'll discuss the first four methods in this section. The two sections that follow focus on detection fusion—a method that generates your most valuable alerts.

Atomic detection

Atomic detection is relatively simple in its methodology and execution. One type of atomic detection is based on traditional signature-based detection, while the other is based on very simple, well-defined, and unequivocal behavior.

Signature-based atomic detection

If you've used common antivirus and antimalware solutions, then you're familiar with atomic detection. *Atomic*, in this instance, means very granular—like an atom. Atomic detection is very granular and very specific. It uses hash values (also called signatures) for malicious code images. If the scanner finds an image on disk or in memory that matches the hashed value, it logs a hit and the offender is removed. Atomic detection is very effective and has an almost perfect hit rate. This is because the hash value almost guarantees a unique find. (There is such a thing as a hash collision, but this typically isn't a problem with virus scanning.)

The problem with atomic scanning is that it's relatively easy for an attacker to change one bit in an image. When that one bit is changed, the hash value of the file is also changed, necessitating the calculation of a new hash value and the updating of the collection of signatures used by the antivirus scanner. This leads to a lot of problems—not least of which is that the system bogs down and becomes painfully slow. Although atomic detection is a powerful tool with very high fidelity, it's also relatively easy for an attacker to circumvent it. For this reason, interest in signature-based detection has decreased. Even large antivirus/antimalware (AV/AM) vendors are signaling the end of the AV/AM era.

Single-finding atomic detection

The second type of atomic detection is based on a single finding in a log file entry on a VM, a single packet logged in a firewall, or any other single-simple event logged or detected somewhere on the system. This type of atomic detection is more effective than signature scanning for the following reasons:

- It does not depend on image hashes, so a single changed bit does not invalidate the pattern.
- It focuses on known-bad, or unequivocal, behaviors.
- It has a very low false-positive rate because it is defined by known-bad behavior.

For example, consider the SID on a user account. There is no reason for someone to change this SID. Therefore, a changed SID on a user account is a known-bad event. Such an event will appear in the event log of a Windows operating system. A single-finding atomic-detection threat-detection module will know to scan this event log for this kind of change, and generate an alert if it detects such a change.

The downside of single-finding atomic detection is that it can be circumvented by an attacker who makes a very small change in the known-bad behavior. Although this is not as easy as circumventing signature-based atomic detection, it remains relatively simple for a skilled attacker.

Threat-intelligence feeds and integrated security solutions

A threat-intelligence feed is a report that contains the IP addresses of internet nodes that are suspected of some type of malevolent behavior or activity, such as the following:

- Sending spam
- Performing brute-force attacks
- Hosting a command-and-control (C&C) server for a botnet
- Sending out traffic as part of a distributed denial-of-service network (botnet)
- Hosting copyrighted material
- Hosting websites that have been compromised by malware
- Hosting dangerous websites—for example, sites for terrorist groups

There are several threat-intelligence feeds, and Microsoft subscribes to many of them. This is helpful not only in terms of increasing the chances you'll become aware of a dangerous internet node, but also in terms of Microsoft's ability to assess the value of these feeds. Microsoft also maintains its own threat-intelligence feeds and checks their alignment (or lack thereof) with other feeds on the market. Figure 6-2 shows an example of how Azure Security Center surfaces findings from traditional threat-intelligence feeds.

Network communication with a malicious machine detected vm4	
◑ Investigation not available [⚙] Playbooks not abvailable	
DESCRIPTION	Network traffic analysis indicates that your machine (IP 1.2.3.5) has communicated with what is possibly a Command and Control center for a malware of type AldiBot at IP 183.95.154.13. AldiBot is an HTTP-controlled denial-of-service bot - it offers HTTP and TCP DDoS capabilities along with Firefox, Pidgin and jDownloader credential theft, the creation of a SOCKS5 proxy on infected machine, and the ability to download and execute malicious code of the attacker's choice.
DETECTION TIME	Tuesday, November 28, 2017 6:01:00 PM
SEVERITY	⚠ Medium
STATE	Active
ATTACKED RESOURCE	vm4
SUBSCRIPTION	ASC DEMO (212f9889-769e-45ae-ab43-6da33674bd26)
DETECTED BY	▦ Microsoft
ACTION TAKEN	Detected
ENVIRONMENT	▦ Azure
RESOURCE TYPE	▣ Virtual Machine
ATTACKER PORT	80
VICTIM PORT	23132

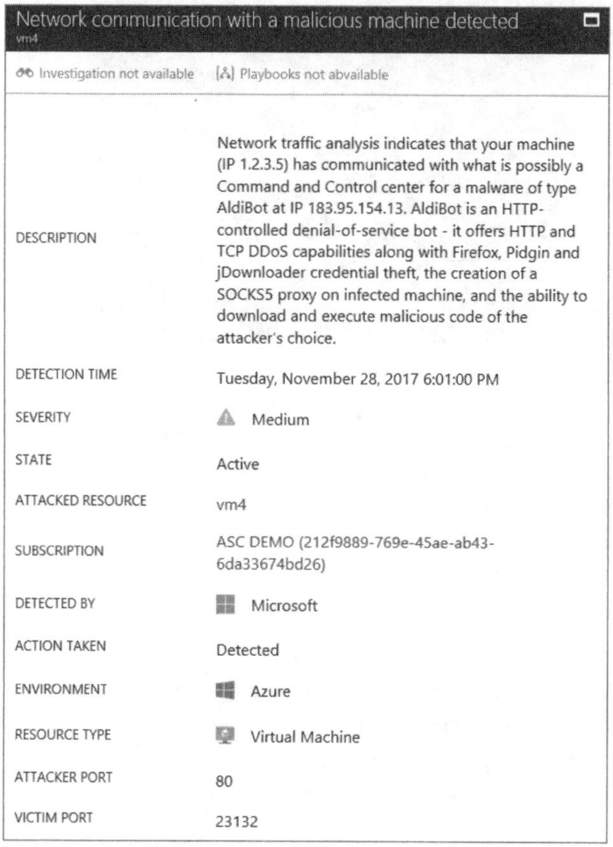

FIGURE 6-2 A threat-intelligence feed alert.

In addition to information received from traditional threat-intelligence feeds, Azure Security Center can surface security event information from numerous other types of resources. For example, if you integrate your firewall solution with Azure Security Center, security event information in the firewall logs will appear as alerts in the Azure Security Center console. The same goes for Azure Active Directory, Azure antimalware, and other Azure and partner-integrated services. (See Figure 6-3 on the next page.)

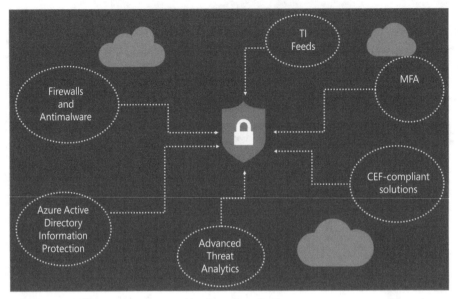

FIGURE 6-3 Intelligence resources used by Azure Security Center.

In addition to triggering alerts, Microsoft can use information in threat-intelligence feeds to better secure your overall deployment. For example, suppose one of your VMs has been compromised and is connecting to a botnet C&C server. Azure can detect this because it has access to some aspects of network communications, especially those that are not encrypted. Azure can then take over the DNS of the compromised VM and use that information to gain more detailed insights about the botnet and the C&C framework that's driving it.

> **NOTE** One security advantage of using the public cloud is that the cloud service provider has access to threat intelligence from hundreds, thousands, or even millions of machines, and can use this information to help protect your deployments. This type of information sharing is incredibly helpful in ensuring that all users on the cloud are secure.

Behavioral analysis

Atomic detection and threat intelligence are both very useful for identifying specific attacks and related dangerous activities. Both are usually correct in their assessments. However, by their very nature, both these types of threat detection require you to be aware of very specific behaviors in advance, and to then narrowly define the detection parameters. This allows for their high fidelity but also limits their effectiveness in detecting potential security events that might develop into major security incidents.

As noted, your goal is to be able to detect security events as quickly as possible. Although detecting signature-attack behaviors is useful, the definitions of these events are too narrow. You need some way to reliably detect suspicious behavior before it progresses to a full-blown compromise. One excellent way to do this is to use behavioral analysis. When you use behavioral analysis, you are not concerned with *how* the attacker accomplishes his or her tasks. You're more interested in the behavior that caused the attacker's actions.

Here's an example. Suppose you know that most (or all) of your line-of-business applications should not spawn external processes. If you find an application that *is* spawning external processes, you know that this is a bad behavior caused by an attack, regardless of how the attacker was able to provoke it.

With that said, behavioral analysis can be tricky business. For example, suppose you consider four failed logon attempts within 90 seconds to be a known-bad behavior. While it is true that it *could* be suspicious, it's also true that it might not be—for example, if the user's fingers aren't lined up properly on the keyboard and the user therefore mistypes his or her password several times. In other words, although four failed logon attempts within 90 seconds is suspicious, you might want to gather more information before issuing an alert.

You must avoid alert fatigue, which is what happens when your system surfaces too many marginal alerts. Alert fatigue can cause security analysts to ignore or temporize alerts—sometimes with disastrous consequences. To help prevent alert fatigue, Azure Security Center might not immediately generate an alert in a case like the one described here. Instead, it will note the behavior and, if some other event occurs that can be correlated with the behavior, generate a fusion alert. (The section "The cyber kill chain and fusion alerts" later in this chapter discusses fusion alerts in detail.)

Leveraging machine learning and the power of the cloud to prevent threats

The majority of security solutions have historically focused more on preventing threats and less on sophisticated ways to detect them as quickly as possible. This assume-breach mindset remains important. But if attacks continue to increase in sophistication and complexity, then attempting to reduce the attack surface also becomes necessary.

One of the biggest problems facing organizations that seek to improve their prevention solutions is a lack of manpower and time to sift through the huge amounts of data produced and to enforce ongoing policies. To mitigate this, Azure Security Center uses machine-learning algorithms on data collected by its agents (for example, security events and network traffic logs) to recommend tailored security policies (for example, application control rules) to its customers. These algorithms not only use data generated by a specific customer but also enrich it with insights gleaned from similar environments. The unique policies produced and enforced by Azure Security Center enable customers to rapidly apply accurate preventive mechanisms. This lowers the exposure of their environments to various risks and helps the customer focus on the most important issues in his or her environment.

Ben Kliger, Senior Program Manager, Azure Security Center Team

Anomaly detection

Security professionals must understand what is normal to be able to understand what is *not* normal—that is, to detect an anomaly. You need a baseline that defines normal—or at the very least, precedented—from a security standpoint. This baseline must consider the following:

- **The amount of time used to determine the baseline values**   Taking a long time to determine these values will lead to a more accurate baseline. Taking less time will enable you to put protections into place more quickly; it might also result in a baseline that is more sensitive to very short-term patterns that might disappear or get lost (or at least be very hard to find) when samples become too large.

- **The factors to be baselined**   It might be a bit of a stretch to say that there is an almost infinite number of factors that can be baselined from a security perspective. Still, the number is significant—too large to provide the type of information you want. It's best to focus on key areas that will provide the most impactful information when subjected to statistical analysis.

- **An adequate level of granularity for the baselined values**   The baseline must allow for the right level of granularity. If it is too coarse, the baseline will be less effective because smaller changes in values will be lost, leading to false negatives.

Azure Security Center creates baselines for VMs across an array of parameters that have been deemed useful for determining the current security state. The parameters used, and the details of how baselines are configured and calculated, is a trade secret—one of the many "secret sauces" that make Azure Security Center today's superior security solution. However, we can tell you that for most of your VMs, the baseline period will be 30 days—although, again, this will vary. Security defenders cannot be bound by strict adherence to orthodoxy. After all, their opponents are not similarly constrained. To do so would put the good guys at a fatal disadvantage.

With your baselines set, you can now use them in a variety of statistical algorithms to determine what is normal and what is not. "Normal" is expected and consistent with previous findings and is assumed to be good. "Not normal" means findings are unexpected and not consistent with previous findings.

> **NOTE** "Not normal" doesn't automatically equate to "bad" or "dangerous." It just means that further investigation and additional supportive evidence are required before the anomaly will be flagged as a possible security event.

Not all anomalies are security issues, but all security issues are anomalies (unless your security architecture and implementation is so bad that security events are the norm in your environment—in which case you have problems that must be addressed well before you attempt to leverage the subtle power of anomaly detection). Figure 6-4 provides a view of what anomalies might look like.

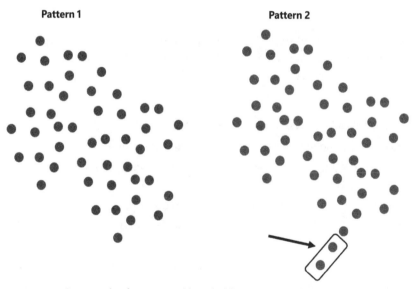

FIGURE 6-4 An example of a pattern with and without an anomaly.

Pattern 1 consists of a collection of blue dots that appear in particular positions along the X/Y axis. (We're measuring on three dimensions: X/Y/color). This is the baseline pattern. Pattern 2 represents a slice of time after the baseline was set. There is one obvious difference: the color of the dots. Another anomaly is the presence of two extra dots in Pattern 2.

NOTE The change of color in Figure 6-4 shows the importance of data visualization in anomaly detection and the process of converting data to information.

With anomaly detection, you progress from detecting things you already know are bad to detecting things you're not sure are bad. Isolated events often appear to be innocuous, but when a certain combination of isolated events occurs in a particular order, it may be a signal that something very bad is taking place. Anomaly detection algorithms are designed to detect these combinations. In addition, as you'll discover in the next section, these algorithms can be used in a process of correlation or reassessment to reveal very high-fidelity findings and trigger alerts related to those findings.

The cyber kill chain and fusion alerts

The cyber kill chain is a threat model described in 2011 by analysts from Lockheed Martin. The model was designed to help security teams and researchers organize their thinking about detecting and responding to threats. The model is now generally accepted and is part of the general lexicon of all security professionals.

NOTE If you are not a security professional and don't want to be one, don't worry. You don't need to remember the details of the cyber kill chain to understand how Azure Security Center uses it to help secure your assets.

The original cyber kill chain was divided into numerous phases:

1. **Reconnaissance** During this phase, the attacker identifies the best targets.

2. **Weaponization** Here, files are altered to make them weapons against a target system and are used to install malicious code.

3. **Delivery** At this point, weaponized files are placed on the target.

4. **Exploitation** During this phase, weaponized files are detonated—that is, they're run on the victim system.

5. **Installation** At this point, a back door is installed on the compromised system, giving the attacker persistent access.

6. **Command and control (C&C)** Here, malware on the compromised system communicates with a C&C system that gives the attacker access to the resources required to carry out his or her objective.

7. **Actions on objectives** At this point, the attacker carries out his or her objectives, which may be predefined or have evolved based on discovery.

The cyber kill chain was defined when on-premises computing was the norm. Now that cloud computing is considered a better option, the cyber kill chain must be re-evaluated and updated. A reconfiguration of the cyber kill chain might include the following phases:

1. **Active recon**   In this phase, the attacker uses numerous footprinting methods to identify the operating system or services being used, which will be the focus of the attack.

2. **Delivery**   Because most public cloud assets lack a logged-on user, attackers will need to hack the system—typically by finding unpatched exploits that can be leveraged against the system or service.

3. **Exploitation**   This phase focuses on problems on the server side instead of the client side.

4. **Persistence**   Unlike client-side systems, which are rebooted often, server- and service-specific systems are rarely rebooted. To remain persistent within the system, the exploit code will need to remain in memory. That is the focus of this stage.

5. **Internal recon**   Attacks against cloud-based systems are server-based. Therefore, rather than installing new tools, the attacker can simply use the server's built-in tools to conduct the attack. This helps the attacker remain undiscovered, as installing new tools could trigger an alert.

Now that you have a basic understanding of the cyber kill chain and its intent, let's consider how you can use it to create high-fidelity alerts with Azure Security Center. Azure Security Center has a type of alert called a security incident, which is raised in the console whenever the system identifies multiple alerts that, when correlated with each other, indicate an active attack. A security incident is sometimes referred to as a fusion alert because the alert represents a fusion of various alerts that appear to be related to each other.

Figure 6-5 shows an example of what such an attack campaign might look like and what alerts might be raised at the various stages of a cyber kill chain. (The figure shows a highly simplified version of the cyber kill chain outlined earlier to make it easier to understand how fusion alerts work.)

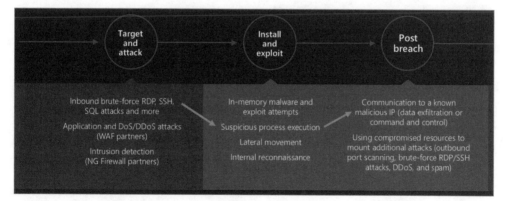

FIGURE 6-5   A simplified version of the cyber kill chain.

The sequence in the figure goes like this:

1. **Target and attack**   In this phase, Azure Security Center detects what appears to be a brute-force attack against the Remote Desktop Protocol (RDP) server on a VM. This determination is made by comparing a baseline of RDP connections to the VM and the current rate of RDP logon attempts, along with other factors related to RDP logons.

2. **Install and exploit**   Here, Azure Security Center detects the execution of a suspicious process on the VM. This suspicious process could be predefined (known-bad malware) or it could be a process that wasn't executed on the machine during previous baselines and is therefore unrecognized. (For example, maybe the process is launched by software recently installed by the admin.) You'll have to correlate this event with other events to find out.

3. **Post breach**   At this point, Azure Security Center has detected what appears to be a communication channel established between the VM and a known malicious IP address (probably flagged by a threat-intelligence feed). There's a very good chance that this is bad, but there is still a chance that it isn't. For example, maybe a security researcher or a red-team member working for the customer connected to the address on purpose. Yes, a connection to a known-bad IP address is serious, but it doesn't guarantee that the VM has been compromised.

Each phase of the cyber kill chain taken by itself indicates that something bad may be happening—but cannot offer you complete certainty. However, when you correlate these findings, you can be almost 100 percent sure that the VM has been compromised by a brute-force RDP attack, that the attacker has installed and run new malware on the machine, and that the malware is communicating with a C&C server (likely identified by a threat-intelligence feed). Figure 6-6 shows the resulting Security Incident Detected alert (top), while Figure 6-7 shows the collection of alerts that were correlated, or fused, to trigger the fusion alert.

DESCRIPTION	COUNT	DETECTED BY	ENVIRONME...
Security incident detected	1	Microsoft	Azure
Security incident detected	1	Microsoft	Azure
Suspicious SVCHOST process executed	21	Microsoft	Azure
Suspicious command execution	21	Microsoft	Azure

FIGURE 6-6 A list of security incidents, including the one generated from the scenario outlined here.

Alerts included in this incident

	DESCRIPTION ↑↓	COUNT ↑↓	DETECTION TIME ↑↓	ATTACKED RESOURCE ↑↓	SEVERITY ↑↓
🛡	Suspicious double extension file executed	16	12/12/17 02:22 AM		ⓘ High
🛡	Suspicious Volume Shadow Copy Activity	16	12/12/17 02:23 AM		ⓘ High
🛡	Suspicious command execution	16	12/12/17 02:23 AM		ⓘ High
🛡	Suspicious SVCHOST process executed	16	12/12/17 02:23 AM		ⓘ High
🛡	Windows registry persistence method detec...	16	12/12/17 02:23 AM		ⓘ Low
🛡	Suspicious process executed	15	12/12/17 02:36 AM		ⓘ High

FIGURE 6-7 The details of the top fusion alert from Figure 6-6.

Application whitelisting: adaptive application controls

Application whitelisting involves defining a list of applications that should, and do, run on a particular machine, with the understanding that any process run on that machine by an application *not* on the whitelist represents a possible threat. Windows Server supported application whitelisting for on-premises computers for many years. However, the complexity involved in configuring and maintaining a whitelist prevented it from being the success it could have been.

Azure Security Center also supports application whitelisting, although it refers to it by another name: application control. And it seems that this time, it might take. The internals of application control are somewhat complex, but you won't have to worry about them. Azure Security Center examines processes running on the VMs in your resource groups, develops a list of allow rules, and surfaces the list as a recommendation that you can choose to accept or reject.

> **NOTE** Be prepared to receive a lot of these recommendations, as each recommendation refers to a single process or file. You can choose to accept all recommendations in the list, some but not all of the recommendations, or just one.

It's up to you whether you want to monitor for whitelist violations and actively block them. In most cases, users monitor for these violations over a period a time. In this way, they develop confidence in the whitelist and can determine whether disabling processes not on the whitelist will interfere with the normal function of applications.

To explore this feature, select **Azure Security Center** in the left pane of the Azure Portal. Then select **Application Control**. The main application control screen explains what application control is and how it works. It also contains three tabs under a Resource Groups heading:

- **Configured** The Configured tab is shown in Figure 6-8. In this example, the Configured tab shows that an application whitelist has been configured and applied to two resource groups—one with two VMs and the other with four. If you click one of these resources, you'll see its whitelisting mode—Audit or Enforcement.

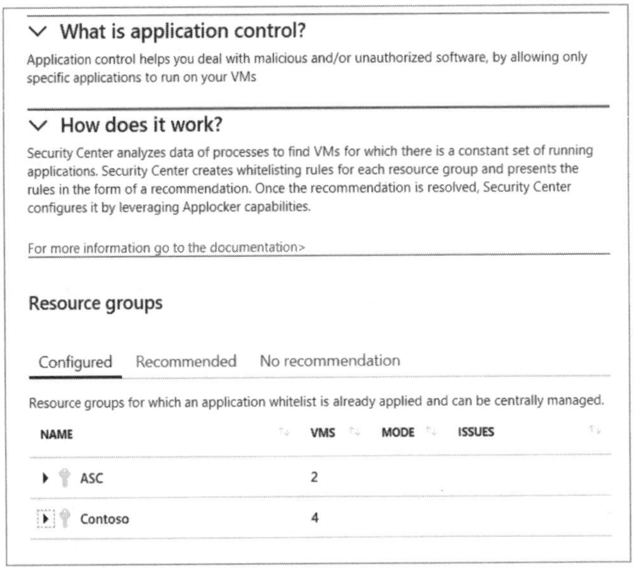

∨ **What is application control?**

Application control helps you deal with malicious and/or unauthorized software, by allowing only specific applications to run on your VMs

∨ **How does it work?**

Security Center analyzes data of processes to find VMs for which there is a constant set of running applications. Security Center creates whitelisting rules for each resource group and presents the rules in the form of a recommendation. Once the recommendation is resolved, Security Center configures it by leveraging Applocker capabilities.

For more information go to the documentation>

Resource groups

| Configured | Recommended | No recommendation |

Resource groups for which an application whitelist is already applied and can be centrally managed.

NAME	VMS	MODE	ISSUES
▸ 🔑 ASC	2		
▸ 🔑 Contoso	4		

FIGURE 6-8 Resource groups configured for whitelisting.

- **Recommended** This tab, shown in Figure 6-9, shows resource groups that, according to Azure Security Center, should be configured to support whitelisting. When you select a resource group, you'll see VMs that you can configure for application whitelisting as well as a list of top-level paths. (See Figure 6-10.) You can expand these paths to see processes that the system has identified as candidates for whitelisting. (For the best view, maximize the window.) Figure 6-11 shows processes in the program files—many of which you're probably familiar with—that Azure Security Center has flagged for whitelisting.

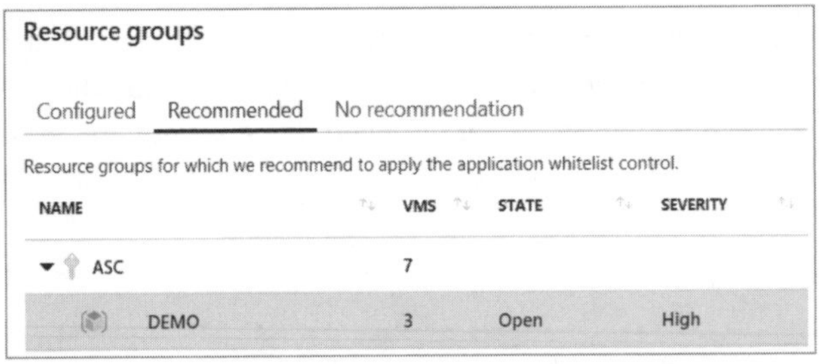

Resource groups

| Configured | Recommended | No recommendation |

Resource groups for which we recommend to apply the application whitelist control.

NAME	VMS	STATE	SEVERITY
▾ 🔑 ASC	7		
🔳 DEMO	3	Open	High

FIGURE 6-9 Selecting a resource group recommended for whitelisting.

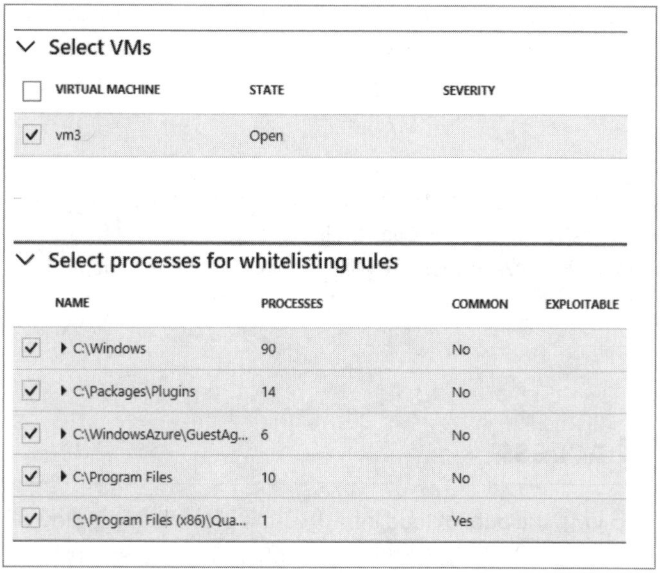

FIGURE 6-10 Viewing the high-level paths to processes flagged for whitelisting.

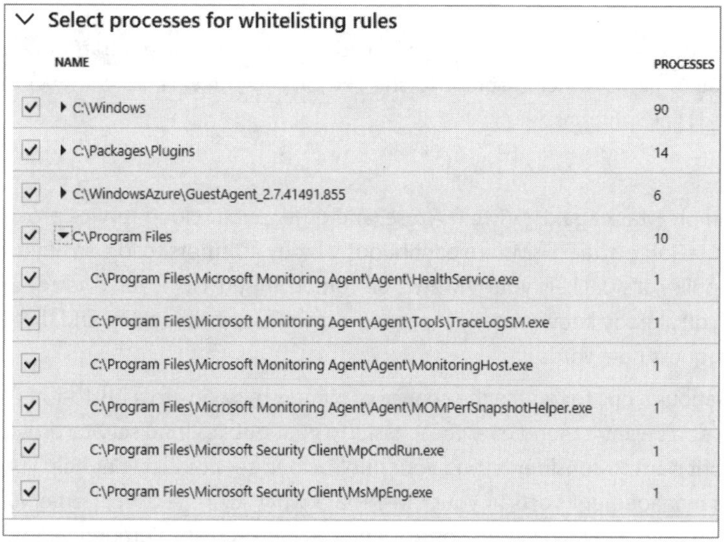

FIGURE 6-11 Specific processes flagged for whitelisting.

- **No Recommendation**   No recommendations are available for these because of compatibility issues.

Application whitelisting is a powerful tool that you can use to protect your Windows VMs running in Azure. Unlike configuring application whitelisting for on-premises machines, setting it up in Azure Security Center is quite easy. Indeed, you'll find it to be an effective and easy-to-manage solution.

> **NOTE** To learn more about application whitelisting (adaptive application controls), check out the article "Adaptive Application Controls in Azure Security Center" at https://docs.microsoft.com/en-us/azure/security-center/security-center-adaptive-application.

Just-in-time VM access

To provide remote access to VMs, the public cloud infrastructure provider must allow all remote management traffic to those VMs. To do this, it uses RDP, SSH, and remote PowerShell. Using these tools is easy—and nothing beats easy. Unfortunately, easy is often the enemy of security, so it's a difficult balancing act.

> **NOTE** There are alternative methods for providing remote management traffic access to VMs. Such methods include point-to-site VPN, site-to-site VPN, and varieties of dedicated WAN link solutions.

The most common attack against VMs in Azure (and other public cloud service providers) is an RDP or SSH brute-force attack. VMs are continuously hit by attempts to log on. If you have a strong password policy, it's unlikely your VMs will be compromised. However, if you're a security professional, you already know that most password policies are not strong and that users often use easy-to-guess passwords.

You can take various steps to reduce the chance of compromise due to a brute-force attack, but you probably don't want to hand over these tasks to your public cloud service provider. However, you might want to consider letting your public cloud service provider help you with network access to management ports to your VMs. That's what Azure Security Center just-in-time (JIT) VM access does. It allows you to control who can gain access to predefined management ports on a VM, when, and for how long. This control—which is enabled through Azure network capabilities rather than through any feature or system on the VM itself—is exerted over incoming connections from the internet.

The Azure Security Center JIT VM access feature is fairly simple. Here are the key points:

- The primary goal of Azure Security Center JIT is to protect VM management ports, such as RDP, SSH, and remote PowerShell ports.

- JIT limits the amount of time a port is open. The port will be open for only as long as is needed to get the work done. (You define the duration.)

- Network security group (NSG) rules control access to the management ports defined in the JIT policy.

- Only ARM VMs support Azure Security Center JIT VM access.

- We recommend that you enable JIT on all VMs that support it. Indeed, the only times we do *not* recommend using JIT are when no existing NSG is associated with the VM or when the VM is a classic VM.

- Sometimes, when a VM might be a candidate for JIT VM access, Azure Security Center doesn't issue a recommendation to that effect. This occurs when the JIT solution is disabled via a security policy set at the subscription or resource-group level, when the VM doesn't have a public IP address, and when the VM is not associated with an NSG.

- JIT VM access provides a collection of default management ports that you can use to enable access. You can also create new ports and remove existing ports.

- An administrator sets the JIT policy, which defines which ports can be used. When a user requests access to JIT, he or she can use only those ports defined in the policy. To increase security, the user can remove all ports except the one required to gain remote administrative access.

- You can use PowerShell to configure JIT policy as well as to request access.

- When users request JIT access, Azure Security Center checks their RBAC permissions. If the user has write access to the VM, JIT access will be granted. At that point, Azure Security Center will dynamically create NSG rules to allow inbound management traffic. When JIT access expires, the NSG rules will be removed. Note that connections are *not* actively reset, so a user who is connected will remain so until the connection is dropped by the user or for some other reason.

To explore this feature, select **Azure Security Center** in the left pane of the Azure Portal. Then select **Just-in-Time Access**. The main screen for JIT VM access explains what the feature is and how it works. It also contains three main tabs under a Virtual Machines heading. (See Figure 6-12 on the next page.)

∨ What is just in time VM access?

Just in time VM access enables you to lock down your VMs in the network level by blocking inbound traffic to specific ports. It enables you to control the access and reduce the attack surface to your VMs, by allowing access only upon a specific need.

∨ How does it work?

Upon a user request, based on Azure RBAC, Security Center will decide whether to grant access. If a request is approved, Security Center automatically configures the NSGs to allow inbound traffic to these ports, for the requested amount of time, after which it restores the NSGs to their previous states.

For more information go to the documentation >

Virtual machines

Configured   Recommended   No recommendation

VMs for which the just in time VM access control is already in place. Presented data is for the last week.

21 VMs   [Request access]

🔍 Search to filter items...

■	VIRTUAL MACHINE	APPROVED	LAST ACCESS	LAST USER	
✓ 🖥	redhat	0 Requests	N/A	N/A	...
🖥	ubuntu	0 Requests	N/A	N/A	...
🖥	CheckPoint-	0 Requests	N/A	N/A	...
🖥	vm	0 Requests	N/A	N/A	...

FIGURE 6-12   JIT VM access.

- **Configured**   The Configured tab is shown in Figure 6-13. It shows a list of VMs that have been configured to support Azure Security Center JIT. It also indicates how many times users have logged in to the VMs.

Virtual machines

Configured   Recommended   No recommendation

VMs for which the just in time VM access control is already in place. Presented data is for the last week.

FIGURE 6-13   The Configured tab of the JIT VM Access screen.

- **Recommended**   This tab, shown in Figure 6-14, contains a list of VMs that aren't currently configured to use Azure Security Center JIT—but perhaps should be.

Virtual machines

Configured   Recommended   No recommendation

VMs for which we recommend you to apply the just in time VM access control.

52 VMs   [Enable JIT on 52 VMs]

🔍 Search to filter items...

✓ VIRTUAL MACHINE		STATE	SEVERITY
✓	Linux	Open	ⓘ High

FIGURE 6-14   VMs recommended for JIT access.

- **No Recommendation** As mentioned, JIT VM access is not recommended for classic VMs or for VMs that are not associated with an NSG. The No Recommendation tab lists these VMs. To view the list of classic VMs, expand the Classic Virtual Machine category. To see VMs that are not associated with an NSG, expand the Missing Network Security Group category. Note that there is also an Other category. (See Figure 6-15.)

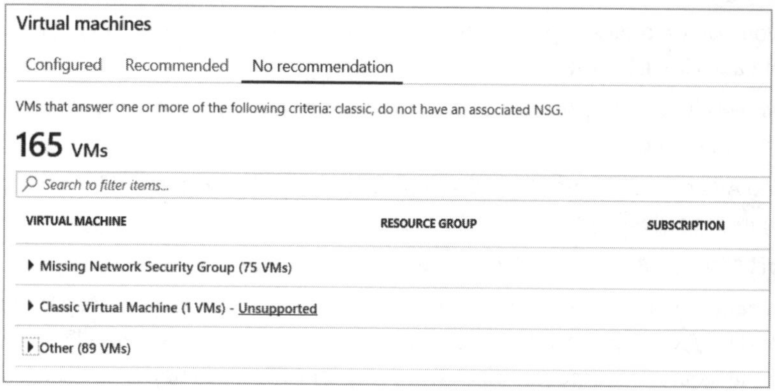

Virtual machines

Configured   Recommended   No recommendation

VMs that answer one or more of the following criteria: classic, do not have an associated NSG.

165 VMs

🔍 Search to filter items...

VIRTUAL MACHINE	RESOURCE GROUP	SUBSCRIPTION
▶ Missing Network Security Group (75 VMs)		
▶ Classic Virtual Machine (1 VMs) - Unsupported		
▶ Other (89 VMs)		

FIGURE 6-15 Adding management ports.

To configure VMs for JIT access, follow these steps:

1. In the **Recommended** tab, select the VMs you want to configure for JIT access.

2. Click the **Enable JIT on X VMs** button. The **JIT VM Access Configuration** page opens. (See Figure 6-16).

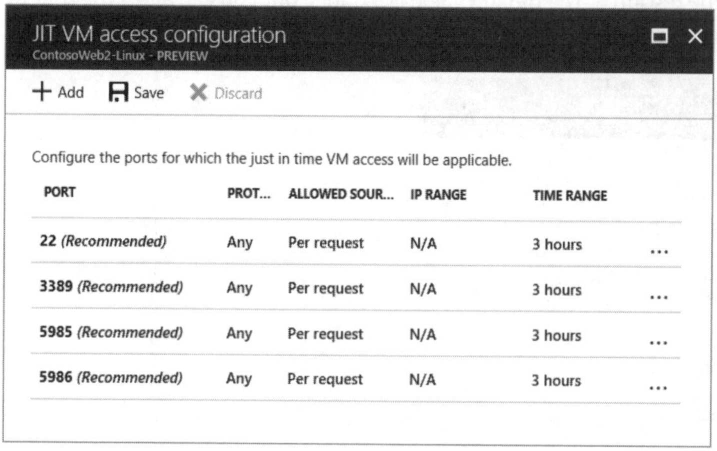

JIT VM access configuration
ContosoWeb2-Linux - PREVIEW

➕ Add   💾 Save   ✖ Discard

Configure the ports for which the just in time VM access will be applicable.

PORT	PROT...	ALLOWED SOUR...	IP RANGE	TIME RANGE	
22 *(Recommended)*	Any	Per request	N/A	3 hours	...
3389 *(Recommended)*	Any	Per request	N/A	3 hours	...
5985 *(Recommended)*	Any	Per request	N/A	3 hours	...
5986 *(Recommended)*	Any	Per request	N/A	3 hours	...

FIGURE 6-16 VMs that do not meet recommendation specs.

The JIT VM Access Configuration screen enables you to specify the ports and protocols to which JIT VM access will apply. The default ports and protocols are as follows:

- Port 22 (SSH)
- Port 3389 (RDP)

- Port 5985 (Remote PowerShell)
- Port 5986 (Remote PowerShell)

3. Do one of the following:

   - If these are all the ports you want available for JIT VM access, click the **Save** button to save the configuration as is.

   - If you want to omit any ports and protocols from the list, click the entry you want to omit and click **Discard**.

   - If you want to add a port and protocol, click **Add**. The following steps assume you chose this option.

4. Clicking Add opens the **Add Port Configuration** page. (See Figure 6-17.) Here, you configure the following settings:

   - **Port** This is the TCP or UDP port used by the protocol.

   - **Protocol** Typically, you'll choose TCP or UDP, but you can also click Any to configure non-UDP/TCP IP protocols. However, it would be unusual to use these IP protocols for management purposes—except possibly for GRE, which uses IP protocol 47.

   - **Allowed Source IPs** You have two options for this setting: Per Request and CIDR Block. If you choose Per Request, whatever IP address is currently assigned to the client system will be allowed access to the VM. If you choose CIDR Block, you can define a collection of IP addresses that client systems must have before they can connect to the resource.

   - **Max Request Time** This is the maximum amount of time the user can request access to the resource. The default value is 3 hours, but you can allow the user to ask for more (or less) time.

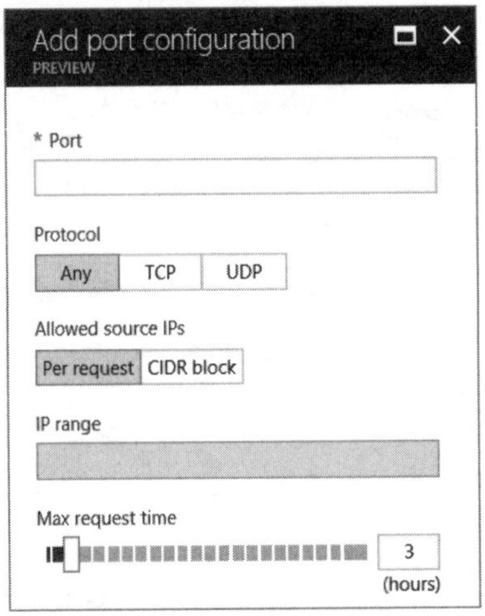

FIGURE 6-17 The JIT VM Access Configuration screen.

5. Having configured the JIT VM access policy, it's time to request access. To begin, click the **Configured** tab and select the check box next to the VM for which you want remote access. Then click the **Request Access** button. (See Figure 6-18.)

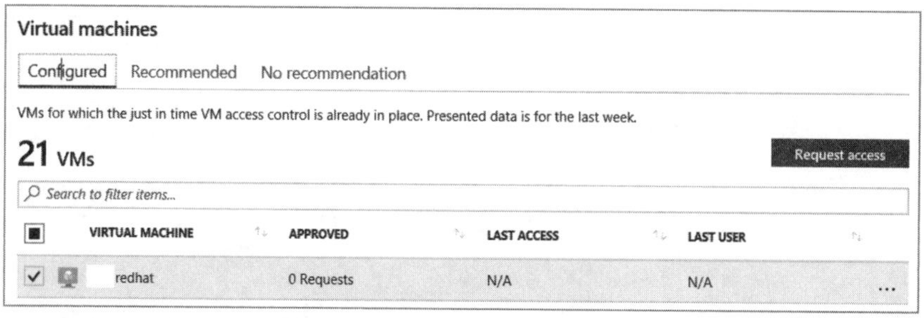

Virtual machines

| Configured | Recommended | No recommendation |

VMs for which the just in time VM access control is already in place. Presented data is for the last week.

21 VMs   Request access

🔍 Search to filter items...

☑	VIRTUAL MACHINE	↑↓	APPROVED	↑↓	LAST ACCESS	↑↓	LAST USER	↑↓
☑ 🖥	redhat		0 Requests		N/A		N/A	...

FIGURE 6-18 Requesting access to a VM.

6. The Request Access page opens. (See Figure 6-19.) Its contents vary depending on the policy settings assigned to the VM. For added security, toggle off any ports that are not required.

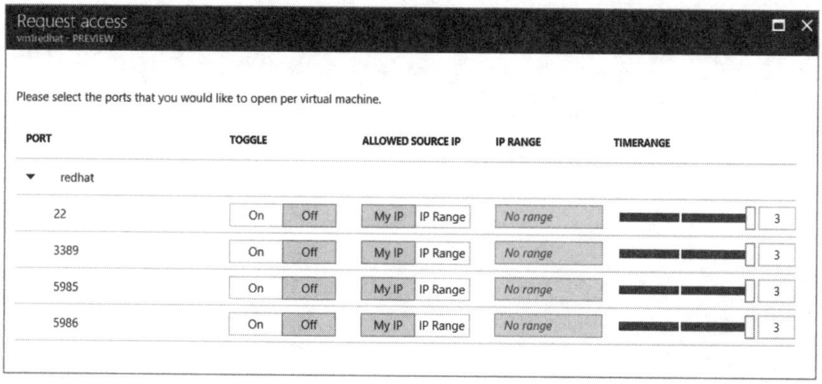

Request access
vmredhat - PREVIEW   ☐ ✕

Please select the ports that you would like to open per virtual machine.

PORT	TOGGLE	ALLOWED SOURCE IP	IP RANGE	TIMERANGE
▼ redhat				
22	On Off	My IP IP Range	No range	▬▬▬▬▬ 3
3389	On Off	My IP IP Range	No range	▬▬▬▬▬ 3
5985	On Off	My IP IP Range	No range	▬▬▬▬▬ 3
5986	On Off	My IP IP Range	No range	▬▬▬▬▬ 3

FIGURE 6-19 Configuring the access request.

7. Back in the Configured tab, click the dots to the right of the VM entry to view the options shown in Figure 6-20. These options are as follows:

- **Properties** This shows the properties of the entry.
- **Activity Log** This shows the related activity log entries.
- **Edit** This enables you to edit information about the entry.
- **Remove** Select this to remove the entry.

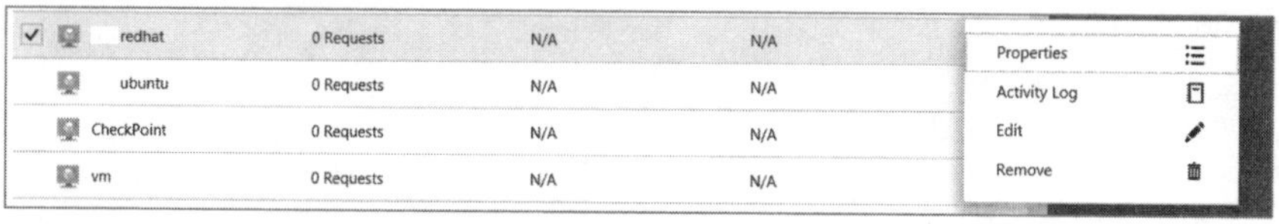

☑ 🖥	redhat	0 Requests	N/A	N/A	Properties	☰
🖥	ubuntu	0 Requests	N/A	N/A	Activity Log	🗒
🖥	CheckPoint	0 Requests	N/A	N/A	Edit	✏
🖥	vm	0 Requests	N/A	N/A	Remove	🗑

FIGURE 6-20 Additional options.

Chapter 7

Security incident and event management (SIEM) integration with Splunk

In this chapter you will learn how to integrate Azure Security Center with Splunk so that information gathered by Azure Security Center can be integrated into your on-premises Splunk deployments.

Figure 7-1 provides a high-level view of the overall architecture of the solution. The key enabling features for the solution include Azure Event Hubs, Azure Monitor, and a Security incident and event management (SIEM) connector add-on that enables the SIEM to poll the event hub to bring the information into the on-premises SIEM.

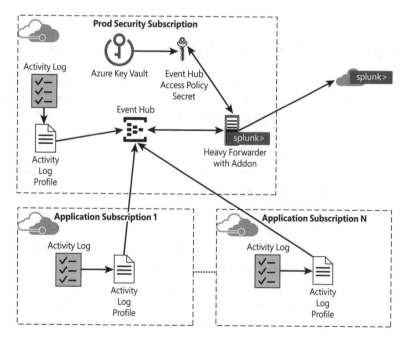

FIGURE 7-1 A high-level view of the overall architecture of the Azure Security Center and Splunk integration solution.

Streaming logs

Prior to Azure Monitor, each Azure service provided its own method of accessing monitoring data. Collecting log and metric data from Azure services involved a variety of methods, including querying REST APIs, reading from Azure Storage accounts, or even connecting to FTP servers. To help navigate this complexity, the Azure Security team created the Azure Log Integrator tool, which collected security data from a variety of sources, standardized and formatted the data, and passed it along to SIEMs. Soon after that, Azure Monitor was introduced—a platform-monitoring service that offered a common way for all Azure services to expose their monitoring data.

Azure Monitor operates at enterprise cloud scale and simplifies the management of routing log data into SIEMs using a single schema and access point across all Azure services. This dramatically simplifies Azure log integration with SIEM tools and includes the alerts available from Azure Security Center. Azure Monitor is Azure's central logging pipeline going forward and provides several out-of-the-box integrations with popular SIEM tools such as Splunk and IBM QRadar.

John Kemnetz, Program Manager

Integrating SIEM solutions

Azure Security Center alerts are published to the Azure activity log. Azure activity logs are considered data plane–level logs, which separates them from Azure diagnostic logs (which allow you to get insight into services and troubleshoot those services).

Azure Monitor can consume or integrate Azure activity logs. This enables you to use Azure Monitor to route Azure Security Center data into an on-premises SIEM solution. To do this, data collected by Azure Monitor from the activity logs can be streamed into event hubs. The streamed information can then be pulled into an on-premises SIEM using a connector tool provided by SIEM vendors.

The general process is simple:

1. Create an event hub that will be the destination for your Azure Security Center data (for more information, see https://docs.microsoft.com/en-us/azure/event-hubs/event-hubs-create).

2. Stream the Azure activity logs into the event hub (for more information, see https://docs.microsoft.com/en-us/azure/monitoring-and-diagnostics/monitoring-stream-activity-logs-event-hubs).

3. Install and configure the SIEM solution vendor's connector (for more information, see https://docs.microsoft.com/en-us/azure/monitoring-and-diagnostics/monitor-stream-monitoring-data-event-hubs#what-can-i-do-with-the-monitoring-data-being-sent-to-my-event-hub).

Splunk integration with Azure Security Center

To get a better idea of how to integrate with a SIEM system, we'll see how to integrate Azure Security Center with Splunk. The configuration process isn't trivial—there are a lot of steps, and you need to make sure to get each one right.

Splunk integration involves the following processes:

1. Confirm there are accessible logs in Azure Monitor.

2. Configure required permissions in a subscription for the SIEM pipe.

3. Create and configure a resource group for the SIEM pipe.

4. Set up an Azure AD application to provide an access control identity.

5. Create a key vault to contain credentials.

6. Put the app password into the key vault.

7. Make an event hub.

8. Create a shared access key for event hub access control.

9. Put the event hub shared access key in Azure Key Vault.

10. Hook up the event hub to Azure Monitor.

11. Spin up the virtual machine that hosts the Splunk enterprise VM.

12. Install and configure the Azure Monitor add-on for Splunk.

Before you can begin, you need to be sure you have the prerequisites for integration. The required components are as follows:

- An Azure subscription (with administrative access)
- Resource groups to contain the required resources
- An Azure Active Directory (AAD) application for service access
- A key vault in which to store required credentials
- An event hub namespace (event hubs will be created automatically as needed)
- A Splunk server (in the cloud or on-premises)
- Microsoft's Splunk add-on to read logs from event hubs

Confirming accessible logs in Azure Monitor

To confirm there are accessible logs in Azure Monitor, open the Azure portal's **Monitor** blade and click **Activity Log**. Run a simple query to confirm that the data is usable. (See Figure 7-2.)

Activity log

FIGURE 7-2 Activity Log option in Monitor blade.

Configuring the subscription for the Splunk SIEM pipe

If you have an existing subscription, make sure you have Owner, Administrator, or Co-Administrator access. If not, request access to that subscription to create the pipe. In this example, the subscription is named **ContosoSub**.

Creating and configuring a resource group for the Splunk SIEM pipe

To create and configure a resource group for the Splunk SIEM pipe, follow these steps:

1. Open the Azure Portal **ResourceGroup** blade. Confirm that the subscription for the SIEM pipe is selected in the filter at the top (**ContosoSub**, in this example).

2. Click the **Add** button at the top of the screen. (See Figure 7-3.) A new blade will open and enable you to configure the resource group. (See Figure 7-4.)

FIGURE 7-3 Click the Add button in the ResourceGroup blade.

3. Enter a unique resource group name (for example, **SiemPipeRG**).

4. Click the **Subscription** drop-down list and select the desired subscription (in this case, **ContosoSub**).

5. Click the **Resource Group Location** drop-down list and select a location for your resource group (we recommend that you place all the resources in this example in the same location).

6. Click the **Create** button at the bottom to save the changes.

FIGURE 7-4 Configure the resource group.

Setting up an Azure AD application to provide an access control identity

You must set up an Azure Active Directory (AAD) application to provide an identity that can be used to enable access control for the solution. Follow these steps:

1. Open the Azure portal's **Active Directory** blade and then click **App Registrations**. (See Figure 7-5.)

FIGURE 7-5 Click App Registrations.

2. Click **New Application Registration** at the top. (See Figure 7-6.) The Create blade opens.

FIGURE 7-6 Click New Application Registration.

3. In the **Create** blade (see Figure 7-7), enter the name of your app—for example, **contoso.siem.example**.

4. Select **Web App/API** in the **Application Type** drop-down list.

5. In the **Sign-on URL** box, type **https://contoso.siem.example**.

> **NOTE** This does not have to be a real, fully qualified domain name for the purposes of this SIEM pipe. You just need to enter a value here to support app creation.

6. Click the **Create** button at the bottom of the blade to create the application.

FIGURE 7-7 Create a registration for your application.

7. In the Azure Active Directory blade, click the **App Registrations** button again. (See Figure 7-8.)

FIGURE 7-8 Click the App Registrations button.

8. In the search box, enter the name of the new app you just created—as shown in this example, **contoso.siem.example**—and click the app when you find it.

9. Select **Keys**. (See Figure 7-9.)

FIGURE 7-9 Select the Keys option to create an access key.

> **NOTE** If you do not see that option, it means you are not an administrator for the key. If you're not an administrator, contact an admin and request access.

10. In the **Keys** blade (see Figure 7-10), enter a descriptive name for the key in the Description field—for example, **siemapppass**.

11. In the **Expires** box, select the duration for which the secret will be available.

12. Click **Save** at the top of the Keys blade.

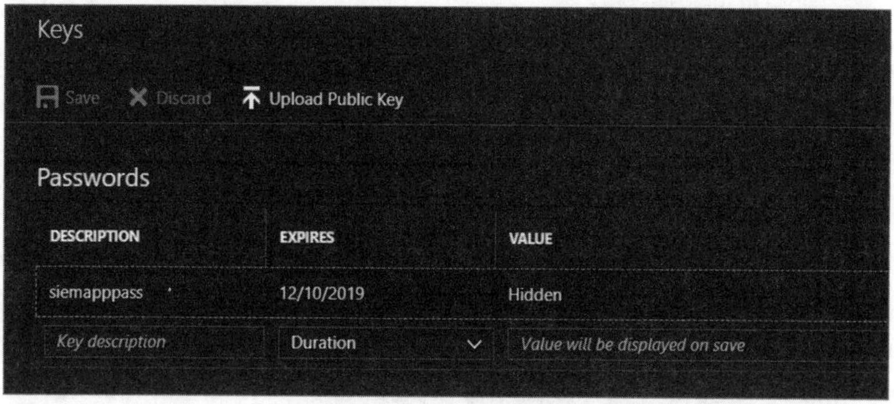

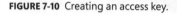

Keys

💾 Save   ✕ Discard   ⬆ Upload Public Key

Passwords

DESCRIPTION	EXPIRES	VALUE
siemapppass	12/10/2019	Hidden
Key description	Duration ⌄	Value will be displayed on save

FIGURE 7-10 Creating an access key.

13. Copy the base64 string value that appears in the **Value Will Be Displayed on Save** box in the **Value** column. You will store this value in your key vault, as described in the next section.

> **IMPORTANT:** Once you click Save, quickly copy the base64 string value (to store in your key vault; see the next section). When you leave this page, the value will be hidden and will not be retrievable by the UI. We refer to this secret as "AppPassword" as we move forward in this example.

Creating an Azure key vault

Authentication credentials are required for the Azure Active Directory application. Those credentials are stored in the key vault to optimize security. To create the key vault, follow these steps:

1. Open the Azure portal's **Key Vault** blade. Confirm that the subscription for the SIEM pipe is selected in the filter at the top (**ContosoSub**, in this example).

2. Click the **Add** button at the top of the screen. (See Figure 7-11.)

FIGURE 7-11 Click the Add button in the Azure portal.

The **Create Key Vault** blade opens. (See Figure 7-12.)

3. Enter a name for the key vault, such as **SiemPipeKV**. Then select the desired subscription, such as **ContosoSub**.

4. Click the **Use Existing** button, and select the **SiemPipeRG** resource group you created earlier in this chapter.

5. In the **Location** drop-down list, select the location of the resource group.

6. Select the pricing tier for this key vault. In the example we're working with, both Standard and Premium tier options will work. (We recommend using the Premium tier for additional capabilities.)

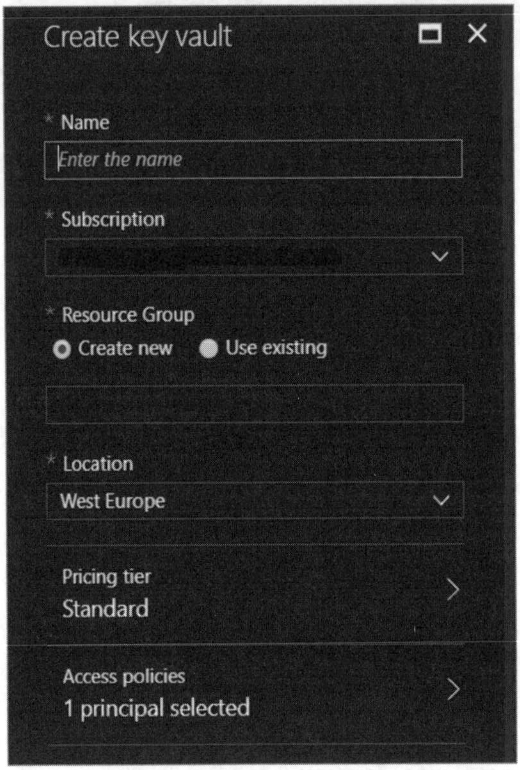

FIGURE 7-12 Create a key vault.

7. Click the **Access Policies** button. The **Access Policies** blade opens.

8. Click the **Add New** button. (See Figure 7-13.)

Access policies
Click to show advanced access policies
Add new

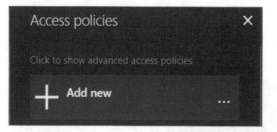

FIGURE 7-13 Click the Add New button to configure privileged access to the key vault.

9. The **Access Policies** blade opens with additional configuration capabilities so that you can configure privileged access to the key vault. (See Figure 7-14.)

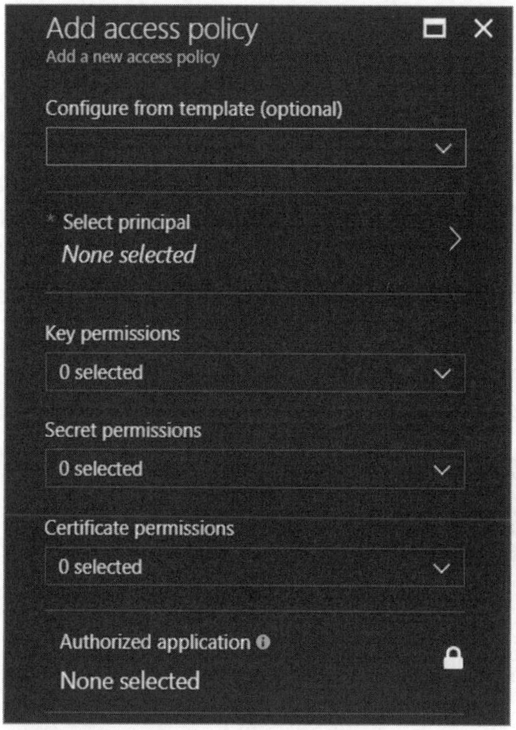

Add access policy
Add a new access policy
Configure from template (optional)
* Select principal
None selected
Key permissions
0 selected
Secret permissions
0 selected
Certificate permissions
0 selected
Authorized application
None selected

FIGURE 7-14 Configure a new access policy.

10. To ensure that the AAD application you created has access to this key vault, open the **Configure from Template** drop-down list and choose **Secret & Certificate Management.**

11. Click the **Select Principal** button. (A principal is an AAD entity for which access may be configured.)

12. The **Principal** blade opens. In the **Select** box, type the name of your AAD app—in this case, **contoso.siem.example**—and click the **Select** button at the bottom of the blade. (See Figure 7-15.)

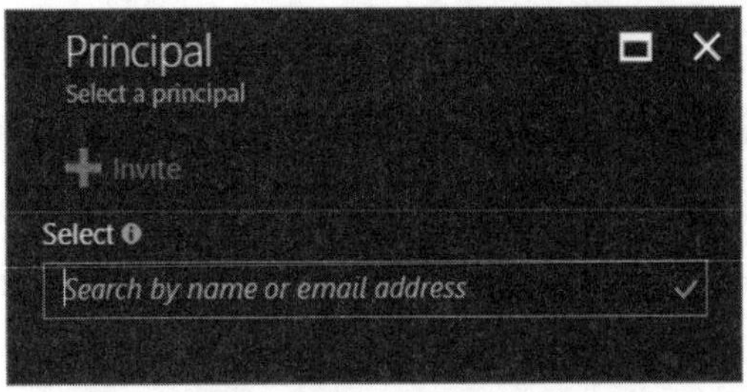

FIGURE 7-15 Select a principal.

13. Click the **Create** button at the bottom of the Add Access Policy blade, and then click the **Create** button at the bottom of the Create Key Vault blade.

Copying the app password into Key Vault

Now that we have a vault, we can put the key in it.

1. Open the **Key Vault** blade and confirm that the subscription for the SIEM pipe is selected in the filter at the top (**ContosoSub**, in this example).

2. Select the **SiemPipeKV** key vault.

3. Click **Secrets**. (See Figure 7-16.)

FIGURE 7-16 Click the Secrets button to start the process of putting a key into the vault.

4. In the **Secrets** blade, click **Add** at the top. (See Figure 7-17.)

FIGURE 7-17 Click Add in the new blade.

5. The **Create a Secret** blade opens. (See Figure 7-18.)

6. In the **Upload Options** drop-down list, select **Manual**.

7. In the **Name** field, enter a name for the secret—for example, **AppPassword**.

8. In the **Value** field, paste the value you copied from the Azure Active Directory app creation process. The value we used was **AppPassword**.

9. In the **Content Type** field, enter **text/plain**. Make sure that you type it exactly as it is written here; it is case sensitive. Leave the check boxes **Set Action Date** and **Set Expiration Date** unselected.

10. Confirm that **Enabled** is set to **Yes**.

11. Click the **Create** button at the bottom of the blade.

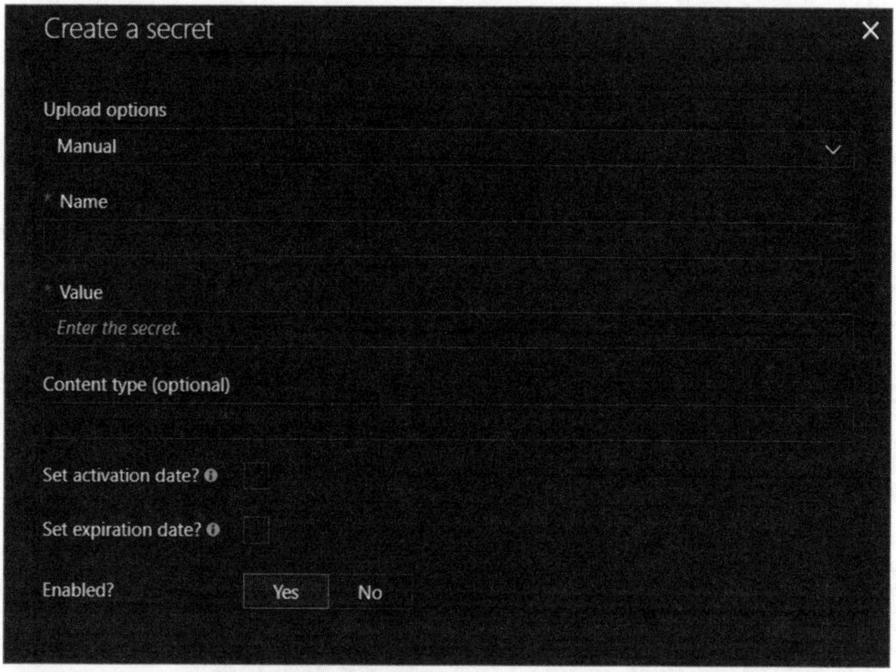

Create a secret   ✕

Upload options

Manual   ⌄

* Name

* Value

Enter the secret.

Content type (optional)

Set activation date? ⓘ ☐

Set expiration date? ⓘ ☐

Enabled?   Yes   No

FIGURE 7-18 Enter the information to create a secret.

Making an event hub

At this point we have an identity and a secret. Let's now create the event hub that we'll use to support the SIEM pipe.

1. Go to the **Event Hubs** blade. Confirm that the **ContosoSub** subscription for the SIEM pipe is selected in the filter at the top.

2. Click the **Add** button at the top of the screen. (See Figure 7-19.)

FIGURE 7-19 Click the Add button.

3. The **Create Namespace** blade opens to enable you to create an event hub namespace. (See Figure 7-20.) Enter a name for the event hub—for example, **contososiem-ns**.

4. Select a pricing tier based on your throughput requirements.

5. Select the **ContosoSub** subscription.

6. Select **Use Existing** in the Resource Group section, and then select the **SiemPipeRG** resource group.

7. Select the location of the resource group.

8. Select the number of throughput units required based on your expected reporting load. Start with 1 and increase this in the future if needed.

9. Select **Enable Auto-Inflate** if you would like Azure to manage the scale of your event hub based on throughput load. If you select the check box (as shown in the image), you will need to specify an upper limit (maximum) number of throughput units to automatically create (scale out). The maximum allowed is 20 per event hub namespace. You may leave this at 20 for now and change it in the future based on scale and cost requirements.

10. Click the **Create** button at the bottom of the Create Namespace blade.

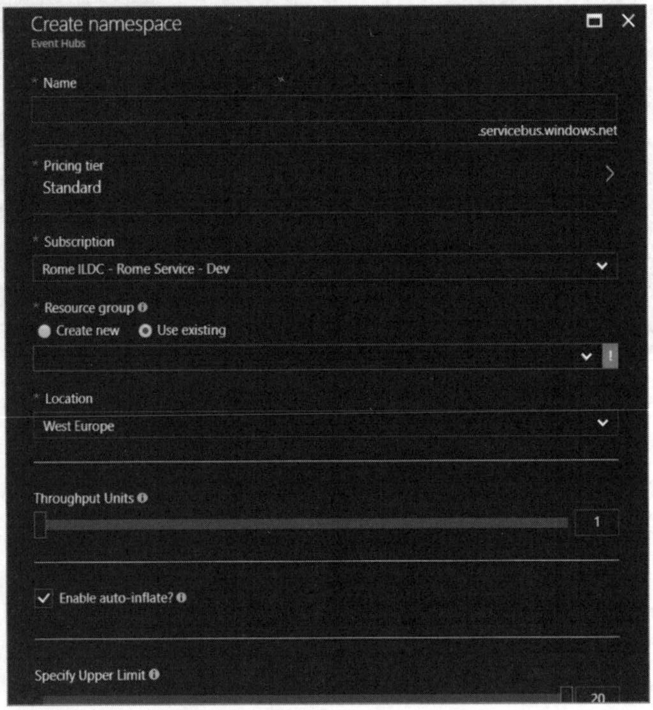

FIGURE 7-20   Create an event hub namespace.

Creating a shared access key for event hub access control

1. Go to the Azure portal's Event Hubs blade. Make sure that the **ContosoSub** subscription for the SIEM pipe is selected in the filter at the top.

2. Select the **contososiem-ns** event hub.

3. Click **Shared Access Policies**. (See Figure 7-21.)

FIGURE 7-21 Click Shared Access Policies in the Event Hubs blade.

4. A new blade opens where you will create a shared access key for event hub access. (See Figure 7-22.)

FIGURE 7-22 Create a shared access key for event hub access.

5. Click the **Add** button, as seen in Figure 7-23.

FIGURE 7-23 Click the Add button to add an SAS policy.

6. The **Add SAS Policy** blade opens. (See Figure 7-24.)

7. Enter a descriptive name for the access policy (for example, **ListenOnlySharedAccessKey**).

8. Click the check box next to **Listen** to give it only listen access.

9. Click the **Create** button. Wait for the policy to be created.

FIGURE 7-24 Add the SAS policy and wait for it to be created.

10. After the policy is created, click it (**ListenOnlySharedAccessKey**, in this example) and the **SAS Policy** blade opens. (See Figure 7-25.)

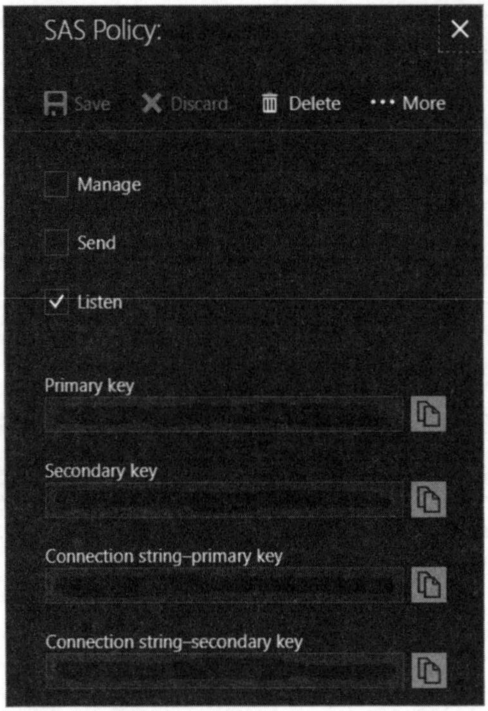

SAS Policy: ×

💾 Save   ✖ Discard   🗑 Delete   ••• More

☐ Manage

☐ Send

☑ Listen

Primary key

Secondary key

Connection string–primary key

Connection string–secondary key

FIGURE 7-25 The SAS Policy blade.

11. Click the blue button next to the primary key, and copy the secret value from that line (we will refer to it as **EventHubPrimaryKey**). (See Figure 7-26.)

FIGURE 7-26 Copy the secret value.

The next step is to store this value in Azure Key Vault as a secret.

Placing the event hub shared access key in Azure Key Vault

1. Open the **Key Vault** blade and confirm that the **ContosoSub** subscription for the SIEM pipe is selected in the filter at the top.

2. Select the **SiemPipeKV** key vault.

3. Click **Secrets**. (See Figure 7-27.)

FIGURE 7-27 The Secrets selection in the Key Vault blade.

4. In the **Secrets** blade that opens, click **Add**. (See Figure 7-28.)

FIGURE 7-28 Click the Add button in the new blade.

5. The **Create a Secret** blade opens, in which you can configure the new secret. (See Figure 7-29.)

6. From the **Upload Options drop-down list**, select **Manual**.

7. Enter a name for the secret in the Name field. In this example, use **ProdEventHub Credential**.

8. Under **Value**, paste the value you copied from the AAD app creation process, which is **EventHubPrimaryKey**.

9. Under **Content Type**, enter **ListenOnlySharedAccessKey** (make sure that you enter it exactly as it is written here, as it is case sensitive). Leave the **Set Activation Date** and **Set Expiration Date** check boxes unselected.

10. Confirm that **Enabled** is set to **Yes**.

11. Click the **Create** button at the bottom of the Create a Secret blade.

Create a secret   ✕

Upload options

Manual

Name

Value

Enter the secret.

Content type (optional)

Set activation date? ⓘ

Set expiration date? ⓘ

Enabled?   Yes   No

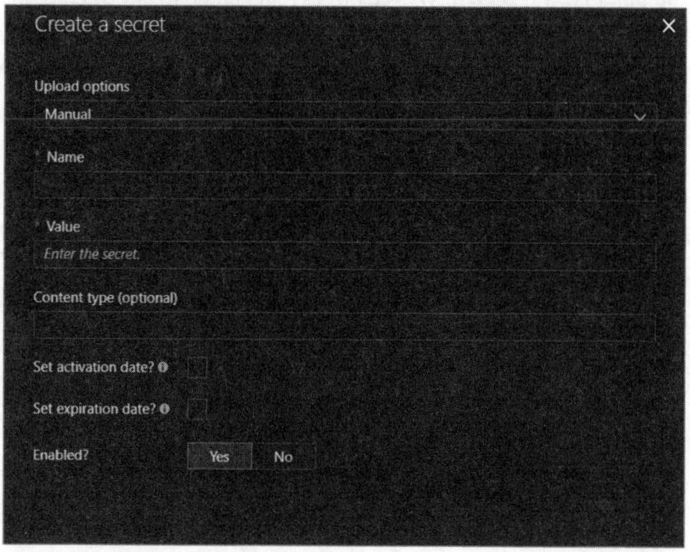

FIGURE 7-29 Configure the new secret.

Hooking up the event hub to Azure Monitor

1. Open the **Azure Portal Monitor** blade, and click **Activity Log**. (See Figure 7-30.)

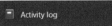

FIGURE 7-30 Click Activity Log in the Monitor blade.

2. Click the **Export** option at the top of the Monitor blade. (See Figure 7-31.)

FIGURE 7-31 Click Export.

3. A new blade opens on which you can configure the data streaming to a SIEM. (See Figure 7-32.)

4. Select the **ContosoSub** subscription.

> **IMPORTANT** Be aware that the SIEM must be configured on a per-subscription basis, so each subscription that has data to transmit to the SIEM will need to be configured manually.

5. Under **Regions**, make sure that all regions are selected.

> **NOTE** We recommend that you keep this check box as is (meaning to have all regions selected). The filter is exclusive regarding the regions selected. Any selection here means that only activities marked for those selected regions will arrive. Most activities do not note region and are reported globally, and so any specific selection will negate the arrival of global items.

6. Select the check box **Export to an Event Hub** to enable the data stream into the event hub (from an activity log).

7. Click the **Service Bus Namespace** button, and select the event hub created in the previous step.

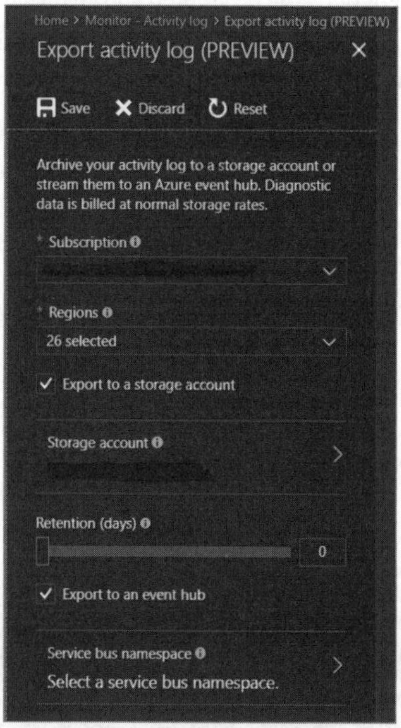

FIGURE 7-32 Configure the data streaming to a SIEM.

8. Select **ContosoSub** from the **Subscription** drop-down list for the SIEM pipe. (See Figure 7-33.)

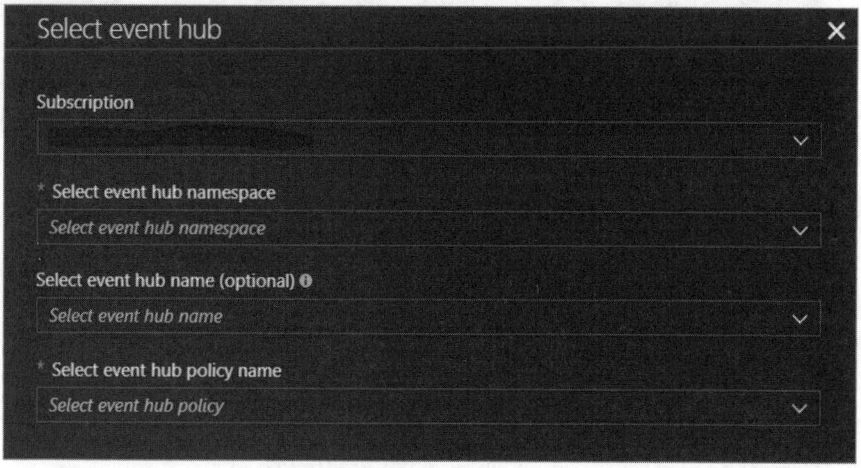

FIGURE 7-33 Configure to select the event hub.

9. Select **contososiem-ns** from the **Select Event Hub Namespace** drop-down list. Leave **Select Event Hub Name** empty. (This is optional in case you want your event to go to a specific event hub. If you leave this blank, event hubs will be created automatically.)

10. From the **Select Event Hub Policy Name** drop-down list, select a policy with an all-access pass, which in this example is **RootManageSharedAccessKey**.

11. Click **OK** at the bottom of the blade.

Spinning up the virtual machine that hosts the Splunk enterprise VM

1. Go to the Azure portal's **Virtual Machine** blade and click the **Add** button. (See Figure 7-34.) The **Compute** blade opens.

FIGURE 7-34 Click the Add button in the Virtual Machine blade.

2. In the search box, enter **Splunk enterprise** and select the Splunk Enterprise template VM. (See Figure 7-35.)

Compute

▼ Filter

🔍 Splunk enterprise

Results

NAME	PUBLISHER
> Splunk Enterprise	Splunk

FIGURE 7-35 Select Splunk Enterprise.

3. Read the documentation carefully and set up any required licenses as detailed.

4. Click **Create** when ready.

5. On the **Basic** page, select a VM user name and password (we recommend **Store All Passwords in Key Vault**).

6. Select the **ContosoSub** subscription for the SIEM pipe.

7. Under **Resource Group**, select the **Create New** option button.

8. Name the new resource group **SiemPipeSplunkVmRG**.

9. Open the **Location** drop-down list and select the location associated with the resource group.

10. Mark the address space (for example, use the 10.2.0.0./16 mask for 65,536 addresses). The **Create Subnet Configuration** page opens.

11. Enter a **Head Subnet** name (use any meaningful name, such as **shsubnet**).

12. In the **Search Head Subnet Address Prefix Field**, select an address prefix that matches the address space (for example, use **10.2.0.0/24** for 32,768 addresses).

13. Enter the index subnet name—for example, **idxsubnet**.

14. Enter the index subnet address prefix, **10.2.0.0/24**.

15. Select a deployment type for the Splunk VM (select based on expected load).

16. Select a VM size (select based on expected load).

17. Select a new IP name. Click the button and create a new name. This can be either static or dynamic. (Note that static names may incur additional charges.)

18. Set up a unique domain name (network unique) for the Splunk VM (for example, **contoso.splunk.example.vm**).

19. Set up an admin password (the user will be admin—that is, preconfigured in the VM). Recommendation: Store the password in Key Vault (see the steps earlier in this chapter). The **Optional** page opens.

20. Configure the SSH source to reduce access (for security reasons).

21. Configure the IP range to receive data (for security reasons).

22. Review all data before proceeding and save a screenshot of the configuration summary for later reference. The **Buy** page opens.

23. Click the **Create** button when done to complete the purchase. Be aware that this will incur regular payment based on the configuration chosen in the previous steps.

> **NOTE** The template will create the VM with the name **standalone-vm** by default.

Installing and configuring the Azure Monitor add-on for Splunk

To install and configure the Azure Monitor add-on for Splunk, please follow the instructions maintained by Splunk at https://github.com/Microsoft/AzureMonitorAddonForSplunk.

Chapter 8

Monitoring identity and access

These days, security monitoring goes beyond assessing the security state of your workloads. You must take a broader approach that also includes identity and access. When an adversary can compromise one user's credentials, that adversary can leverage the legitimate account for a much larger attack campaign. Regardless of where your workloads are located—in the cloud or on-premises—it is imperative to monitor your users' behaviors, their access, and how their credentials are used.

In this chapter, you will learn how to use Azure Security Center to monitor your users' identity and access requests, to integrate with Azure AD Identity Protection, and to customize your search when investigating credentials that were potentially compromised.

Monitoring identity-related activities

Your users' authentication patterns can provide great insight into what's happening in your environment. Fortunately, Azure Security Center has an entire dashboard dedicated to this type of activity: the Identity & Access dashboard. Follow these steps to access this dashboard:

1. Open the **Azure Portal** and sign in as a user who has **Security Admin** privileges.

2. In the left pane, click **Security Center**.

3. In the left pane of the Security Center window, under **Prevention**, click **Identity & Access**.

4. If you have multiple workspaces, you'll be prompted to select the one you want to monitor. (See Figure 8-1.) Click the desired workspace. The **Identity & Access** dashboard opens. (See Figure 8-2.)

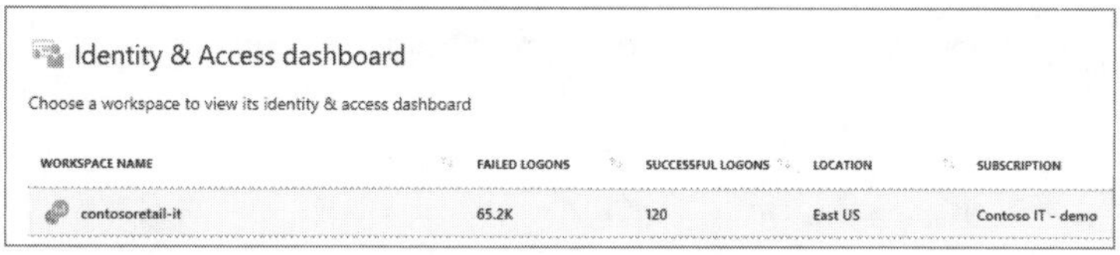

FIGURE 8-1 Choose which workspace you want to monitor.

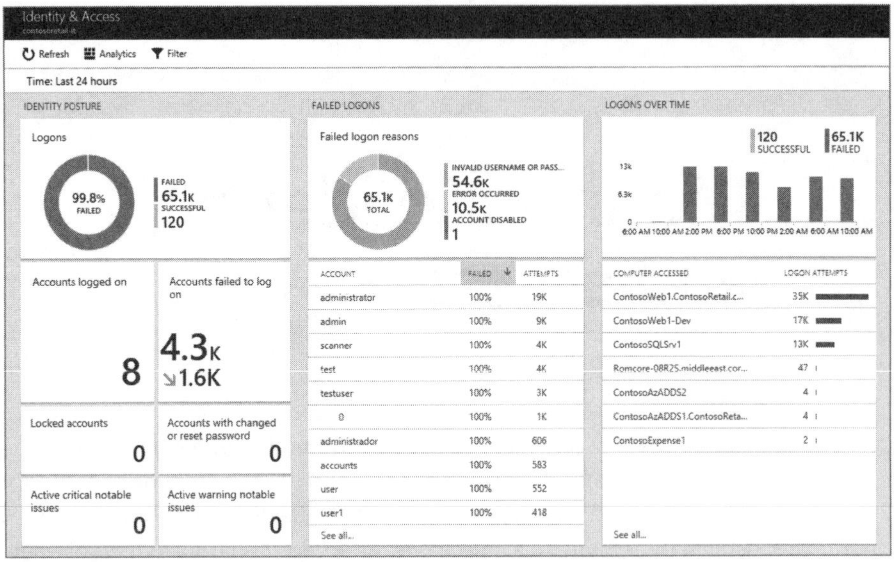

FIGURE 8-2 The Identity & Access dashboard.

This dashboard has a great summary of all identity-related activities monitored by Security Center. Security operations personnel should visit this dashboard multiple times throughout the day to quickly assess the current identity state.

This dashboard contains three major sections:

- Identity Posture
- Failed Logons
- Logons Over Time

The following sections discuss these dashboard features in more detail.

One dashboard for all your identity-related events

Monitoring and analyzing identity and access on your machines is crucial. It enables you to take proactive action before an incident occurs. Azure Security Center collects logon events from your machines. The Identity & Access dashboard then surfaces the number of failed attempts to log on and the associated accounts, accounts that were locked out, accounts that changed passwords, and more.

Koby Koren, Azure Security Center Program Manager

Identity posture

The Identity Posture section of the Identity & Access dashboard conveys various analytics representing the last 24 hours of data, which can help you better understand your users' authentication patterns. These analytics include the following:

- **Logons**   This pie graph shows the number of failed and successful logons.

- **Accounts Logged On**   This counter shows the number of user accounts that are currently logged on.

- **Accounts Failed to Log On**   This counter shows the total number of accounts that failed to log on, along with an arrow pointing up or down. In Figure 8-2, the arrow is pointing down, signaling that the number of failed logons has dropped by 1.6K since the last update.

- **Locked Accounts**   This counter conveys the number of accounts that are currently locked.

- **Accounts with Changed or Reset Password**   This counter shows the total number of accounts whose passwords have been changed or reset.

- **Active Critical Notable Issues**   Notable issues are critical events. In the context of identity, they are critical identity events. This counter reflects the active notable issues that require immediate attention.

- **Active Warning Notable Issues**   This is the same as the previous counter, but for medium-priority issues rather than critical ones.

You can click each tile for more information about its corresponding analytic. For example, to see more details about logons, click the Logons tile. The **Log Search** dashboard opens with a custom query result, as shown in Figure 8-3.

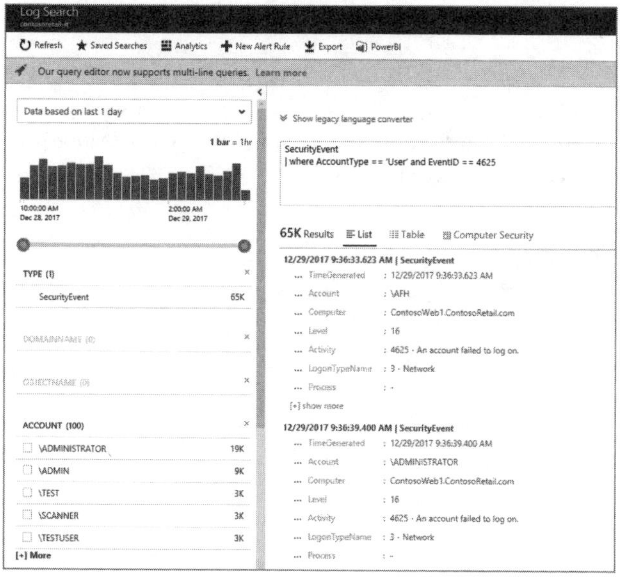

FIGURE 8-3 The Log Search page.

In the left pane of the **Log Search** page, you can customize your results by filtering for the accounts you want to see. For example, to see only administrator account activity, select the Aministrator check box. You can also filter by selecting the process that initiated the logon attempt, the logon type (network or service), and the computer's name.

Failed logons

The Failed Logons section of the Identity & Access dashboard conveys at a glance the main causes of failed logons.

When a user fails to authenticate, Windows generates an event called event 4625. To investigate why a particular logon failed, click it in the list in the Failed Logon Reasons section. As shown in Figure 8-4, an Event 4625 window opens that shows the reason for the failure. (See the Failure Information section.)

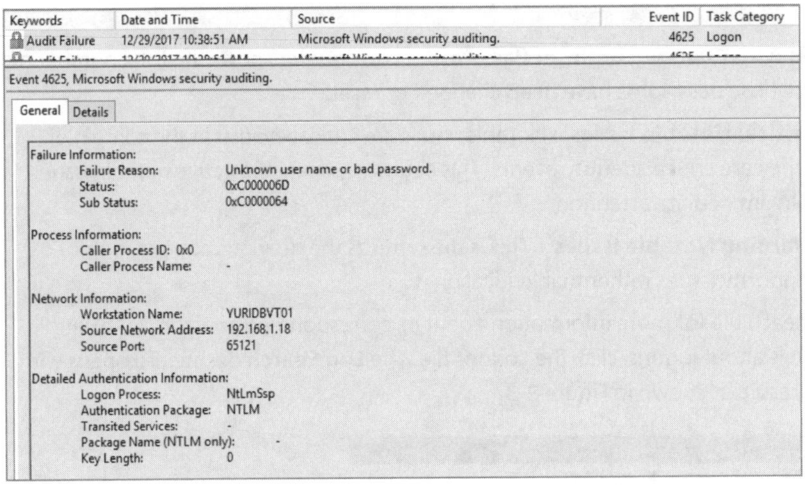

FIGURE 8-4 A description of event 4625.

The information available in the Event 4625 window may vary depending on the failure reason. Table 8-1 lists some of the most common reasons.

TABLE 8-1 Common reasons for logon failures

Error code (status/substatus)	Description
0xC0000064	Unknown user name or bad password
0xC0000234	Account locked out
0xC0000072	Account currently disabled
0xC0000193	The specified user account has expired
0xC0000071	Expired password

TIP For a complete list of logon failure reasons, see https://aka.ms/AccountLogon.

When reviewing the Event 4625 window, pay close attention to the LogonTypeName field. If this field is set to 3, it means the logon attempt came from the network. In this case, you'll also see an IPAddress field with the corresponding IP address. If LogonTypeName is set to 5, it means the logon attempt is coming from a service or process. A Process field will contain the process name. The following code contains the entire contents of the screen shown in Figure 8-4:

```
Log Name:       Security
Source:         Microsoft-Windows-Security-Auditing
Date:           2/19/2018 9:08:29 AM
Event ID:       4625
Task Category:  Logon
Level:          Information
Keywords:       Audit Failure
User:           N/A
Computer:       ARGOS
Description:
An account failed to log on.
Subject:
                        Security ID:                    NULL SID
                        Account Name:                      -
                        Account Domain:                    -
                        Logon ID:                               0x0
Logon Type:                                             3
Account For Which Logon Failed:
                        Security ID:                            NULL SID
                        Account Name:
YURIDBVT01$
                        Account Domain:
NORTHAMERICA
Failure Information:
                        Failure Reason:
Unknown user name or bad password.
                        Status:
0xC000006D
                        Sub Status:             0xC0000064
Process Information:
                        Caller Process ID:      0x0
                        Caller Process Name:    -
Network Information:
                        Workstation Name:       YURIDBVT01
                        Source Network Address:         192.168.1.254
                        Source Port:            53407
```

Detailed Authentication Information:

        Logon Process: NtLmSsp

        Authentication Package: NTLM

        Transited Services: -

        Package Name (NTLM only):   -

        Key Length: 0

This event is generated when a logon request fails. It is generated on the computer where access was attempted.

The Subject fields indicate the account on the local system which requested the logon. This is most commonly a service such as the Server service, or a local process such as Winlogon.exe or Services.exe.

The Logon Type field indicates the kind of logon that was requested. The most common types are 2 (interactive) and 3 (network).

The Process Information fields indicate which account and process on the system requested the logon.

The Network Information fields indicate where a remote logon request originated. Workstation name is not always available and may be left blank in some cases.

The authentication information fields provide detailed information about this specific logon request.

        - Transited services indicate which intermediate services have participated in this logon request.

        - Package name indicates which sub-protocol was used among the NTLM protocols.

        - Key length indicates the length of the generated session key. This will be 0 if no session key was requested.

Event Xml:

```
<Event xmlns="http://schemas.microsoft.com/win/2004/08/events/event">
  <System>
    <Provider Name="Microsoft-Windows-Security-Auditing" Guid="{54849625-5478-4994-A5BA-3E3B0328C30D}" />
    <EventID>4625</EventID>
    <Version>0</Version>
    <Level>0</Level>
    <Task>12544</Task>
    <Opcode>0</Opcode>
    <Keywords>0x8010000000000000</Keywords>
    <TimeCreated SystemTime="2018-02-19T15:08:29.580037100Z" />
    <EventRecordID>60107528</EventRecordID>
    <Correlation />
    <Execution ProcessID="724" ThreadID="16256" />
```

```
      <Channel>Security</Channel>
      <Computer>ARGOS</Computer>
      <Security />
   </System>
   <EventData>
     <Data Name="SubjectUserSid">S-1-0-0</Data>
     <Data Name="SubjectUserName">-</Data>
     <Data Name="SubjectDomainName">-</Data>
     <Data Name="SubjectLogonId">0x0</Data>
     <Data Name="TargetUserSid">S-1-0-0</Data>
     <Data Name="TargetUserName">YURIDBVT01$</Data>
     <Data Name="TargetDomainName">NORTHAMERICA</Data>
     <Data Name="Status">0xc000006d</Data>
     <Data Name="FailureReason">%%2313</Data>
     <Data Name="SubStatus">0xc0000064</Data>
     <Data Name="LogonType">3</Data>
     <Data Name="LogonProcessName">NtLmSsp </Data>
     <Data Name="AuthenticationPackageName">NTLM</Data>
     <Data Name="WorkstationName">YURIDBVT01</Data>
     <Data Name="TransmittedServices">-</Data>
     <Data Name="LmPackageName">-</Data>
     <Data Name="KeyLength">0</Data>
     <Data Name="ProcessId">0x0</Data>
     <Data Name="ProcessName">-</Data>
     <Data Name="IpAddress">192.168.1.254</Data>
     <Data Name="IpPort">53407</Data>
   </EventData>
</Event>
```

The **Failed Logon Reasons** section of the dashboard also contains a list of the top 10 accounts that failed to log on. Also, as with the Logons section of the dashboard, clicking a tile opens the **Log Search** dashboard with a relevant query result.

Logons over time

The Logons Over Time section contains a timeline of logon attempts, which can be very useful for understanding your users' authentication patterns. If you see an authentication spike every day at 6 AM—a time when your environment shouldn't be receiving a significant number of authentication requests—it certainly suggests a suspicious behavior requiring further investigation.

This section also contains a list of the 10 most frequently accessed computers (assuming you have accessed at least that many). Selecting a computer from this list opens a Log Search screen like the one shown in Figure 8-5.

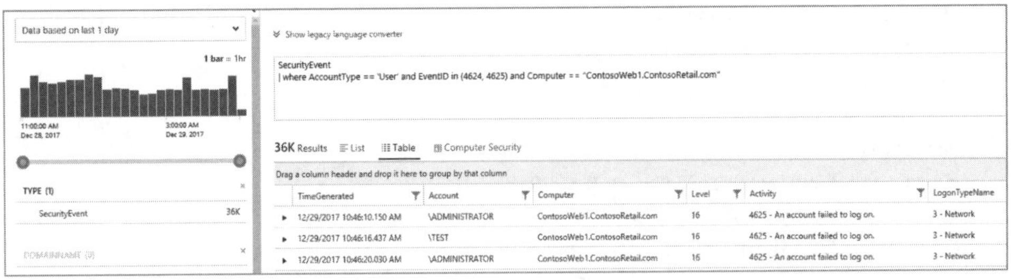

FIGURE 8-5 Most frequently accessed computer query results.

Integrating Security Center with Azure Active Directory Identity Protection

Security Center can integrate with Microsoft Azure AD Identity Protection. This allows for the visualization of Microsoft Azure AD Identity Protection alerts and data correlation. And because this combines low-fidelity detections across all your security data, it is likelier that attacks will be detected. Microsoft Azure AD Identity Protection comes with Azure Active Directory Premium P2 and the EMS E5 license, resulting in extra costs on your Azure invoice.

To perform this integration, follow these steps:

1. Open the **Azure Portal** and sign in as a user who has **Global Admin** or **Security Admin** privileges.

2. In the left pane, click **Security Center**.

3. In the left pane of the Security Center window, under **Prevention**, click **Security Solutions**.

4. In the **Discovered Solutions** section, under **Azure AD Identity Protection**, click **Connect**. (See Figure 8-6.) The **Integrate Azure AD Identity Protection** page appears. (See Figure 8-7.)

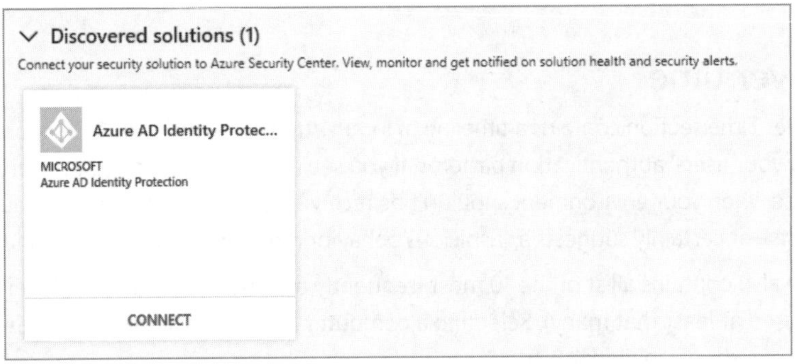

FIGURE 8-6 Integrating with Azure AD Identity Protection.

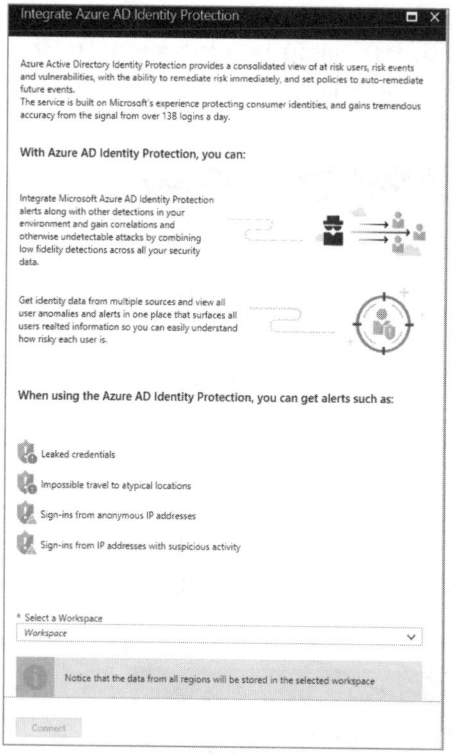

FIGURE 8-7 The Integrate Azure AD Identity Protection page.

5. In the **Select a Workspace** drop-down list, select the workspace you want to monitor.

6. Click **Connect**.

After the connection is made, you will use the Azure AD Identity Protection dashboard to configure this service and to manage users. To learn more about the capabilities offered by Azure AD Identity Protection, visit https://aka.ms/riskyuser.

Customizing your search

Clicking any of the tiles in the Identity & Access dashboard opens the Log Search page, with the search results generated by a built-in query displayed. Although these built-in queries are very useful, you can extract information that is more relevant to your needs by customizing your search. Security Center uses Azure Log Analytics to retrieve and analyze your security data. To access this feature, follow these steps:

1. Open the **Azure Portal** and sign in as a user who has **Security Admin** privileges.

2. In the left pane, click **Security Center**.

3. In the left pane of the Security Center window, under **General**, click **Search**.

4. Select the workspace that you want to search for information. The **Log Search** page appears. (See Figure 8-8.) This page includes suggested search terms and strings. It also provides a box in which you can type a custom query, as well as three buttons: Refresh, Saved Searches, and Analytics.

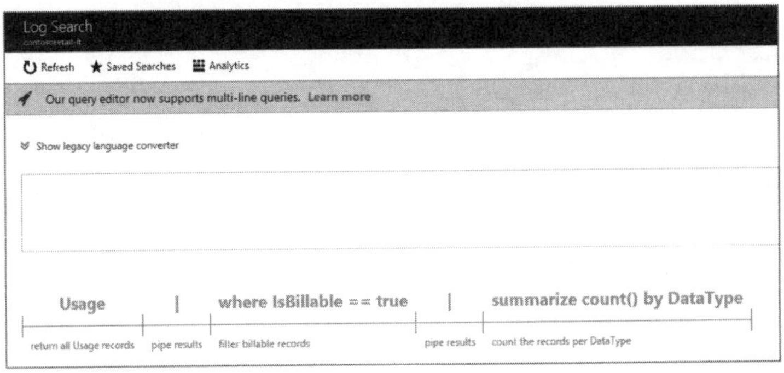

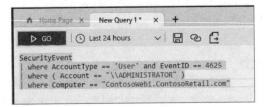

FIGURE 8-8 Customizing your log search.

5. Click the **Analytics** button. The **Azure Log Analytics** page opens.

6. Click the plus sign to open a new tab. (See Figure 8-9.)

FIGURE 8-9 The Azure Log Analytics page.

7. In the **New Query 1** tab, type the query shown in Figure 8-10, but change the computer name to one that is relevant to you. Then click **Go**.

FIGURE 8-10 Custom query using Log Analytics.

The query in Figure 8-10 searches for user accounts that failed to authenticate (Event ID == 4625), where the account name is ADMINISTRATOR and the computer is ContosoWeb1. ContosoRetail.com. If the query yields results, a table containing all matches will appear.

8. Each entry in the table contains information about a particular match. Click an entry to view additional details.

9. You don't have to be an expert in the Log Analytics query language to create custom queries. The left pane in the Azure Log Analytics page contains information about query structure. In this case, because the intent of the query is to look for authentication-related events, expand the **Security** entry and then click **SecurityEvent** to reveal additional attributes. (See Figure 8-11.)

FIGURE 8-11 Attributes that contains relevant data.

10. Type **SecurityEvent** in the New Query 1 tab. Azure's IntelliSense feature suggests various SecurityEvent-related attributes. (See Figure 8-12.) This makes it even easier to create custom queries.

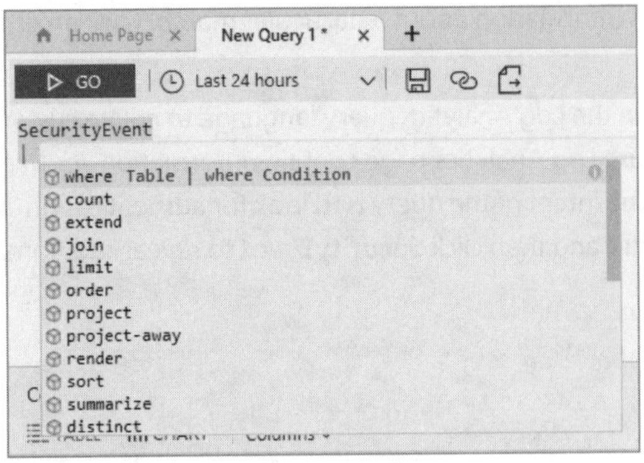

FIGURE 8-12 Log Analytics IntelliSense.

The following scenarios provide more examples of how queries can be useful when investigating authentication-related issues:

- **Account enumeration** Suppose you are investigating a potential lateral movement in your environment. One way to perform this lateral movement is through account enumeration. Every time a security-enabled local group is enumerated, it triggers event 4799. The following query returns computers that have experienced this event, enabling you to identify all computers that were a target of the enumeration:

```
SecurityEvent | where EventID == 4799
```

- **Process creation** Imagine you are investigating the use of non-authorized software in your environment to determine when this software was launched. You aren't sure of the exact command line for the software, but you know it starts with cm. You also know that every time a new process is created, it triggers event 4688. To find software that contains cm in the command line and triggers event 4688, try the following query:

```
SecurityEvent | where EventID == 4688 and CommandLine contains "cm"
```

- **Successful anonymous authentication** Suppose you receive a request to report all successful anonymous logon attempts from the network. You know that each successful logon triggers event 4624. You can therefore use the following query to locate instances of event 4624 made by anonymous users from the network (indicated by the string LogonType == 3):

```
SecurityEvent | where EventID == 4624 and Account contains "anonymous logon" and
LogonType == 3
```

Chapter 9

Using threat intelligence to identify security issues

The famous Chinese military strategist and philosopher Sun Tzu once said, "Every battle is won before it is fought"—meaning that in order to win, you must gather intelligence so that you know your enemy, their strategies, and how best to enhance your defense. These days threat intelligence is a requirement to stay on top of new threats, how those threats behave, and who the threat actors are. Security Center leverages the Microsoft Threat Intelligence Center (MSTIC) to improve its detection capabilities, enhance its accuracy to avoid false positive alerts, and enable customers to make proactive cybersecurity decisions. In this chapter, you will learn how to use MSTIC to identify security issues in your environment.

What is threat intelligence and why use it?

For threat intelligence to be useful, you need to draw from a large, diverse set of data and you must apply it to your processes and tools. The good news is that MSTIC does both. Telemetry flows into MSTIC from multiple sources, such as Azure, Office 365, Microsoft CRM online, Microsoft Dynamics AX, outlook.com, MSN.com, the Microsoft Digital Crimes Unit (DCU), and the Microsoft Security Response Center (MSRC). Researchers also receive threat intelligence information that is shared among major cloud service providers and subscribe to threat intelligence feeds from third parties.

The data collected by Microsoft from these various sources passes through three phases. (See Figure 9-1.) The first phase involves ensuring that data is used only in ways that Microsoft customers have agreed to. The data crosses this strict privacy/compliance boundary before entering the second phase: data collection and analysis. Here the data is normalized, various analytics (machine learning, detonation, behavior) are applied to identify relevant security insights and findings, and the data is published to an internal API. In the third phase, each product consumes this data, combs over it to uncover insight, and feeds these new insights back into the system to enrich other product findings.

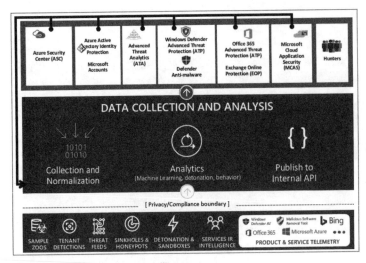

FIGURE 9-1 Microsoft threat intelligence.

Notice that Figure 9-1 contains an entry for "hunters." These hunters—which are simply human teams—play a significant role: identifying attacks, helping improve analytics, and feeding information back into the product. Hunters search constantly for adversaries in various environments (Azure, Office 365, Microsoft IT, Windows ATP Customers, and so on) as well as creating, tuning, and validating new analytics to improve the overall detection capability.

How Security Center powered by Microsoft Threat Intelligence helps detect advanced attacks

Microsoft manages hundreds of products and services that must be protected from attacks. As customers onboard to the cloud platform, their adversaries may follow. To protect customers and services from cyberattacks, threat intelligence is a key pillar of security strategy.

Microsoft tracks an enormous number of threat actors, and each threat is handled by a virtual team. Products are instrumented to provide security-relevant data with privacy and compliance in mind. This data is used in analytics to identify abnormal behaviors. Security analysts perform investigations to understand the scope and scale of cyberthreats through log analysis, forensics, data mining, and detonation of malware samples.

Microsoft connects with customers to help them understand what's going on, and in the process, gains new insights. Partnerships with other threat intel providers and partner organizations enhance research and help develop additional intelligence and context. This knowledge is used to classify and track threat actors, create new analytics, and improve threat intelligence in all products and services.

After an attack, customers want to know why they were attacked, the attack's origin, and who conducted it. Without this context, an alert is just a piece of information. Using threat intelligence data, Security Center provides technical, activity group, and campaign reports that identify adversary goals, tactics, techniques, procedures, and targeted industries. This best-in-class threat intelligence is used to protect all Security Center customers. Understanding the scope, nature, and intent of attacks acquired through threat intelligence helps customers make informed and timely cybersecurity decisions.

Ajeet Prakash, Senior Program Manager, Microsoft Threat Intelligence Team

Security Center can use threat intelligence information to alert you to threats from known bad actors—for example, an outbound communication from a virtual machine (VM) to the IP address of a known botnet or darknet. This behavior would indicate that your resource has been compromised and an attacker is attempting to execute commands on that resource or perform data exfiltration.

> **NOTE** At the time of this writing, the Security Center integration with Windows Server Defender Advanced Threat Protection (ATP) is in preview. This integration enables you to go beyond what Security Center finds to see more details about what happened at the endpoint. The user interface (UI) experience in this preview includes in the Security Center Investigation dashboard a hyperlink to Windows Defender Security Center.

Using threat intelligence reports in Security Center

In Chapter 5, you learned how to use security alerts and security incidents for incident response. Security alerts in which the source of the attack is a known malware or threat actor provide a link to a threat intelligence report that contains more details. An example of a report link appears at the bottom of Figure 9-2.

☑ Learn more

⌃ General information

DESCRIPTION	Network traffic analysis detected suspicious outgoing traffic from vm1lin. This traffic may be a result of a spam activity. If this behavior is intentional, please note that sending spam is against Azure Terms of service. If this behavior is unintentional, it may mean your machine has been compromised.
DETECTION TIME	Tuesday, January 30, 2018 11:02:00 PM
SEVERITY	ⓘ Low
STATE	Active
ATTACKED RESOURCE	vm1lin
SUBSCRIPTION	
DETECTED BY	▦ Microsoft
ACTION TAKEN	Detected
ENVIRONMENT	▦ Azure
RESOURCE TYPE	🖥 Virtual Machine
REPORTS	Report: Spambots and email flooders

FIGURE 9-2 This security alert contains a link to an extra report.

Clicking the link shown in Figure 9-2 opens a new browser window with a report, in PDF format, about spambots and email flooders. This report contains information you can use to better understand how to defend against this type of attack. Figure 9-3 shows the front page of this report.

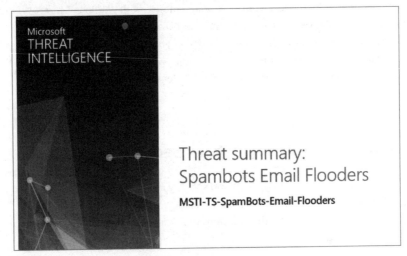

FIGURE 9-3 Microsoft threat intelligence report.

Using the Threat Intelligence dashboard in Security Center

The threat intelligence report discussed in the previous section isn't the only way to use Security Center to obtain threat intelligence. For a better vision of potential compromises on your environment based on threat intelligence data, you can use the Threat Intelligence dashboard. This dashboard contains the following:

- **Threat intelligence map**   This map can help you determine whether any of your systems have become nodes in a botnet and identify potential threats coming from underground communication channels, such as the darknet.
- **Pie chart**   This gives a breakdown of the current threats in your environment.
- **Traffic report**   This shows information about incoming and outgoing traffic according to its location on the world map.

To open the Threat Intelligence dashboard, follow these steps:

1. Open the **Azure Portal** and sign in as a user who has **Security Admin** privileges.
2. In the left pane, click **Security Center**.
3. In the left pane of the **Security Center** window, under **Detection**, click **Threat Intelligence**.
4. If you have multiple workspaces, select the workspace for which you want to obtain more information. The **Threat Intelligence** dashboard opens. (See Figure 9-4.)

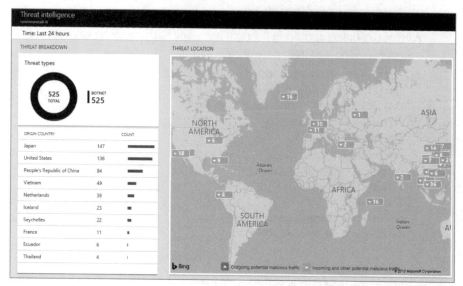

FIGURE 9-4   The Threat Intelligence dashboard.

NOTE The details of this map may vary depending on your environment, which means it might not look exactly like Figure 9-4.

5. Click the pie chart or click a country in the list below it. Log Analytics opens the query result for your selection. Figure 9-5 shows the query result for the pie chart.

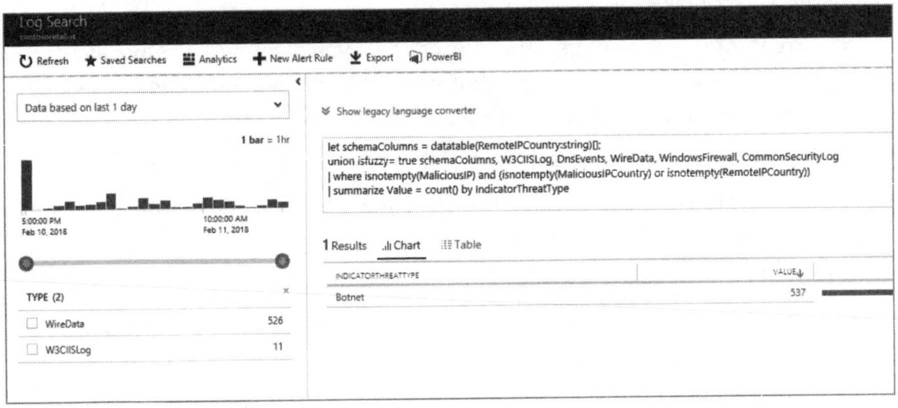

FIGURE 9-5 Log Analytics query result.

6. In the left pane, select the **WireData** (network traffic) or **W3CIISLog** (Internet Informa-tion Services logs) check box to filter the data.

7. To find out which systems were compromised and are now part of a botnet, click **Botnet**.

   A list of computers appears in the right pane, and each computer has a set of fields and values. Following is an example with W3CIISLog:

```
2/11/2018 4:02:29.000 PM | W3CIISLog
...RemoteIPCountry:United States
...TimeGenerated:2/11/2018 4:02:29.000 PM
...sSiteName:Default+Web+Site
...sIP:10.6.0.5
...csMethod:HEAD
...cIP:XXX.XXX.XXX.XXX
...scStatus:404
...TimeTaken:30
...Computer:ContosoWeb1.ContosoRetail.com
...MaliciousIP:XXX.XXX.XXX.XXX
...Severity:2
...SourceSystem:OpsMgr
...csUriStem:/phpmyadmin/scripts/setup.php
```

```
...sPort:80
...csUserName:-
...csUserAgent:-
...csReferer:-
...scSubStatus:0
...scWin32Status:2
...IndicatorThreatType:Botnet
...Confidence:75
...FirstReportedDateTime:2018-02-10T20:11:34.0000000Z
...LastReportedDateTime:2018-02-11T21:44:26.3696180Z
...IsActive:true
...RemoteIPLongitude:-82.46
...RemoteIPLatitude:27.99
...ManagementGroupName:AOI-b438b4f6-912a-46d5-9cb1-b44069212abc
```

These entries contain much useful information, including the malicious IP, the computer name, the source IP (in the case of outgoing traffic, this represents the compromised system), the threat type, and the dates when the threat was first and last reported. This information can be used to do the following:

- Determine the nature of the attack.

- Determine the point of origin of the attack.

- Identify the systems that have been compromised.

- Identify the files that have been accessed and determine the sensitivity of those files.

Threat intelligence data, which includes a list of malicious IPs, is updated frequently and adapted to fast-moving threats. Due to its nature, it should be combined with other sources of security information while investigating a security alert.

> **TIP** Visit https://youtu.be/QK3qxheUdBA to watch a presentation delivered by co-author Yuri Diogenes at Ignite 2016 that demonstrates how to use the threat intelligence map in an investigation scenario.

Hunting security issues in Security Center

Part of a successful investigation, or *hunt*, is using different tools to narrow down the root cause of the issue. Throughout this book you've learned about several different Security Center capabilities that can be used during an incident response process; the Threat Intelligence dashboard is simply the last one in this arsenal.

This section steps you through a real-world investigation scenario to show you how all these features work together to help you respond to an incident. In this scenario, suppose one Azure VM has been compromised, and there has been an attempt to perform lateral movement from the compromised VM to another VM. In response, Security Center has created a new security incident that contains three high-priority security alerts. (See Figure 9-6.)

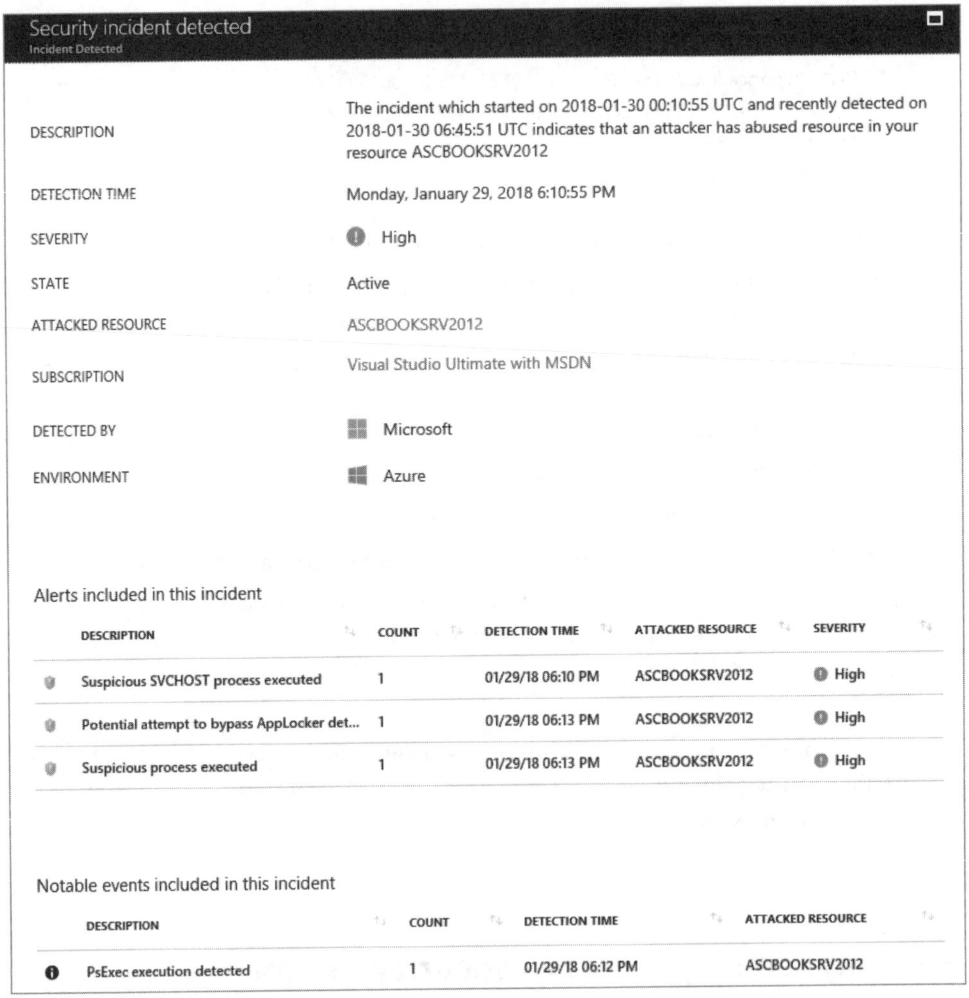

Security incident detected
Incident Detected

DESCRIPTION	The incident which started on 2018-01-30 00:10:55 UTC and recently detected on 2018-01-30 06:45:51 UTC indicates that an attacker has abused resource in your resource ASCBOOKSRV2012
DETECTION TIME	Monday, January 29, 2018 6:10:55 PM
SEVERITY	❶ High
STATE	Active
ATTACKED RESOURCE	ASCBOOKSRV2012
SUBSCRIPTION	Visual Studio Ultimate with MSDN
DETECTED BY	▦ Microsoft
ENVIRONMENT	▦ Azure

Alerts included in this incident

	DESCRIPTION	COUNT	DETECTION TIME	ATTACKED RESOURCE	SEVERITY
🛡	Suspicious SVCHOST process executed	1	01/29/18 06:10 PM	ASCBOOKSRV2012	❶ High
🛡	Potential attempt to bypass AppLocker det...	1	01/29/18 06:13 PM	ASCBOOKSRV2012	❶ High
🛡	Suspicious process executed	1	01/29/18 06:13 PM	ASCBOOKSRV2012	❶ High

Notable events included in this incident

	DESCRIPTION	COUNT	DETECTION TIME	ATTACKED RESOURCE
❶	PsExec execution detected	1	01/29/18 06:12 PM	ASCBOOKSRV2012

FIGURE 9-6   A security incident showing three high-priority security alerts.

The first alert shows a suspicious process execution of SVCHOST. To see the details of this alert, shown in Figure 9-7, simply click it. In a real investigation, you would take note of the command line, process name, user name, and detection time. At this point you would also review the threat intelligence report for this alert—in this case, the suspicious SVCHOST report.

> **NOTE** In a real investigation, you would click all the security alerts in the security incident. In this example we've clicked only the first one.

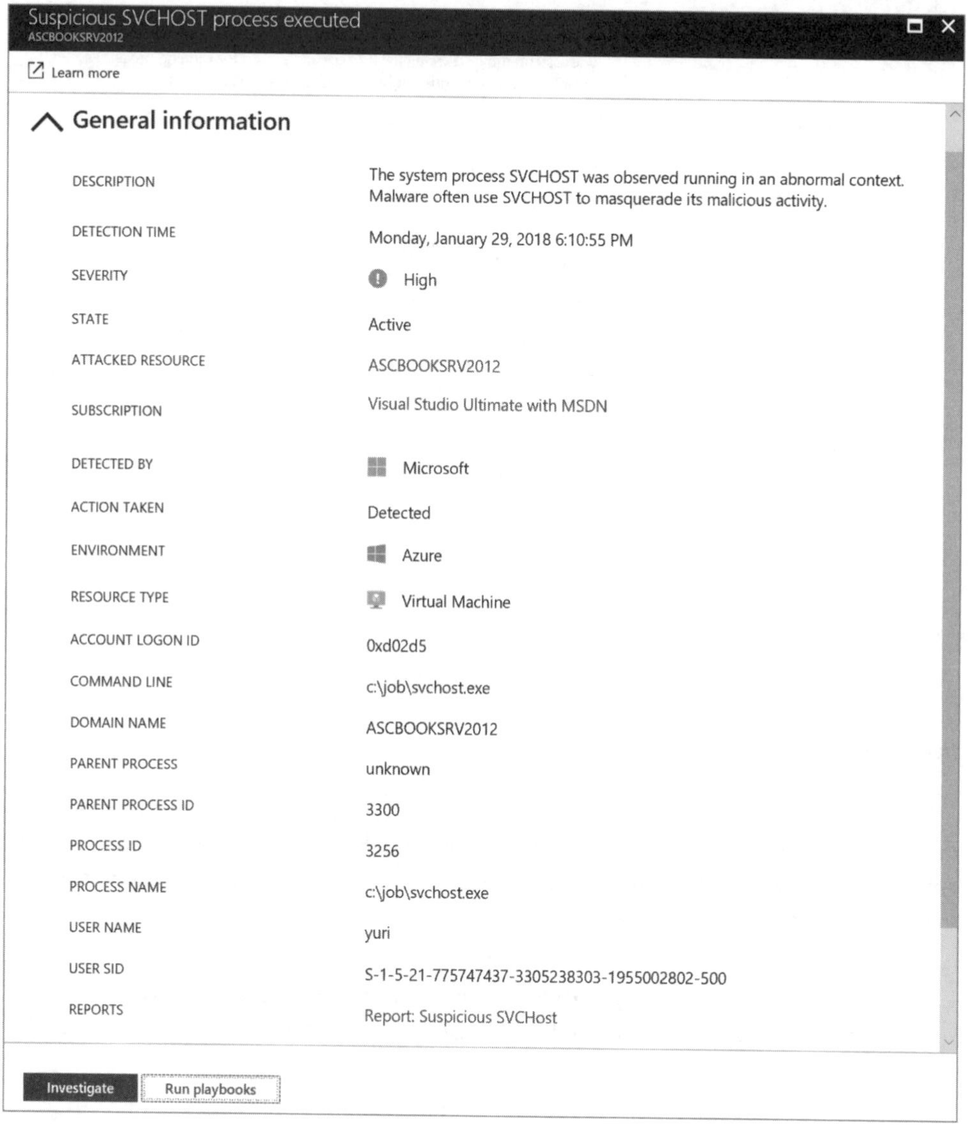

Suspicious SVCHOST process executed
ASCBOOKSRV2012

☐ ✕

☑ Learn more

⋀ General information

DESCRIPTION	The system process SVCHOST was observed running in an abnormal context. Malware often use SVCHOST to masquerade its malicious activity.
DETECTION TIME	Monday, January 29, 2018 6:10:55 PM
SEVERITY	❗ High
STATE	Active
ATTACKED RESOURCE	ASCBOOKSRV2012
SUBSCRIPTION	Visual Studio Ultimate with MSDN
DETECTED BY	⊞ Microsoft
ACTION TAKEN	Detected
ENVIRONMENT	⊞ Azure
RESOURCE TYPE	🖥 Virtual Machine
ACCOUNT LOGON ID	0xd02d5
COMMAND LINE	c:\job\svchost.exe
DOMAIN NAME	ASCBOOKSRV2012
PARENT PROCESS	unknown
PARENT PROCESS ID	3300
PROCESS ID	3256
PROCESS NAME	c:\job\svchost.exe
USER NAME	yuri
USER SID	S-1-5-21-775747437-3305238303-1955002802-500
REPORTS	Report: Suspicious SVCHost

Investigate   Run playbooks

FIGURE 9-7 The suspicious process executed alert.

Notice that the security incident in Figure 9-6 contains extra information at the bottom, under Notable Events Included In This Incident. Click the notable event to learn more about it. The notable event in this incident report tells you that the PsExec tool was used against the ASCBOOKSRV2012 machine, but it doesn't tell you the source. (See Figure 9-8.)

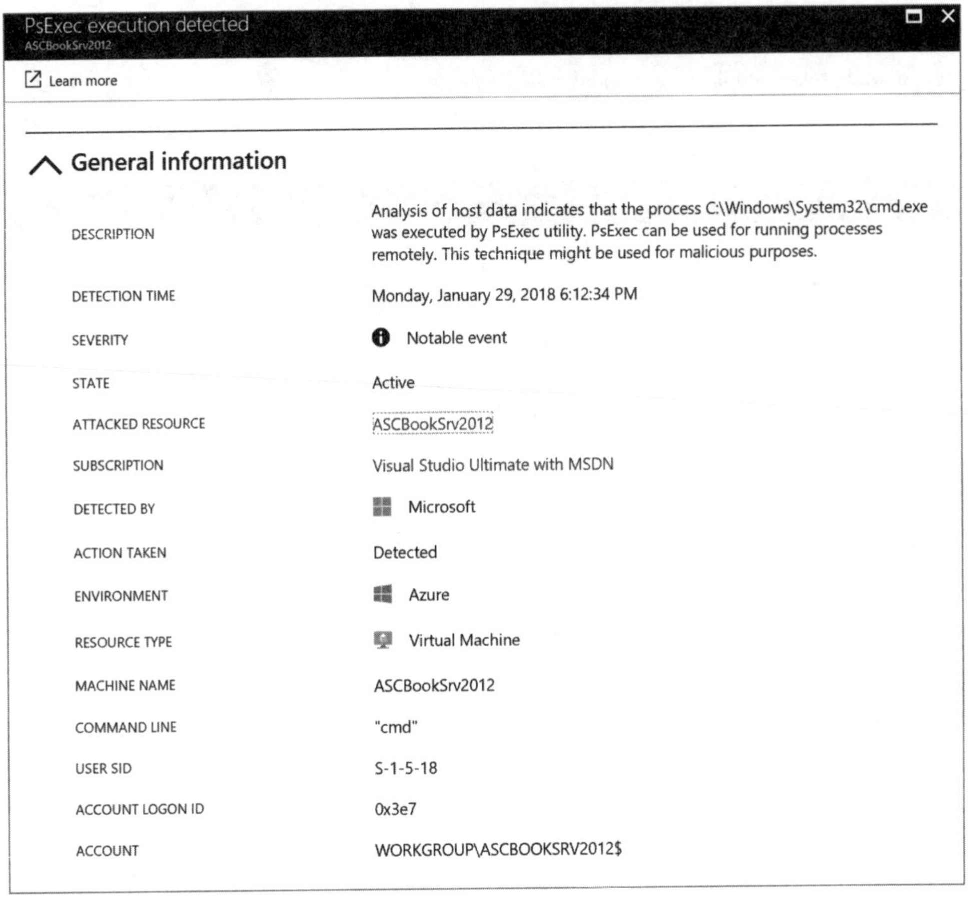

FIGURE 9-8 The notable event.

Although this is valuable information, you still need to understand which machine initiated this operation. For that you can use Security Center's **search** feature. In this scenario, you might enter a query like **SecurityEvent | where CommandLine contains "psexec"**. (For more on the search feature, refer to Chapter 8.)

> **TIP** To simulate these security alerts in your own environment, follow the instructions in the Azure Security Center Security Incident Playbook, at https://aka.ms/ASCSecPlaybook.

Virtual Analyst

At the time of this writing, a feature called Virtual Analyst (VA) is in private preview. The goal of VA is to automate human analyst expert knowledge by generating a custom, rich entity-based hunting graph for each security alert to extract meaningful insights. VA runs this online automated investigation on security alerts and assigns them confidence scores. A confidence score gives security operations personnel more (or less) confidence in the alert and helps them decide whether to move forward in the investigation. Confidence scores can also be used to help prioritize alerts and make risk assessments.

Using multiple workspaces in Security Center

In Chapter 2, you learned what a workspace is and how it works, and you explored some design considerations to determine how many workspaces you might need for your environment. In this appendix, you will learn how to create a new workspace and how to configure computers managed by Security Center to use this workspace as their main repository.

Creating a new workspace

As you learned in Chapter 2, there are many reasons to create more than one workspace. One scenario in which multiple workspaces are needed is when you need to isolate data—for example, if a company wants a separate workspace for each branch office. (See Figure A-1.)

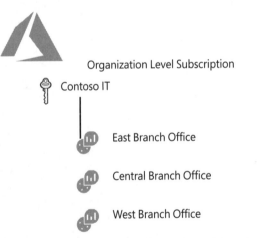

FIGURE A-1 Using a separate workspace for each branch office.

Whatever the reason may be, if you determine during the design process that you need more than one workspace, you can use Log Analytics to create one. Follow these steps:

1. Open the **Azure Portal** and sign in as a user who has **Security Admin** privileges.

2. In the left pane, click **More Services**, and type **Log Analytics**.

3. In the **Log Analytics** page, click the **Add** button.

4. In the **Workspace** page, click **Create New**, and type a name for the new workspace in the **Workspace** box.

5. Open the **Subscription** drop-down list and choose the subscription that will be used for this workspace.

6. Under **Resource Group**, select the resource group you want to use, or create a new one.

7. Under **Location**, select the geo-location for this workspace.

8. If your workspace is on the free pricing tier, you can send only 500 MB of data per day. When you reach the daily limit, data collection stops until the next day. To switch to the paid tier, click the **Pricing Tier** option and choose **Per Node**. Then click **OK**.

9. Click **OK** to create the workspace.

10. Your new workspace should appear in the Log Analytics page under the default workspace created by Security Center. (See Figure A-2.) If you don't see it, click **Refresh** to update the page.

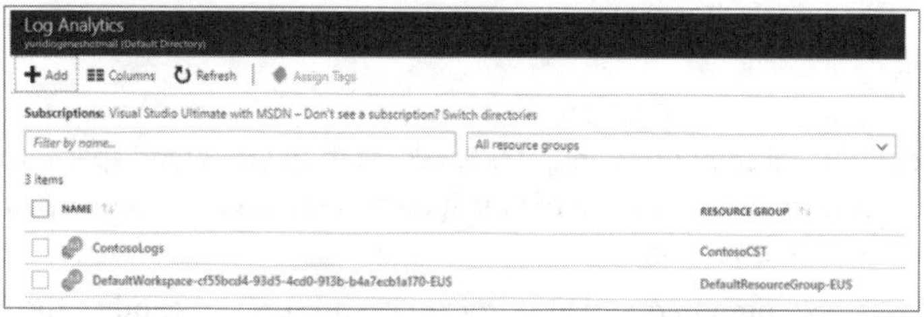

FIGURE A-2 New workspace created.

Moving computers and VMs to a new workspace

All computers and virtual machines (VMs) with the Security Center agent installed store data in the default workspace. You can move some or all computers and VMs to a different workspace. (The same basic processes work for both Azure VMs and on-premises computers.)

1. Open the **Azure Portal** and sign in as a user who has **Security Admin** privileges.

2. In the left pane, click **Security Center**.

3. In the left pane of the Security Center window, under **General**, click **Security Policy** and select your subscription.

4. In the **Security Policy – Data Collection** page, select **Use Another Workspace**. Then select the desired workspace from the drop-down list. (See Figure A-3.)

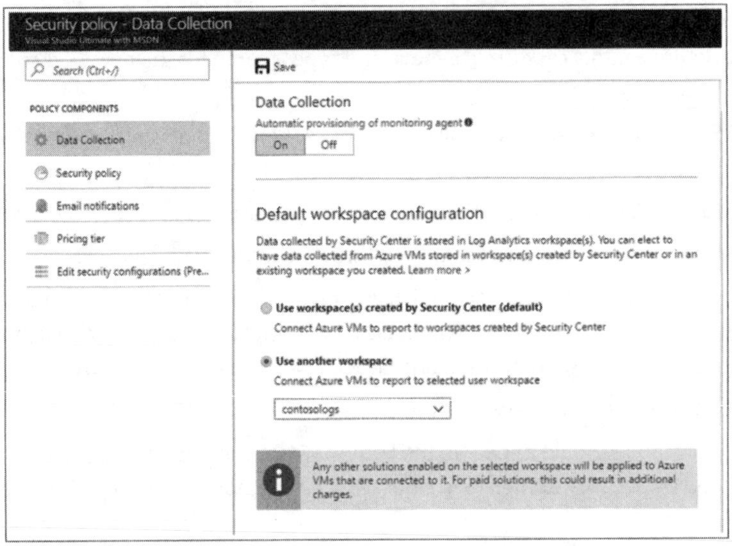

FIGURE A-3 Changing the default workspace.

5. Click **Save**.

Security Center will configure all computers and VMs to report to this new workspace. This remapping might take some time. The amount of time it takes depends on how many computers and VMs you have in your environment.

If you need to move just a few computers and VMs from one workspace to another, the easiest way to do so is via Log Analytics.

1. Open the **Azure Portal** and sign in as a user who has **Security Admin** privileges.
2. In the left pane, click **More Services**, and type **Log Analytics**.
3. In the **Log Analytics** page, click the workspace containing the VMs you want to move.
4. In the workspace's page, under **Workspace Data Source**, click **Virtual Machines** to view a list of machines in that workgroup, as shown in Figure A-4.

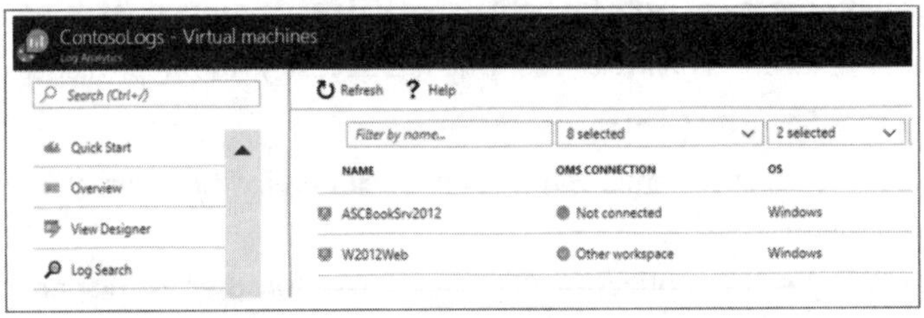

FIGURE A-4 Viewing the VMs that have (and have not) been moved to the new workspace.

5. As shown in Figure A-4, you have one VM that belongs to another workspace (the default one), and another VM that is not connected to any workspace. You can connect this VM to this workspace by clicking on the VM, and then clicking **Connect**.

You can also use PowerShell to obtain the VM's attribute, which includes the extension (in this case MicrosoftMonitoringAgent) and the workspace ID, by using the *Get-AzureRmVMExtension* command. Listing A-1 shows a sample PowerShell script.

LISTING A-1 PowerShell script for to obtain a VM's attribute.

```
PS C:\> Get-AzureRmVMExtension -ResourceGroupName "CONTOSOCST" -VMName "W2012Web" -Name
"MicrosoftMonitoringAgent"
ResourceGroupName       : CONTOSOCST
VMName                  : W2012Web
Name                    : MicrosoftMonitoringAgent
Location                : centralus
Etag                    : null
Publisher               : Microsoft.EnterpriseCloud.Monitoring
ExtensionType           : MicrosoftMonitoringAgent
TypeHandlerVersion      : 1.0
Id                      : /subscriptions/XXXXXXXXXX-b4a7ecb1a170/resourceGroups/
CONTOSOCST/providers/Microsoft.Compute/virtualMachines/W2012Web/extensions/
MicrosoftMonitoringAgent
PublicSettings          : {
                            "workspaceId": "XXXXXXXXXX-XXXXXXXXX",
                            "azureResourceId": "/subscriptions/XXXXXXXXXXXXXXXX-
b4a7ecb1a170/resourcegroups/contosocst/providers/microsoft.compute/virtualmachines/
w2012web",
                            "stopOnMultipleConnections": true
                          }
ProtectedSettings       :
ProvisioningState       : Succeeded
Statuses                :
SubStatuses             :
AutoUpgradeMinorVersion : True
ForceUpdateTag          :
```

If you need to move just a couple of VMs from workspace to another, the easiest way to do it is via Log Analytics, as shown previously in step 5. However, if you need to move many more VMs, you should use PowerShell. You can start with the following PowerShell sample script:

```
$ASCId = "<Replace with your Azure Security Center Workspace Id>"
$ASCKey = "<Replace with your Azure Security Center key>"
Set-AzureRmVMExtension -ResourceGroupName myResourceGroup `
   -ExtensionName "Microsoft.EnterpriseCloud.Monitoring" `
   -VMName YourVM `
   -Publisher "Microsoft.EnterpriseCloud.Monitoring" `
   -ExtensionType "MicrosoftMonitoringAgent" `
   -TypeHandlerVersion 1.0 `
   -Settings @{"workspaceId" = $ASCId} `
   -ProtectedSettings @{"workspaceKey" = $ASCKey} `
   -Location YourLocation
```

Customizing your operating system security baseline assessment

In Chapter 4, you learned how to remediate operating (OS) system vulnerabilities based on Common Configuration Enumeration (CCE) recommendations. Azure Security Center monitors security configurations by applying a set of recommended rules for hardening the OS. Although these recommendations are important, in some scenarios organizations might want to create their own set of security configurations to validate that their servers are compliant with it. In this appendix, you will learn how to customize the OS security configuration in Security Center.

> **NOTE** At the time of this writing, this feature is in preview (released in January 2018) and the only supported Operating Systems are Windows Server 2008, 2008 R2, 2012, and 2012 R2.

General considerations

Review the following considerations before making changes to the OS security configuration

- **Permission**   To perform this customization you need to belong to the Subscription Owner, Subscription Contributor, or Security Administrator role.
- **Tier**   The customization capability is available only in the Security Center standard tier
- **Affected resources**   The customization applies to all virtual machines (VMs) and computers that are connected to all workspaces under the selected subscription. Plan carefully before making changes that will have a broad impact.

- **Backup**   Before making changes to the original baseline policy, be sure to save the original baseline configuration file and keep it in a safe location for backup purposes.

- **Planning**   Before making changes to the original baseline policy, be sure you plan which changes you want to make and why those changes are necessary to your environment. Also, be sure to align the business needs with the recommendations that you want to implement.

Azure Security Center support for custom security assessments

Azure Security Center monitors security configurations by applying a set of more than 150 recommended rules for hardening the OS, including rules related to firewalls, auditing, password policies, and more. If a machine is found to have a vulnerable configuration, Security Center generates a security recommendation.

By customizing the rules, organizations can control which configuration options are more appropriate for their environment. You can customize the OS security configuration rules by enabling and disabling a specific rule, changing the desired setting for an existing rule, or adding a new rule that's based on the supported rule types (registry, audit policy, and security policy). This ensures you have a desired security assessment that fits your organization environment.

Miri Landau, Senior Program Manager, Azure Security Center team

Customizing operating system configuration

To customize the OS configuration, you need to download the JSON file, manually make the necessary changes to it, and then upload it.

Downloading the JSON file

Follow these steps to download the default configuration file:

1. Open the **Azure Portal** and sign in as a user who has the necessary privileges to perform this operation.

2. In the left pane, click **Security Center**.

3. In the left pane of the Security Center, under **General**, click **Security Policy**.

4. Select the subscription whose OS configuration you want to customize.

5. Click **Edit Security Configurations** to open the **Edit Security Configurations** blade. (See Figure B-1.)

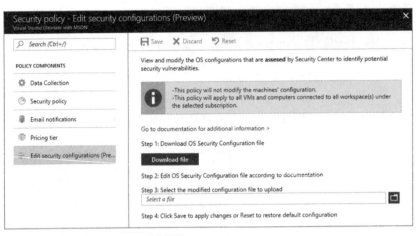

FIGURE B-1 Downloading the configuration file.

6. Click the **Download File** button.

7. Select the location where you want to save the *BaselineConfiguration.json* file and click **Save**.

8. After downloading the file, save a copy of it in a safe location before making changes.

9. Optionally, rename the new file to reflect the changes that you want to make—for example, **NewOSConfig.json**.

Editing the JSON file

To edit this file, you can use tools like *Visual Studio Code* or *Notepad++*. (You can download Notepad++ from https://notepad-plus-plus.org.) When you open this file, you will see the structure shown in Figure B-2.

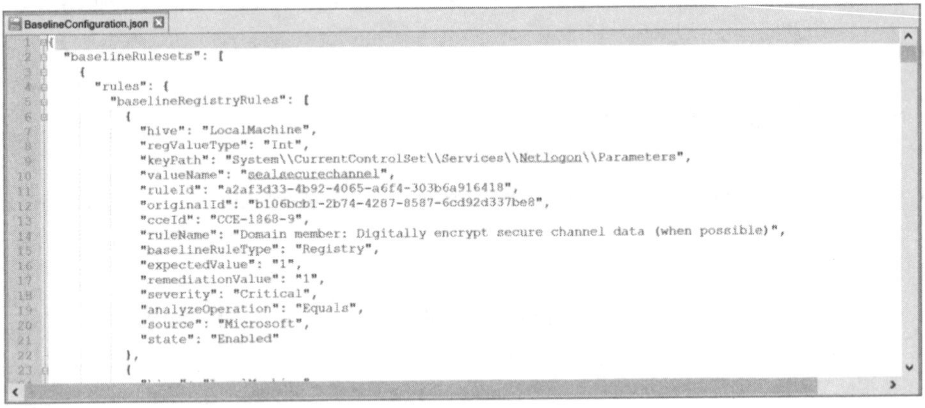

FIGURE B-2 Baseline configuration file.

The second line of this JSON code contains a `baselineRulesets` entry, which goes on to define many rules. These rules are divided into three categories: `baselineRegistryRules`, `baselineAuditPolicyRules`, and `baselineSecurityPolicyRules`. The registry rules (`baselineRegistryRules`) contain a set of attributes. Some correspond to registry fields and others to the Security Center baseline assessment, as shown in the following example:

```
        "hive": "LocalMachine",
        "regValueType": "Int",
        "keyPath": "System\\CurrentControlSet\\Control\\Lsa\\MSV1_0",
        "valueName": "NTLMMinClientSec",
        "ruleId": "b4b001c2-fe3d-470f-908a-9c533de6b187",
        "originalId": "9969a7db-5fd1-4713-9a26-9862c15359e9",
        "cceId": "CCE-1767-3",
        "ruleName": "Network security: Minimum session security for NTLM SSP based
(including secure RPC) clients",
        "baselineRuleType": "Registry",
        "expectedValue": "537395200",
        "remediationValue": "537395200",
        "severity": "Critical",
        "analyzeOperation": "Equals",
        "source": "Microsoft",
        "state": "Enabled"
```

Not all attributes are customizable. Only the following attributes can be changed:

- **expectedValue**   This attribute's field data type must match the supported values per rule type. For example:

  - **baselineRegistryRules**   This value must match the `regValueType` defined in that rule. (See this article for more information about registry values types: https://aka.ms/registrytypevalue.)

  - **baselineAuditPolicyRules**   Use one of the following supported string values for this value:

    - `Success and Failure`

    - `Success`

  - **baselineSecurityPolicyRules**   Use one of the following supported string values for this value:

    - `No one`

    - `Administrators`, `Backup Operators`, or any other values from the list of allowed user groups

- **state**   The string can contain the options `Disabled` or `Enabled`. In the preview release, the string was case-sensitive. Review the latest documentation (https://aka.ms/CustomOSSec) to confirm that this still applies.

The audit policy rules (`baselineAuditPolicyRules`) contain a set of attributes. Some of these correspond to Windows audit policies, such as `Audit Policy: Account Management: Other`

Account Management Events. Others correspond to the Security Center baseline assessment, as shown in the previous example.

The security policy rules (baselineSecurityPolicyRules) also contain a set of attributes. Some of these correspond to Windows security policies, such as Increase a process working set. Others correspond to the Security Center baseline assessment, as shown in the previous example.

You can use these guidelines to keep track of what you can change on the default rules. You can also create your own custom rules. When creating your own rules, comply with the following requirements:

- baselineId and baselineName can't be changed.
- A ruleset cannot be removed.
- A ruleset cannot be added.
- The maximum number of rules allowed (including default rules) is 1,000.
- For registry rules, the hive must have LocalMachine.
- The originalId attribute can be null or empty. If it is not empty, it should be a valid GUID.
- The cceId attribute can be null or empty. If it is not empty, it must be unique.
- The ruleType attribute can be Registry, AuditPolicy, or SecurityPolicy.
- The severity attribute can be Unknown, Critical, Warning, or Informational.
- The analyzeOperation attribute must be Equals.
- The auditPolicyId attribute must be a valid GUID.
- The regValueType attribute can be Int, Long, String, or MultipleString.

To create a new rule, simply copy the entire block of an existing rule and paste it under the last rule or in between existing rules. Here is a sample of a custom rule. (Be sure to change the values in *italic*.)

```
{
"hive": "LocalMachine",
"regValueType": "Int",
"keyPath":
"System\\\\CurrentControlSet\\\\Services\\\\Netlogon\\\\MyCustomKey",
"valueName": "MyCustomValue",
"originalId": "",
"cceId": "",
"ruleName": "My custom registry rule", "baselineRuleType": "Registry",
"expectedValue": "12345", "severity": "Critical",
"analyzeOperation": "Equals",
"source": "MyCustomizedSource",
"state": "Enabled"
}
```

Uploading the new rule

After making the desired changes in the JSON file, return to the **Edit Security Configurations** page (refer to Figure B-1), select the file, and click **Save**. If the upload process succeeds, you will see a green check mark and a message that reads "Save action finished successfully." If it fails, you won't be able to upload, and a red exclamation mark accompanied by a message that reads "Please upload a valid JSON configuration file" will appear. The error code will vary. To interpret the error code, see the "Error Code" section in this article: https://aka.ms/CustomOSSec.

Index

A

AAD (Azure Active Directory),
125–127
access and identity
    activities, 141–142
    Failed Logons, 144–147
    Identity Posture, 143–144
    Logons Over Time, 147–148
    management, 9
    restricting, 61–63
Access Control (IAM), 22
ACLs (access control lists), 12
Activity Log, 78
AD Identity Protection,
    integration with ASC, 148–149
Adaptive Application Controls,
    38, 111–114
agents
    installing, 26–30
    missing and not
        responding, 52
    removing, 35
Amazon EC2 keys, theft, 7
analytics. See Log Analytics
anomaly detection, 20, 106–108
Antimalware installation, 55
application controls, 111–114
application whitelisting, 111–114
applications. See also logic app
    firewalls, 68–71
    as malware, 5

ASC (Azure Security Center).
    See also security; SIEM
    (Security Incident and Event
    Management); Splunk
    integration solution
  access control, 22
  analytics, 20
  architecture, 18–21
  assessment, 30–32
  connectivity, 18
  considerations, 22–24
  dashboard, 21–22, 142
  detection capabilities, 20–21
  event evaluation, 20
  Failed Logons, 144–147
  features, 15–16
  Identity Posture, 143–144
  incorporating, 24–25
  intelligence resources, 104
  JIT VIM access
    feature, 115–119
  Logons Over Time, 147–148
  Monitoring Agent, 19
  next-generation
    policy, 38–43
  onboarding resources, 25–30
  overview, 17–18
  permissions, 49–50
  RBAC (role-based access
    control), 22–23d
  recommendations, 23–24
  security operations, 24–25
  security policy, 23

  storage, 23
  subscription, 17–18
  tiers, 17–18
assume-breach mentality, 6. See
    also attacks
atomic detection, 101–102
ATP (Advanced Threat
    Protection, 155
attack vectors, identifying, 2–3
attacked resources, listing, 77–78
attacks. See also assume-
    breach mentality; detection
    capabilities; Trojans
    brute force, 85
    drive-by download sites, 4
    IP addresses, 7
    local privilege escalation, 3
    RDP brute force, 114
    SSH brute-force, 114
attributes, obtaining
    for VMs, 167
authentication-related issues,
    investigating, 152
Azure AD Identity Protection
    customizing search, 149–152
    integration, 148–149
Azure Automation and
    PowerShell, 30
Azure Log Analytics
    customizing searches,
        149–152
    IntelliSense, 152
    query language, 83

query result, 158
website, 19
Azure Monitor add-on
accessible logs, 124
event-hub connection,
136–138
and Splunk, 139
Azure Policy. *See also* policies;
security policies
customizing, 49
definitions and assignments,
44, 48
elements, 47
exploring, 45–48
initiative definitions and
assignments, 44–45
JSON configuration, 48
overview, 43–44
scope, 44
Azure Portal, 11–12
Azure security. *See also* security
Disk Encryption, 14
host protection, 12
network protection, 12–13
overview, 11–12
storage protection, 14

B

behavioral analytics, 20, 104–105
blades, security policies, 35–36
BLOBs (binary large objects), 37
botnets, defined, 2
breaches. *See* assume-breach
mentality; attacks
brute-force attacks, 85

C

C2 (command and control)
servers, 4
CAV (counter-antivirus) services, 2
CCE (Common Configuration
Enumeration), 25, 52, 56–58

cloud defense
cyber kill chain, 108–111
fusion alerts, 108–111
JIT VM access, 114–119
threat detection, 100–108
threat prevention vs.
detection, 99–100
cloud security, rethinking, 31–32
cloud threats
access management, 9
compliance, 8–9
data protection, 10
endpoint protection, 10
identity management, 9
and machine learning, 105–106
operational security, 9
overview, 7–8
risk management, 9
compliance, 8–9
compute recommendations
CCE (Common Configuration
Enumeration), 56–58
endpoint protection, 52–56
overview, 51–52
security configurations, 56
compute recommendations,
accessing, 30–31
configuration flaws, 7
contextual information alerts, 74
crash-dump analysis, 76
CSPs (cloud solution
providers), 8–9
cyber kill chain, 2–4, 108–111
cybercrime, 1–2

D

data and storage
encryption, 66–67
overview, 63–64
protection, 10
server auditing, 64–66
threat detection, 64–66
Data Collection blade, 38–40

database auditing, 64
DCU (Digital Crimes Unit), 153
defense layers, 11
detect, security posture, 5–6
detection capabilities, 74,
154–155. *See also* attacks
DevOps, 7
DiCola, Nicholas, 71
Disk Encryption policy, 37, 52
domain dominance, 3
drive-by download sites, 4

E

Email Notifications blade, 41–42
encryption, 14. *See also* Storage
Encryption policy
Endpoint Protection policy, 10,
37, 52–56
entities and incidents, 87–88
error codes, website, 173. *See
also* WER (Windows Error
Reporting)
ETW (Event Tracking for
Windows), 19
Event 4625, 145–147
event hub
connecting to Azure
Monitor, 136–138
creating for SIEM, 122, 131–132
shared access key, 133–136
events. *See also* notable events
correlating with entities, 87
evaluating, 20
filtering, 39

F

Failed Logons section, 144–147
Fender, Sarah, 31–32
financial losses, 1
firewalls, 58, 68–70

G

GitHub public secret attack, 7–8

H

Healthy Databases, 64
host protection, 12
Hunter, Laura E., 15–16
hunting security issues, 159–162
Hyper-V virtualization solution, 12

I

IaaS (Infrastructure as a
    Service), 17
IAM (Access Control), 22
IC3 (Internet Crime Complaint
    Center), 1–2
Identity & Access, customizing
    search, 149–152
identity and access
    activities, 141–142
    Failed Logons, 144–147
    Identity Posture, 143–144
    Logons Over Time, 147–148
    management, 9
    restricting, 61–63
Identity Posture section, 143–144
IExpress self-extractor, 29
inbound security rules, 62–63
Incident Playbook, 162. *See also*
    playbooks
incident response. *See* security
    incidents
    crash-dump analysis, 76
    detection scenarios, 75–76
    security alerts, 73–75
    spam activity, 75
InfoSec Institute, lurking statistic, 5
initiative definitions and
    assignments, 44–45

install and exploit, 109–110
intel, obtaining, 3
IntelliSense, Log Analytics, 152
internet-facing endpoints,
    59, 61–63
Investigation feature, using, 84–88
IP addresses, attacks, 7
IPFIX (Internet Protocol Flow
    Information Export), 74
IT assets, securing, 99–100

J

JIT Network Access, 37–38, 52
JSON configuration
    OS customization, 169–172
    policies, 48
Just-in-Time VM access, 114–119.
    See also VMs (Virtual
    Machines)

K

Kemnetz, John, 122
Key Vault blade
    app password, 130–131
    creating, 127–130
Kliger, Ben, 106
Koren, Koby, 142

L

Landau, Miri, 169
legacy security policy, 33–38
Linux agents, installing, 27
local privilege escalation attack, 3
Log Analytics
    customizing searches, 149–152
    IntelliSense, 152
    query language, 83
    query result, 158
    website, 19

log search, customizing, 150
logic app, creating, 90. *See also*
    applications
logon failures, reasons for, 144
Logons Over Time
    section, 147–148
lurking statistic, 5

M

machine learning and
    cloud, 105–106
malware
    Antimalware installation, 55
    apps as, 5
Microsoft
    Antimalware installation, 55
    Monitoring Agent, 19
    Security Intelligence Report/
        IP-address attacks, 7
Missing Disk Encryption, 52
Missing Scan Data, 52
Missing System Updates, 52
Monitoring Agent, 19
MSRC (Microsoft Security
    Response Center), 153
MSTIC (Microsoft Threat
    Intelligence Center), 153

N

network analysis alerts, 74
network protection, 12–13
network recommendations
    internet-facing
        endpoints, 61–63
    NSGs on subnets not
        enabled, 59–61
    overview, 58–59
    restricting access, 61–63
NGFW (Next-Generation
    Firewall) policy, 37, 58
Nitol botnet, 2

notable events, 162. *See also* events

Notepad++, downloading, 170

NSGs (network security groups), 12, 37, 59–61,

O

omsagent daemon, 19

onboarding resources, 25–30

operational security, 9

OS hardening, rules, 169, 172–173

OS security configuration considerations, 168–169 customizing, 169–173 JSON file, 169–172 uploading rule, 173

OS Version Not Updated, 52

OWASP documentation for cyberattacks, 68

P

permissions and OS customization, 168 and RBAC, 49–50

Petya ransomware, 1

playbooks. *See also* Incident Playbook; security alerts auditing execution, 95–97 creating, 89–91 executing, 94–95 website, 162 workflows, 91–93

policies. *See* Azure Policy; security policies

Policy Management blade, 40–41

post breach, 109–110

Potential SQL Injection alert, 74. *See also* SQL databases

PowerShell, script to obtain VM's attribute, 167

Prakash, Ajeet, 155

prevention, importance of, 71

Pricing Tier blade, 42–43

Privileged Access Workstations, 10

protect, security posture, 5–6

public key secret, 7

Q

QKSee installation, 3 Trojan, 4

R

ransomware complaints, 1 financial loss, 1 Petya, 1 WannaCry, 1

RBAC (role-based access control), 11, 22–23, 49–50

RDP brute-force attacks, 114

recon, internal and external, 3

red/blue team simulations, 6

Remediate Security Configurations, 52, 56–58

removing agents, 35

reports, linking to security alerts, 156

resource analysis alerts, 74

resources, onboarding, 25–30

respond, security posture, 5–6

Restart Pending, 52

risk management, 9

rules, OS hardening, 169, 172–173

S

scan data, 52

SDL (Security Development Lifecycle), 68

SecOps (security operations), 24

securing IT assets, 99–100

security. *See also* ASC (Azure Security Center) cloud threats, 7–11 incidents, 79–81 resources, 12

security admin role, 22

security alerts. *See also* playbooks accessing, 77–84 categories, 74 customizing, 81–84 displaying, 160–161 linking to reports, 156 overview, 73–74 responding to, 89

security assessments, customizing, 169

Security Center access control, 22 analytics, 20 architecture, 18–21 assessment, 30–32 connectivity, 18 considerations, 22–24 dashboards, 21–22, 142 detection capabilities, 20–21 event evaluation, 20 Failed Logons, 144–147 features, 15–16 Identity Posture, 143–144 incorporating, 24–25 intelligence resources, 104 JIT VIM access feature, 115–119 Logons Over Time, 147–148 Monitoring Agent, 19 next-generation policy, 38–43

onboarding resources, 25–30
overview, 17–18
permissions, 49–50
RBAC (role-based access
control), 22–23
recommendations, 23–24
security operations, 24–25
security policy, 23
storage, 23
subscription, 17–18
tiers, 17–18
Security Configurations policy, 36
security data, analyzing, 149–152
security incidents, 110, 160–161.
See incident response
security issues
hunting, 159–162
investigating, 84–88
security playbooks. *See also* Incident Playbook; security alerts
auditing execution, 95–97
creating, 89–91
executing, 94–95
website, 162
workflows, 91–93
security policies. *See* Azure
Policy; policies
blades, 35–36
customizing, 49
legacy, 33–38
overview, 23
security posture, 5–6
security reader role, 22
security rules, 62–63
server auditing, 64–66
SIEM (Security Incident and
Event Management), 121–123.
See also Splunk integration
solution
Slack, integrating playbooks, 97
social engineering, 3
spam activity, detecting, 75

Splunk integration solution.
See also ASC (Azure
Security Center); SIEM
(Security Incident and Event
Management)
app password for Key
Vault, 130–131
Azure AD application, 125–127
Azure Key Vault, 127–130,
134–135
Azure Monitor add-on, 139
confirming accessible logs, 124
event hub and Azure
Monitor, 131–132, 136–138
processes, 123
shared access key, 133–134
Splunk SIEM pipe, 124
VM (Virtual Machine), 138–139
SQL Auditing & Threat
Detection, 38
SQL databases, threat detection,
66. *See also* Potential SQL
Injection alert
SQL Encryption, 38
SSE (Storage Service
Encryption), 14
SSH brute-force attacks, 114
storage
considering, 23
encryption, 66–67
storage and data
encryption, 66–67
overview, 63–64
protection, 10
server auditing, 64–66
threat detection, 64–66
Storage Encryption policy, 37.
See also encryption
storage protection, 14
streaming logs, 122
suspicious process executed
alert, 161
System Updates policy, 36, 52

T

target and attack, 109–110
TDE (Transparent Data
Encryption), 64
Teller, Tomer, 74
threat detection
anomaly detection, 106–108
atomic, 101–102
behavioral analytics, 104–105
methods, 101
vs. prevention, 64, 99–100
threat-intelligence
feeds, 102–104
threat intelligence
dashboard in Security
Center, 157–159
hunting security issues, 159–162
integration, 20
overview, 153–155
reports in Security
Center, 155–156
VA (Virtual Analyst), 163
threats, 4–5
TLS (Transport Layer Security), 10
Trojans, 1, 4. *See also* attacks

V

VA (Virtual Analyst), threat
intelligence, 163
VAs (vulnerability
assessments), 36–37
VHD (virtual hard disk), 63
VM Agent Is Missing or Not
Responding, 52
VMBA (Virtual Machine
Behavioral Analysis) alerts, 74
VMs (Virtual Machines). *See also*
Just-in-Time VM access
Azure Portal, 12–13
cloud-weaponization, 7

moving to workspaces, 165–167
obtaining attributes, 167
operations, 12
Splunk enterprise, 138–139
VMware virtualization solution, 12
VNets (virtual networks), 12
vulnerabilities, identifying and
mitigating, 57, 71
Vulnerability Assessment Not
Installed, 52

W

WAF (Web Application Firewall)
policy, 37
web applications, 68–70
websites
Activity Log for security
alerts, 78
agent installation, 29
application whitelisting, 114
ASC detection capabilities, 21
ASC pricing, 18
Azure AD Identity
Protection, 149
Azure network security, 13
Azure Policy, 48

Azure Storage security, 14
CCE rules, 25, 58
cloud threats, 7
compliance, 9
compute recommendations, 51
computer security, 12
cybercrime, 2
Data Collection blade, 39
Disk Encryption, 37
endpoint protection, 53
error codes, 173
event hub for SIEM, 122
IC3 (Internet Crime
Complaint Center), 1
IExpress self-extractor, 29
Incident Playbook, 162
Linux agents, 27
Log Analytics, 83
Log Analytics workspaces, 19
Nitol botnet, 2
Notepad++, 170
OWASP documentation for
cyberattacks, 68
playbook integration with
Slack, 97
Privileged Access
Workstations, 10

RBAC (role-based access
control), 23
SDL (Security Development
Lifecycle), 68
security alerts, 75, 77
Splunk integration solution, 139
SQL database threat
detection, 66
threat intelligence map, 159
VAs (vulnerability
assessments), 36
Welcome to Azure Policy
blade, 46
WER (Windows Error Reporting),
19. *See also* error codes
whitelisting, 111–114
WinZipper Trojan, 4
workflows, creating for
playbooks, 91–94
workspaces
changing defaults, 166
computers and VMs, 165–167
creating, 19, 164–165
data retention, 23
and data storage, 19
ID and primary key, 29
monitoring, 141